T0277412

Paris

Also by Mary McAuliffe

Paris

*Secret Gardens, Hidden Places,
and Stories of the City of Light*

Mary McAuliffe

ROWMAN & LITTLEFIELD
Lanham • Boulder • New York • London

Published by Rowman & Littlefield
An imprint of The Rowman & Littlefield Publishing Group, Inc.
4501 Forbes Boulevard, Suite 200, Lanham, Maryland 20706
www.rowman.com

86-90 Paul Street, London EC2A 4NE

Distributed by NATIONAL BOOK NETWORK

British Library Cataloguing in Publication Information Available

Library of Congress Cataloging-in-Publication Data

Names: McAuliffe, Mary Sperling, 1943– author.
Title: Paris : secret gardens, hidden places, and stories of the City of Light / Mary
    McAuliffe.
Other titles: Secret gardens, hidden places, and stories of the City of Light
Description: Lanham : Rowman & Littlefield, [2023] | Includes bibliographical
    references and index.
Identifiers: LCCN 2022046343 (print) | LCCN 2022046344 (ebook) | ISBN
    9781538173336 (cloth) | ISBN 9781538173343 (epub)
Subjects: LCSH: Paris (France)—Guidebooks.
Classification: LCC DC707 .M4418 2023 (print) | LCC DC707 (ebook) | DDC
    914.4/3610484—dc23/eng/20220930
LC record available at https://lccn.loc.gov/2022046343
LC ebook record available at https://lccn.loc.gov/2022046344

∞™ The paper used in this publication meets the minimum requirements of
American National Standard for Information Sciences—Permanence of Paper
for Printed Library Materials, ANSI/NISO Z39.48-1992.

For All Those Who Love Paris

~

Contents

Illustrations

~

Acknowledgments

One day, as the pandemic was raging, I found myself looking up an old, much-thumbed copy of Frances Hodgson Burnett's *The Secret Garden*, to see if I could still find the wonder and beauty that I had found there as a child.

Indeed, the wonder and beauty remained but on a different level, and it prompted me to reimagine my many explorations of Paris, to look for those secret and hidden places that had come to mean so much to me over the years. After all, my mandate in the first of many writing assignments for *Paris Notes* had been to take my readers off the beaten path, and so I have continued throughout the years—exploring the unknown and the unusual but also finding special places of beauty and meaning even in the midst of the most well-known of Paris destinations. It now seemed time to share my many years of discovery. After all, in this time of pandemic and global distress, the qualities of peace, quiet, and beauty are more necessary than ever. They are small refuges in this ever-more-turbulent world.

Throughout my years of exploring Paris, I have benefited from the knowledge and assistance of many wonderful folks, most especially my editor at *Paris Notes*, Mark Eversman, and my longtime editor at Rowman & Littlefield, Susan McEachern. Now that Susan has retired, I have been blessed with yet another fine editor, Katelyn Turner, whose enthusiasm, good judgment, and ready support have been invaluable. Katelyn is always there for me, and I vastly appreciate her guidance and encouragement. My deepest thanks as well to my longtime production editor Jehanne Schweitzer, who has stayed with me through all my books at Rowman & Littlefield, much to the books' benefit. I know that I can always trust even the most complex of my manuscripts to Jehanne's care.

This book, much like all the others I have written, has been a joint effort with my husband, Jack McAuliffe, whose assistance has smoothed every step of the way. Exploring Paris with him has been an ongoing adventure and a delight, for which I am deeply grateful.

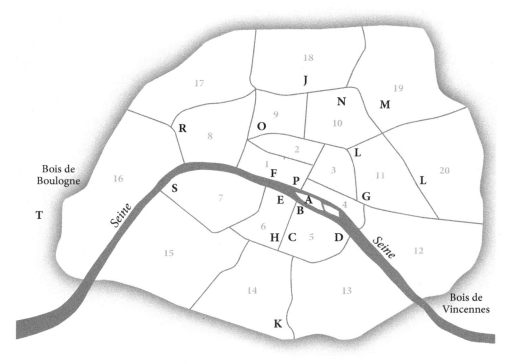

PARIS
Key

A. Ile de la Cité and Notre-Dame
B. Sorbonne and Latin Quarter
C. Panthéon
D. Jardin des Plantes
E. Saint-Germain-des-Prés
F. The Louvre
G. Place de la Bastille
H. Luxembourg Gardens
J. Sacré-Coeur
K. Parc Montsouris
L. Père-Lachaise
M. Parc des Buttes Chaumont
N. Gare de l'Est
O. Opéra Garnier
P. Place du Châtelet
R. Arc de Triomphe and Place Charles-de-Gaulle
S. Eiffel Tower
T. Parc de Saint-Cloud

Paris's twenty arrondissements are indicated by number.

© J. McAuliffe

Paris Coat of Arms, Basilica of Sacré-Coeur. © J. McAuliffe

~

Introduction

Beginnings

Paris, as Victor Hugo once observed, was born on the island of the Ile de la Cité—a small slice of land that he likened to the shape of a cradle, gently rocked by the River Seine. Others, especially those among Paris's powerful medieval guild of water merchants, were more inclined to regard the Ile de la Cité as boat shaped. These folks, who slapped a hefty fee on all incoming goods arriving in Paris by water, held boats in high regard and placed one at the center of the city's coat of arms, where it remains to this day.

Whichever shape you choose, Paris had its beginnings here more than two millennia ago. In this spot—a hill-ringed basin lying at the Seine's confluence with the Oise and the Marne—a Celtic tribe known as the Parisii established themselves around 250 B.C., fishing, boating, and generally prospering in this watery locale. Two centuries later, their settlement caught the attention of the Romans, who understood the area's strategic importance and relentlessly pushed in, incorporating it into the Roman Empire under the name of Lutetia.

Paris's Gallo-Roman years now began, with the Romans building bridges (at the sites of the present Petit Pont and the Pont Notre-Dame) that connected the island with Right and Left Banks and erecting a temple and administrative buildings on the Ile de la Cité. During these years, the conquered Celts mingled with their Roman conquerors, and many even became Roman citizens. The result was a culture that we now call "Gallo-Roman," a term that acknowledges Roman influence on Gaul's conquered people,

1

Ile de la Cité and Ile Saint-Louis from Right Bank. © M. McAuliffe

including those of Lutetia, who became Romanized without entirely losing their Celtic ways.

Unlike the Celts, though, the Romans did not live on the flood-prone island, nor on the soggy marshes of the Seine's banks. Instead, they set up a small metropolis in their usual style, including a forum, public baths, and an amphitheater on the Left Bank hill now known as Montagne Sainte-Geneviève. To boost their water supply, they built an impressive aqueduct bringing in spring water from the south.

Barbarians on the march attacked the Left Bank settlement several times in the third and fourth centuries, at about the same time as the arrival of St. Denis, the town's first Christian bishop, who added a new element to the mix. Although St. Denis' mission to Lutetia ended in martyrdom, he succeeded in creating a foothold for Christianity. And as the Empire crumbled and Roman influence waned, Christianity played an ever-growing role in keeping Lutetia (now called Paris, after the Celtic Parisii) from going under. By the sixth century, following the conversion of Clovis I, King of the Franks, forerunners of some of Paris's most famous churches and abbeys were beginning to appear. Following the Roman precedent of establishing official buildings at the western end of the Ile de la Cité and religious structures to the east, Parisian Christians erected their churches at the eastern end of the island and a royal palace to the west.

By the late ninth century, when Paris had once again begun to prosper, the sails of Viking dragon ships now appeared on the Seine, striking terror as they came. The entire population of Paris retreated to the walled Cité as its men fought the Viking besiegers. After plundering the town and receiving a large ransom, the Vikings moved on, but a century of political disruption and chaos followed.

It took time, but by the twelfth century, Paris had revived and even begun to thrive. And it is from this time that the city of Paris really began.

Square du Vert-Galant. © J. McAuliffe

~

CHAPTER ONE

The Heart of Paris

The Ile de la Cité has been the heart of Paris for more than two millennia, and this is where I would like to begin my tale—at the western tip of this small island, descending down steep stairs to a spot that I treasure, the **Square du Vert-Galant**.

This tiny triangle, located down all those stairsteps from the Pont Neuf, attracts lovers, Parisians in search of quiet, and tourists in the know, especially in the morning hours, when it is at its most peaceful. Classes of schoolchildren may arrive for picnic lunch, and curiosity-seekers from the nearby Vedettes du Pont Neuf sometimes wander in. As the day progresses, university students arrive and gravitate to the island's tip, which culminates at a level somewhat below the park's own point. Marked by a large willow, the view here is spectacular, taking in the Louvre, the Pont des Arts, and the Institut de France in one sweep.

This small park is rightly named for Henri IV, the monarch whose statue rises from the central portion of the Pont Neuf above. "Vert Galant" refers to Henri's amorous reputation, for although he was not a handsome man, he seems to have had a way with the ladies. These in turn were not reluctant to receive his attentions, as a topless portrait of one of his mistresses, Gabrielle d'Estrées (with her sister, in their bath), clearly shows. This rather raunchy painting from the distant past is something you can look for in the Louvre that will take you off its well-trodden path. The last time I looked, Gabrielle and her sister were far from the *Mona Lisa*, in the Richelieu Wing.

As for the bridge above you, the **Pont Neuf**, or New Bridge, has quite a story. Its genesis goes back to the reign of Henri III, who laid its first stone in 1578. Spanning the Seine had never been easy, and this king and his engineers had a wealth of bad examples to avoid. Throughout the centuries, a series of bridges, first of wood, then of stone, had either burned or collapsed under the weight of the multistoried houses and shops that lined their sides. Floodwaters of the Seine did the rest. And so, when the idea of a new span across the Seine arose, Henri III and his engineers decided to embrace a different kind of bridge, one without houses along it, wide enough for pedestrian walkways, and built solidly of stone. It was meant to be a thing of beauty and a source of civic and royal pride.

There certainly was need for a bridge crossing the western tip of the Ile de la Cité. For years, the only way across the Seine in this part of town was a ferry (the name Rue du Bac on the Left Bank retains this memory). But unlike earlier bridges, which spanned the Seine at its narrowest points, this one had a broad stretch of water to cover—in addition to the difficulty of crossing the marshy tip of the Ile de la Cité.

Henri III's elaborate scheme never came to pass. The religious and civil warfare that had been tearing France apart continued unabated, and in 1589, the king himself was murdered. Henri of Navarre, champion of the Huguenots, or French Protestants, claimed the crown, but he had to fight for it. After unsuccessfully besieging Paris, he at length agreed to convert to Catholicism—a shrewd move that ensured him his coronation as Henri IV. Thoroughly pragmatic, this Henri had no problem with a purely political solution to virtual anarchy. Paris, as he so famously remarked, was well worth a Mass.

Not until 1599 did construction on the Pont Neuf really begin—this time under the aegis of a king who dearly loved Paris and who already was embarked on a massive building program to enhance her beauty. Henri IV retained his predecessor's expansive vision, if not his exact specifications, and soon the waterlogged area at the Cité's tip was drained and several islets joined into what now is the Square du Vert-Galant. A massive terrace was then built to support the central portion of the new bridge—a striking stone structure completed in 1607, whose broad promenade, attractive niches, and pedestrian sidewalks (a first) drew crowds of strollers, peddlers, and revelers, who could enjoy anything from a tooth-pulling to fireworks entertaining royalty at the nearby Palais du Louvre.

It's ironic that the Pont Neuf, or New Bridge, is anything but new. Over the course of four hardworking centuries, it has been reconstructed and renovated, most recently in a massive project completed in 2007, the four-hundredth anniversary of the bridge's first inauguration. In design, the Pont Neuf still is old—as close to original as humanly possible. In actual structural materials, it is now mostly new, although perhaps astonishingly, its original wooden piles (well reinforced) still remain.

As does that small triangle of greenery beneath it, that secret spot where one can escape the city's push and shove. From your vantage point in the Square du Vert-Galant, you can see the vast stretch of the Louvre on the Seine's right bank, whose enormous riverside gallery Henri IV built as part of his vision for a breathtaking entrance to Paris from the west. His plan, when completed, included not only this addition to the Louvre and the Pont Neuf, but also Place Dauphine, an innovative open-air triangle of brick-and-stone town houses that rises just to the east of the Pont Neuf.

Henri made his impact on other parts of town as well, as I will explore. "I make war, I make love, and I build," this monarch once remarked, and having established peace, good government, and prosperity throughout France, he devoted his attentions to the vast building program that still defines this and other parts of Paris today.

Henri IV was a popular monarch—"A chicken in every pot every Sunday" he is said to have promised, and he did his best to keep his word. Unfortunately, he was hated as well, by extremists, religious fanatics, and schemers of all sorts. After surviving multiple attacks during his reign (nineteen in all), he was finally assassinated by a religious fanatic gripped by visions, who leaped into Henri's carriage and drove his knife deep into the king's heart. You can still see the place where it happened, marked by a large marble slab in the center of the street at 11 Rue de la Ferronnerie (1st).

Paris and all of France deeply and genuinely mourned his death. Henri le Grand, they call him, one of the greatest, and certainly the most beloved of French kings. One you can remember as you sit on your bench in the tiny park named in his memory, looking out at the boats and barges as they pass slowly by.

～

The Ile de la Cité has undergone vast changes over the centuries, most especially during the mid-nineteenth-century reign of Bonaparte's nephew, Napoleon III. At this time, virtually half the island succumbed to the wrecking ball under the direction of the emperor's right-hand man, Baron Georges Haussmann. Both Pont Saint-Michel (arched, narrow, and once lined with houses) and the equally narrow and shop-lined Pont au Change were completely rebuilt, while the street that took traffic from the Pont au Change onto the island was widened and became the Boulevard du Palais. Another new street, the Rue de Lutèce, extended eastward from it, bordering a newly razed section that became the police prefecture. (Georges Simenon's fictional Inspector Maigret famously had his offices across the way, at 36 Quai des Orfèvres.) Haussmann planned to carry on his demolition westward to the Pont Neuf, leveling Place Dauphine in the process, but he did not get that far. Still, by the time Haussmann had finished with it, the island's population had shrunk by 75 percent, from around twenty thousand to five thousand, and the island itself had become a virtual administrative center.

Dominating the island's eastern end, the great cathedral of **Notre-Dame de Paris** is still, as of this writing, undergoing massive rebuilding and restoration following the fire of 2019 that almost destroyed it. When once again it is restored to its former glory, including a spire that we are promised will look much like its beloved predecessor, the construction work and fences will disappear, and we will be able to view Notre-Dame as before, its façade facing westward across a vast open square.

Notre-Dame of course underwent massive restoration once before, in the mid-nineteenth century, thanks to the prodding of Victor Hugo. His best-selling 1831 novel, *Notre-Dame de Paris* (the original title of *The Hunchback of Notre-Dame*), made a *cause célèbre* of the dying cathedral, which over the course of seven centuries had become dark, dismal, and sadly neglected. Revolutionary mobs had done the most serious damage, making off with or destroying anything within reach, but there were also destructive acts of a more calculated sort, most notably the mutilation of the cathedral's grand central portal, hacked apart to allow easier passage of processionals. Moreover, as an expert on the subject has pointed out, the masonry throughout the structure was in a "lamentable state."[1]

Responding to popular demand, the government agreed to underwrite a huge restoration program, and Jean-Baptiste Lassus and Eugène Viollet-le-Duc won the competition to lead this all-important project (both had previously worked together on restoring the delicate beauty of nearby Sainte-Chapelle). Both men, much like Victor Hugo, were enthusiasts of Gothic rather than neoclassical Greek and Roman architecture, and both were dedicated to remaining true to the original concept behind Notre-Dame. But Lassus died during the early portion of this project, leaving Viollet-le-Duc to carry on alone.

Although Viollet-le-Duc was only thirty years old and with no degree in architecture when he set to work on Notre-Dame (he had flat-out refused to attend the Ecole des Beaux-Arts on the grounds that it was tied too rigidly to neoclassicism and churned out unimaginative architects), he had already established himself in the field of architectural restoration. He had received practical experience at an architectural firm and traveled, drawing extensively (buildings and their ornamentation) before entering on restoration work, starting with the abbey church of Vézelay and moving on to Sainte-Chapelle in Paris as well as the chapel at the Château d'Amboise that held Leonardo da Vinci's tomb.

The restoration of Notre-Dame drew upon Viollet-le-Duc's talent for meticulous research as well as for informed inspiration. He made careful drawings and took photographs of the damaged sculptures, whether on the façade or the interior, most of which had to be removed and re-created from scratch by a large team of sculptors. Those years of careful observation and drawing allowed him to fill in the blanks where only blanks remained, whether gargoyles on the drain spouts and chimeras on the cathedral roof, or statues of saints throughout the edifice. He rebuilt entire sections of the cathedral, repaired and replaced windows, and positioned a taller and more ornate spire over the transept, replacing one that had been removed for safety reasons many years before.

Aiding the effort, fragments of the cathedral's original sculpture began to turn up during the project's early stages, providing essential references for restoration. As for the rest, Viollet-le-Duc's imagination filled the gaps. The work would go on for two decades, and some would complain that not all of Viollet-le-Duc's production was accurate and that his imagination sometimes got the better of him. Yet whether or not the restored Notre-Dame of Viollet-le-Duc is the Notre-Dame of the thirteenth century, the outcome—the result of almost twenty years of meticulous research and inevitable guesswork—was the beloved Notre-Dame that lasted until 2019.

When we once again can visit the newly rebuilt and restored Notre-Dame, be sure to search out its treasures. One of these is the north portal, known as the **Coronation of the Virgin**. Throughout the years, crowds have hastily exited the cathedral through this doorway, one of the cathedral's masterpieces, scarcely giving it a glance. Take the time to give it a good look, at its saints (including Saint-Denis, holding his head, and Sainte-Geneviève, patron saint of Paris), and especially at those tiny figures along the doorposts, which are some of the few surviving figures from the original cathedral of eight centuries ago. I love these, because they show us what the common people looked like then, dressed in tunics and leggings while hauling wood, hammering a beam, or making wine. A single maiden in a long gown represents Virgo, while another woman, huddled in a cloak, represents winter. For those who take the time to look, these richly carved doorposts—a small but significant portion of this magnificently carved doorway—give a glimpse of the long-distant past.

~

When it is once again possible, stand in the Place du Parvis facing Notre-Dame. Stand close, for originally this was the way Notre-Dame was meant to be seen. Before Baron Haussmann flattened an entire neighborhood to create a far vaster cathedral square, or even before Notre-Dame acquired its famed flying buttresses, the people of Paris approached their cathedral through narrow byways, catching glimpses of a portal here or a tower there, until at last they stood before the western façade and looked up. And up and up. For this was a cathedral built to be seen and appreciated from below, not from afar.

You will also be standing on history, for beneath your feet lie the remains of the ancient cathedral that preceded Notre-Dame. Excavations for an underground parking garage have uncovered a dense patchwork of archaeological ruins going back to Gallo-Roman times, including bits and pieces of the foundations of another, older cathedral. Long buried beneath the rubble of the centuries, these dusty bricks and stones help to tell the complex story of this eastern tip of the Ile de la Cité and of Notre-Dame's early years.

You can visit these remnants of a distant past in the nearby **Crypte Archéologique**, which has the distinct advantage of providing a quiet spot below ground in the midst of what often is a bedlam of tourists above.

However, there are some clues aboveground, on the *parvis*, to help you better understand what you are about to view below. You probably are familiar with the octagonal brass plate reading "Point Zero des Routes de France," which marks the center of Paris and from which all distances in France, to or from Paris, are measured. It's a popular place to make wishes, so there usually is a crowd here. But nearby and virtually ignored are the stones and a plaque indicating a portion of the layout of Notre-Dame's predecessor, the ancient (and huge) **Cathedral of Saint-Etienne**. This cathedral, portions of which were first discovered during Viollet-le-Duc's renovations of Notre-Dame, dates from the remote sixth century, and possibly even earlier. Majestically proportioned, it stretched some 118 feet wide by 230 feet long—although its exact length will always remain a question, as this early cathedral's eastern end completely disappeared during Notre-Dame's construction. Dedicated to Saint-Etienne, or Saint Stephen, this extraordinary structure gloried in decorations of marble and mosaic, whose remnants (along with fragments of Notre-Dame's original sculpture) you can find in the nearby Musée du Moyen Age.

No one knows exactly what happened to this ancient cathedral, but it may still have been in reasonably good shape when Maurice de Sully became bishop of Paris in 1160. Sully, a man of humble origins who had begged for food during his student years in Paris, was a dynamo with vision. Bishops throughout France, most especially Abbot Suger of the nearby abbey church of Saint-Denis, were in a building mode by the middle years of the twelfth century, and Sully was not to be outdone. An organizational genius, he quickly realized that to construct a new cathedral in the already-dense urban fabric of the Ile de la Cité would require a major effort in what we today would call urban planning. Not only did he plan, build, and finance an enormous and pathbreaking cathedral within his own lifetime, but he also altered the entire cityscape on this end of the island, erecting and demolishing buildings with tornado force.

By the time of his death in 1196, Sully had leveled the old Bishop's Palace and Hôtel-Dieu (charity hospital) and rebuilt them in far grander style on a strip of land outside the ancient Gallo-Roman walls to the south of his new cathedral—on land that was so marshy that foundations had to plunge thirty feet below the surface for secure footing. To provide sufficient land for the new cathedral's choir and apse, Sully used landfill to extend the Ile de la Cité eastward, joining it with a small island just offshore. And then, with remarkable persistence, he negotiated his way through a welter of irate property-holders to pierce a new street with the then-unheard-of width of twenty feet, right to Notre-Dame's front door. One of these property-holders, a widow by the name of Pétronille, owned several houses along this proposed route and dragged negotiations out for thirty years—almost until Sully's death. In the end, the good bishop won, and Rue Neuve-Notre-Dame was built.

Remnants of the **Rue Neuve-Notre-Dame** are outlined on the Place du Parvis and can be found in the Crypte Archéologique, along with remnants of the fourth-century A.D. **Gallo-Roman walls** built to protect the town, then called Lutetia, from barbarian attacks. Erecting sturdy fortifications around the Ile de la Cité as well as their nearby forum, the Gallo-Romans eventually turned the entire town into a military outpost.

Nothing remains aboveground of the forum or its defensive walls, which encompassed the Left Bank area from Rue Soufflot to Rue Cujas, between Rue Saint-Jacques and Boulevard Saint-Michel. But here in the Crypte Archéologique, you can see the remains of the wall that once encircled the Ile de la Cité. Remember that the Cité was a far smaller and lower place two millennia ago, before Seine silt and human landfill did their work. You can find another trace of Roman wall on Rue de la Colombe, on the Cité's northern side.

The atmosphere here, well below the Cité's present surface, is quiet, as those few who venture down here whisper as they gaze at the remnants of a far different world from our own. We are exploring a tomb that is not a tomb, one that preserves the shells of long-ago lives—their homes and the evidence they left behind, including coins, tools, utensils, and jewelry. Here are the remains of Gallo-Roman streets and heating systems, medieval houses, and buildings built upon other buildings, layer upon layer, century upon century.

It's a good place to let your imagination go to work.

I have not forgotten the shimmering thirteenth-century chapel of **Sainte-Chapelle**, at the heart of the huge structure that at various times in its history has housed royalty and imprisoned others (most famously, Marie Antoinette). The Conciergerie contains a somber fourteenth-century Salles des Gardes and Salle des Gens-d'Armes, the latter having originally served as a refectory. But if you brave the lines of tourists, you can visit the lovely Sainte-Chapelle, built by Louis IX (Saint Louis) as a royal chapel in the courtyard of the royal palace, to house precious relics such as the Crown of Thorns and fragments of the True Cross (later moved to Notre-Dame's sacristy and, since the 2019 fire, to the Louvre).

Emerging from either of the narrow tower staircases into the upper level of Sainte-Chapelle can be a startling experience, like entering the interior of a jewel box. The small but glorious interior seems to consist almost entirely of stained glass, whose colors vibrate in the sunshine (do visit on a sunny day). Originally reserved for the royal family, leaving the lower level to the servants and other lesser beings, this chapel directly connected to Louis's royal chambers. Damaged over the centuries, from fires and during the French Revolution, Sainte-Chapelle was restored over the course of three decades in the mid-1800s by Lassus and Viollet-le-Duc but was severely damaged (along with the gardens and woods of Versailles) by hurricane-force winds that swept through in 1999, leveling millions of trees throughout France. Thankfully, the chapel has been carefully restored.

While in the Palais de Justice, which surrounds Sainte-Chapelle, try to find the **Chambre Dorée**, a historic room that now functions as the First Civil Court of the Court of Appeals (located at one corner of the grand Salle des Pas Perdus). Originally the bedchamber of Louis IX, it was grandly renovated by Louis XII for his marriage to Mary Tudor, daughter of England's Henry VII, and was so magnificent that it earned its name as the Chambre Dorée, or Golden Room.

Ironically, it was here, in these grand surroundings, that the Revolutionary Tribunal condemned Marie Antoinette to death.

After the Palais de Justice burned during the Commune uprising of 1871, the entire building was rebuilt and restored, including this courtroom, reconstructed identically to its original gilded Renaissance décor. It's an unexpected treasure.

~

By now you will be in need of some grass and trees, and although there is a pleasant strip alongside the south and east of Notre-Dame, named for Pope Jean (John) XXIII, this is usually pretty packed. Instead, I recommend that you turn toward the dour and unpromising-looking building to the north of the *parvis*, the **Hôtel-Dieu de Paris**, founded more than a millennium ago—making it the oldest continually operating hospital in the world.

This, of course, is not the original building. Back in the twelfth century, when Bishop Sully was sending Notre-Dame heavenward and rearranging this end of the island, he moved the disparate buildings then constituting the Hôtel-Dieu to a site just to the south of Notre-Dame, along with a new and far-grander Bishop's Palace. This land was marshy, outside the ancient Roman walls, and the new foundations had to plunge deep below the surface for secure footing, but they held firm. The Hôtel-Dieu, a charity hospital that provided the poor with food and shelter as well as caring for the ill, remained on this site for centuries, growing to include large structures on both sides of this small southern arm of the Seine. By the nineteenth century, squashed between Notre-Dame and the river, this by-now enormous structure had become a dark and sinister edifice that crammed some eight hundred patients inside, polluting the river with a deluge of hospital waste. Baron Haussmann, who worried about hygiene, wanted to move it completely from the Ile de la Cité, but the emperor, Napoleon III, preferred to keep it in the city's center. In the end, the Hôtel-Dieu moved to the other side of the island, where it now overlooks the northern (and wider) arm of the Seine.

Remarkably, this building encloses an unexpectedly large and lovely garden in its center. Just inside the front door you will see, straight ahead, this extensive garden at the hospital's core, one of the best-kept secrets in Paris. On its lower level, walkways border elaborate scrolls of clipped boxwood that in turn enclose beds of bright flowers. These lead to a palatial rise of steps, which in turn open onto a magnificently cloistered courtyard. When I have visited, this had a piano at its far end—in addition to a statue that, I understand, is regularly dressed in costume by the hospital interns. The idea is to provide greenery (and humor) in addition to music in support of healing, and it is an admirable addition to the hospital's more usual therapeutic methods.

In addition, you may want to visit the galleries bordering the courtyard, where there are pictures and text giving a fascinating history of medical treatment in this facility from earliest times. You may encounter a doctor

Garden-courtyard of the Hôtel-Dieu. © J. McAuliffe

or two scurrying from one closed door to another as you stroll along, but otherwise these halls are virtually deserted. As I looked carefully at the series of plaques and illustrations, I especially noted one picture that showed the huge and forbidding building that preceded this one, on the south arm of the Seine, and a very early picture showing an arrangement of multiple invalids per bed. They look pleased to be there, and in those days, no one would have found this arrangement at all unusual.

Speaking of beds, I was intrigued to learn that the Hôpital Hôtel-Dieu provides budget overnight accommodations (fourteen rooms) for guests who do not need to be related to any patients currently under care there. The pandemic, of course, may have put a stop to all that.

⌣

Baron Haussmann did not succeed in wiping out all of the Ile de la Cité's ancient past, and as you exit the Hôpital Hôtel-Dieu, you can see remnants of the canonical close that occupied the land north of the cathedral to the river. Here, in a community surrounded by walls, the cathedral canons (clergy) lived in individual houses with their own plots of land, holdings that the industrious residents increased over the years by reclaiming the marshes along the riverside and building up a significant retaining wall. The Musée Carnavalet, the museum of the history of Paris, has a fine painting of this setup dating from around 1755.

The ancient Rue Chanoinesse takes you through the heart of this quarter, with its narrow lanes and astonishing conjunction of rooftops. The medieval canons' houses at 23 and 24 Rue Chanoinesse are especially evocative, as is the corner of Rue des Chantres at Rue des Ursins, which marks the site of the house (9-11 Quai aux Fleurs) belonging to Fulbert, where two medallions representing **Abelard and Heloise** gaze out from above the doors. Fulbert was a cathedral canon and uncle of Heloise, with whom Abelard fell "all in fire with love" in the early years of the twelfth century. Arrogant and attractive, Abelard already was famous as a teacher and disputer (debater), and Fulbert, all unsuspecting, leaped at Abelard's offer to tutor Heloise, who was as brilliant as she was beautiful. This offer came with rooms for Abelard in Fulbert's house, and the inevitable happened. The two fell passionately in love, and Heloise became pregnant.

Abelard promptly spirited her away to his sister in Brittany, where Heloise gave birth to a son, whom the besotted parents named Astrolabe—an unusual name even for those times. (In a footnote to their love affair, their son—raised in Brittany—may have become an abbot.) Fulbert allowed the lovers to wed but then took his revenge, sending thugs to seize and castrate

Abelard—a shocking retaliation, even by medieval standards. Heloise, distraught, became a nun, but she never ceased to yearn for him. In turn, Abelard entered a monastery, but he promptly stirred up one disastrous confrontation after another. For many years the two did not even communicate, but at length, after learning that Heloise's convent was in need of a new home, Abelard unexpectedly offered up the teaching hermitage of Le Paraclet that he had established in Champagne. She accepted, and they met for the first time since the tragedy.

It was a difficult encounter, in which Abelard insisted that Heloise forget the past. Reluctantly, she came to accept his advice and, in time, became a renowned abbess. Abelard returned to teaching in Paris, establishing a school on the Left Bank. His school, along with those of Notre-Dame and the nearby abbey of Saint-Victor, gave Paris a concentration of educational riches that within a century would lead to the founding of the University of Paris. No trace of Abelard's school remains, but a few vestiges of his Paris have survived the centuries.

Among these is the tiny **Chapel of Saint-Aignan**, hidden behind a locked gate at nearby 19 Rue des Ursins. Beyond that gate is a small courtyard and an inconspicuous doorway into what at first looks like the cellar of a house. But behind that door is a small jewel of a chapel, built in the early 1120s by Etienne de Garlande, archdeacon of the cathedral and chancellor to the king. This chapel, near Garlande's house in the canonical quarter, was all that a man of his power and wealth could make it—a miniature masterpiece of early Parisian architecture. Daringly, Garlande had it built just outside the ancient Gallo-Roman city wall. By his time, barbarian and Viking attacks were a thing of the past, and the king had effectively restrained marauding noblemen. But the Seine still flooded regularly, and anything beyond the old walls was particularly vulnerable. Nonetheless, Garlande boldly filled in the marshy area to the north and built his chapel there.

Centuries passed, and after the Revolution (which stripped Saint-Aignan of its ecclesiastical purposes), the chapel fell on hard times. Sadly, it became a storeroom and stable for a house, with both structures plastered over to look like one building. Fortunately, a recent owner recognized the chapel's worth and gave it back to the diocese. After a cleaning and careful restoration, it now serves as a chapel for the nearby Seminaire de Paris.

If you are fortunate enough to be in Paris during Paris's Journées du Patrimoine each September, you may find Saint-Aignan open to visitors. It is also occasionally open for small exhibitions. If so, don't miss the opportunity to enter this tiny space, dimly lit with lamps strategically placed to illumine its Romanesque vaults (reaching fourteen feet above the floor) and its carvings, including stylized leaves, cut confidently and deep, crowning the capitals of the larger columns in the Corinthian manner. Only a master carver could have created these intricate beauties, and some think that he must have been Burgundian, trained in a Cluniac abbey workshop. By the time Garlande began to build his chapel, Cluniac style had come to represent the pinnacle of good taste, and Garlande certainly had both the eminence and the wealth to attract such talent to his door.

Whatever his identity, a talented carver seems to have been responsible for most of the sculpture in Saint-Aignan, although a less deft carver appears to have created the somewhat crude but friendly array of animals that crown the chapel's smaller columns. These include a monkey or monkey-like man with a bulging tummy, a winged griffin, and two friendly lions, their paws just touching. Someone had a good deal of fun with these figures, especially the monkey, which may have closely resembled an associate—possibly even one of the clerics.

Some speculate that Heloise, who lived close by with her uncle Fulbert, may have prayed and met Abelard here, nine centuries ago. Yet even without this *frisson* of romance, Saint-Aignan is extraordinary. Now classified as a *monument historique*, this chapel remains a rare relic from the distant past.

Some time ago, I encountered several medieval Jewish gravestones at Paris's Musée du Moyen Age, and they intrigued me. It was a vivid reminder that there had been a significant Jewish presence in Paris in medieval times and even earlier, under the Gallo-Romans. There originally was a small Jewish community, synagogue, and cemetery on the Left Bank, but in Abelard and Heloise's time, and as Notre-Dame was going up, the main Jewish community in Paris was here on the Ile de la Cité. I have seen conflicting views on where this exactly lay, but best evidence points to the current Rue de la Cité, then called the Rue de la Juiverie (Street of the Jews), along which was a synagogue. By the 1170s there were twenty-four houses in this area occupied by Jews, some of whom may have been bakers, because there were at the time numerous bakeshops there. But this community's most important activity would have been moneylending, and this location, in the heart of the student quarter, would have provided plenty of business.

In theory, this activity would not have been a problem, as officially, under King Louis VII, there was little anti-Semitism in Paris, and this Jewish community was allowed to thrive. But unofficially there must have been festering antagonism towards this prospering community in the shadow of Notre-Dame, because soon after young Philip Augustus came to the throne, he sent the Jews into exile, officially confiscating their twenty-four houses. He brought Paris's Jews back briefly, after which they settled on the Right Bank, in a quarter we will look at shortly, and then he expelled them once again.

A roller-coaster cycle of expulsion and return followed for centuries until the French Revolution, when France's Jews became full citizens. But even the 1905 official separation of church (Roman Catholic) and state in France did not wipe out the latent anti-Semitism there, which boiled up in the Dreyfus Affair (1894 to 1906) and, even more violently, under the Vichy Regime during Germany's Occupation of France (1940–1944). During these horrific years, thousands of Jewish men, women, and children were rounded up and crammed together under ghastly conditions in the infamous Vélodrome d'Hiver, or Vél d'Hiv, a covered cycling arena in the fifteenth arrondissement that the Nazis and their French collaborators used as a staging area for the death camps. (A moving memorial to these victims, the Place-des-Martyrs-Juifs-du-Vélodrome d'Hiver, now rests near this spot.)[2] From there the authorities sent them to the notorious Drancy transit camp just outside of Paris, where boxcars waited to take them to the death camps. A Holocaust Memorial at Drancy includes an old boxcar typical of those used to transport the tens of thousands of French Jews, while a museum dedicated to these victims of the Holocaust is located nearby.

At the eastern tip of the Ile de la Cité is the **Mémorial des Martyrs de la Déportation** (Memorial to the Martyrs of the Deportation), a stark underground memorial to the approximately two hundred thousand people deported to the Nazi death camps from Vichy France during the German Occupation. Many were Jewish immigrants who had fled from Hitler's Germany and Austria, while others were members of the French Resistance or political opponents, such as Léon Blum, France's first Jewish and first Socialist prime minister. He was sent to the Buchenwald death camp—where his wife joined him, and where both miraculously survived.

Walk silently down the stone steps surrounded by harsh concrete walls and you will find yourself facing an oppressive spiked iron portcullis overlooking the Seine, at the island's eastern tip. A narrow, claustrophobic entry leads to a small, dimly lit chamber, which in turn opens onto a long, narrow space, faintly lit with tightly packed crystals, each symbolizing a deportee who died in the death camps. At the foot, in somber silence, lies the tomb of the Unknown Deportee.

This is a memorial to incomprehensible tragedy, but at the chamber's far end is a single bright light representing the eternal flame of hope. The message as you exit is "Forgive, but never forget."

Here in this spot, hollowed out of the island that was the birthplace of Paris, is a memorial that everyone should visit, but few do. It is almost always quiet and peaceful here, a refuge from the nearby crowds. Here you may silently contemplate as you gaze at the Seine, the beating heart of Paris, as it sweeps silently by.

Garden and charnel house of Saint-Séverin. © M. McAuliffe

CHAPTER TWO

~

The Latin Quarter and Beyond

Even back in the twelfth century, Paris's Latin Quarter was a hectic place, with street criers bellowing, beggars begging, carts and horses trampling, and black-gowned students, always late for classes, racing through the crush.

The quarter received its name from the language the teachers and students all spoke, Latin being the only common language among the babble of other languages spoken throughout Western Christendom. Latin provided a form of lingual order, much as the Roman Catholic Church provided an international form of political order during the chaotic early years following the collapse of the Roman Empire—and prior to the emergence of strong nation-states. Remember that France itself, even as late as the eleventh and early twelfth centuries, consisted of little more than the lands around Paris—the Ile de France—which the Capetian monarchs controlled. Even this was under threat from local noblemen, and during the early years of his reign, Louis VI thought carefully before leaving his palace on the well-defended Ile de la Cité.

Wooden houses densely packed the narrow streets and lined the Petit Pont, which connected the Ile de la Cité to the Left Bank. This diminutive bridge looked very different then, with shops and houses along its sides, and with teachers such as the famed Adam du Petit Pont holding forth to students jammed around their doorsteps. At that time, this was the only bridge connecting the Left Bank to the island. Until the fourteenth century, a small but meaningful fortification (the Petit Châtelet) blocked the bridge's southern entrance from traffic arriving along the old Roman road from Orléans, guarding the Ile de la Cité on its southern side. It was Louis VI who erected this fortification as well as another more massive one (the Grand Châtelet) at the Ile de la Cité's northern approach. By the end of this determined monarch's long reign, he had, piece by piece, secured Paris and its immediate environs.

Nowadays, there is no guardhouse, and crowds surge unimpeded across the Petit Pont. Few among them notice the small park nearby, the **Square René-Viviani**, with its splendid views of Notre-Dame. The square also boasts an ancient *robinia* (black locust tree), reputedly planted in 1602, that has survived the centuries to become one of the oldest trees in Paris. But the square's real treasure is the adjoining twelfth-century church of **Saint-Julien-le-Pauvre**, built on the ruins of a far older predecessor. Here students assembled during the University of Paris's earliest days, to hold their disputations. Here as well, centuries of students attended morning Mass before racing off to classes. The church's façade has crumbled, exposing an ancient well to the right of the entry, but jagged remnants of the early structure still hauntingly remain. Originally a Roman Catholic church, St-Julien-le-Pauvre has become an Eastern Catholic Melkite place of worship. It has also become a treasured venue for small classical concerts, a place to sit in peace and quiet contemplation.

The neighborhood, although considerably gentrified, has managed to survive the centuries, including Haussmann's nearby demolitions, and is one of the most ancient in Paris. The rooftops across from the church are among my favorites in the city. And around the corner is tiny **Rue Galande**, a cobbled lane that lies along an early Roman roadway to the south. For centuries it was jammed with tavern-seekers, loiterers, and travelers. Traditionally, many of the quarter's numerous students also congregated here, and while doubtless some of them were up to no good, a respectable number were simply trying to get to classes in the Rue du Fouarre just beyond. There, in the early Middle Ages, students met in the open air, sitting on bundles of straw or whatever was available as they listened to their lecturers.

Pause for a moment at 42 Rue Galande and look up. There you will find a fourteenth-century bas-relief of **St. Julien and his wife** rowing Christ across the Seine. According to legend, St. Julien had an unusually dark history, having been warned in his youth that he would in time kill both his father and mother. To prevent this terrible fate, he departed into exile; but his parents disregarded his pleas and managed to bring him home. Unfortunately, they returned to his house without him (he seems to have been temporarily drawn away on other business). Instead, they were greeted by his new wife, who graciously gave them the newlyweds' bed (being the best in the house).

They promptly fell asleep, where they were found by their son, who thought it was his wife and a lover. In a rage, he killed them.

Bad mistake. In anguish, Julien again went into exile, this time with his repentant wife, and vowed to help the poor, in an effort to assuage his terrible crime. One day the two encountered a leper, who asked them to carry him across the river—which river, we do not know, but long believed by Parisians to be the Seine. Lepers, being highly contagious as well as unpleasant to look upon, were shunned in medieval times, but Julien and his wife had compassion on him. This proved to be their reward, for once in the boat, a halo appeared above the leper's head; it was the Christ, and Julien was forgiven his sins.

In time, sainthood followed, commemorating Julien's goodness in helping the poor (Saint Julien le Pauvre, or the Poor). His wife did not similarly achieve sainthood, but one hopes that she was suitably gratified by this turn of events.

Near Rue Galande is a warren of small streets untouched by Haussmann, including the Rue de la Parcheminerie, home in medieval times of scribes, manuscript copyists, and parchment dealers. At the center of this ancient area is the **Church of Saint-Séverin**, portions of which date from the thirteenth century, including its tower foundations and the first bays of its nave. To especially savor this church's antiquity, enter at the eastern end, or ambulatory, to find yourself in another world. Here, carved columns soar upward into a complex forest of vaults, dimly lit by the surrounding stained-glass windows. Saint-Séverin's bells include one of the oldest in Paris, cast in 1412.

Easy to overlook is the small walled garden adjoining the church, a haven in this heavily touristed and clamorous quarter. Surrounding it is a Gothic covered gallery that once was a charnel house, built around what once was the church's cemetery (because of limited space, bones were removed from the cemetery and stored in the charnel house, to make room for new burials). The cemetery has since disappeared, along with all the others in the city—the remains taken to the Catacombs, then on the city's outskirts, as part of a massive effort to eliminate the city's overflowing burial grounds. What remains is a small peaceful garden, a shady oasis in this colorful but often crowded part of Old Paris.

Remnants of Paris's Gallo-Roman past were scattered throughout medieval Paris, but their meaning was long forgotten by the time long-ago students and their teachers swarmed through the Latin Quarter. These baffling ruins from another time intrigued the people of medieval Paris, who conjured up unlikely tales to explain their presence. The forum, for example, was believed to have been the family home of Ganelon, legendary betrayer of Charlemagne's noble henchman, Roland. Moreover, when it came to practical matters, medieval Parisians could not be bothered with preservation. Many of the stones from these ruins disappeared into Paris's twelfth-century wall, and even the Gallo-Romans helped themselves to stones from their public buildings to bolster Lutetia's third-century fortifications.

Time and neglect buried the rest, and when in 1711 workers digging a vault beneath Notre-Dame's choir discovered five large carved blocks of stone dedicated to the Roman god Jupiter and dating from the reign of Emperor Tiberius, it created a sensation. Those eagerly deciphering the roughly carved Latin inscription learned that these stones, which originally were mounted on top of one another, had been erected early in the first century A.D. by the Nautes, a group of boatmen who controlled river traffic on the Seine. This *Pilier des Nautes*, or *Boatmen's Pillar*, which today is regarded as the oldest surviving sculpture from Gallo-Roman Lutetia, has long been a special prize of the Musée national du Moyen Age.

Antiquities continued to turn up at construction sites, such as the Luxembourg Gardens and the Panthéon, but the antiquarians who collected and even catalogued these rarities did not really know what to make of them. Nor did royalty, even when Louis XVIII came to the rescue of the ruined Roman baths (the Thermes de Cluny) that rise so spectacularly adjoining the Hôtel de Cluny, on the northern slope of Montagne Sainte-Geneviève. Louis cleared out the tradesmen who had set up shop inside and removed some more recent add-ons, such as a garden on the roof. Soon after, King Louis-Philippe had the idea of integrating these baths (part of a sprawling third-century complex including a *frigidarium*) into the museum holding the *Pilier des Nautes*, a forerunner of today's Musée du Moyen Age. Still, despite good intent, the spirit that moved these monarchs seems to have been heavily laced with romanticism and civic pride. Not surprisingly, the story of Paris's origins remained muddled.

It was Baron Georges Haussmann who, around the middle of the nineteenth century, unintentionally uncovered the bulk of Paris's Gallo-Roman past. Baron Haussmann was not interested in the past: he had in mind a city of the future, of broad boulevards and flattened cityscapes as well as a monumental new sewer system. To achieve this, he tore out Paris's narrow winding medieval streets, leveled the city's innumerable hills and rises, and dug deep into the accumulated dirt and rubbish of the centuries. Since so much of Haussmann's projects took place in the center of Paris, directly above ancient Lutetia, the antiquities that the workmen uncovered were frequently Gallo-Roman. As a result, the outlines of Gallo-Roman Paris began to emerge, for the first time in fifteen hundred years.

After digging up the remnants of Gallo-Roman baths, villas, and the forum, the city carted sculptures and other precious bits over to the Musée du Moyen Age and a new Museum of the City (now known as the Musée Carnavalet). Extensive excavation for the Métro system at the turn of the last century turned up more finds, as did a mid-century spate of excavations for underground parking garages.

Finds like this are still going on throughout the heart of what used to be Lutetia. In the early 1990s, the Commission du Vieux Paris discovered a small group of first-century habitations in Place André-Honnorat in the Luxembourg Gardens. More recently, some of the earliest dwellings in Lutetia were located in the courtyard of the Institut Curie, on Rue D'Ulm, south of the Panthéon.

And what has happened to all of these discoveries? After these digs were completed and properly recorded, with transportable elements hauled off to appropriate museums, they then were covered over. A pragmatic but sad decision.

Public outcry did manage to preserve some of these discoveries for our viewing—most notably a portion of the Gallo-Roman amphitheater, the **Arènes de Lutèce** (located along Rue Monge, just to the southeast of the major Gallo-Roman discoveries), although unfortunately this outcry occurred too late to save the other portion, which had been demolished to make way for Rue Monge and a bus depot. Baron Haussmann of course was responsible for the destruction, but an indignant public, led by a very determined Victor Hugo, managed to save the rest. Several decades later, a repentant city of Paris reconstructed the demolished part.

It's an odd story, but one can be grateful that anything remains. As it is, this is an off-the-beaten-track attraction, often virtually empty except for a few schoolchildren playing soccer in the arena's center. Entering through the restored gateway, try to imagine fifteen thousand cheering Gallo-Romans as you come. Christians versus the lions? Well, there at least were lions, or wild animals, for you can still see where what may have been animal cages opened onto the arena. And then you can settle down on the two-thousand-year-old stone seats and enjoy the tranquility.

Stairway into Arènes de Lutèce. © M. McAuliffe

Adding to the calm, the Arènes is surrounded by a narrow but lovely band of dense vegetation, which opens onto an adjoining little park, the **Square Capitan**. There, an elegant double staircase in neoclassical style leads downward to surround a fountain, where neighbors gather to chat and rest in the shade.

⌣

Not far from the Arènes de Lutèce is another small park, the **Square Paul-Langevin** (Rue des Ecoles at Rue Monge), named in honor of the prominent physicist and forming a lovely green space behind the buildings of the former Ecole Polytechnique where he taught. This rarely visited garden comes with a story that even the park's historic marker does not reveal. Langevin had been a doctoral student of Pierre Curie and a close friend of both Marie and Pierre. Langevin and Marie became even closer after Pierre's tragic death, and in time they became lovers.

Langevin's wife (from whom he was estranged) became irate and took her grievances to the public, claiming all sorts of nastiness against Marie Curie. The press took chase and hounded Curie, branding her a brazen foreigner (she was Polish by birth) and doing everything it could to undermine her career. As Langevin's son later wrote, "The xenophobes, the antifeminists, and the ultra-nationalists of the era organized a hateful campaign against Marie Curie and my father."[1] Curie suffered greatly and became quite ill, but eventually she returned to her lab and her work, even as Langevin returned to his wife (and, in time, to a more acceptable mistress). In the aftermath, Marie Curie would win her second Nobel Prize and Langevin would continue his own remarkable career in physics. Their romance was over, but in a romantic conclusion, Langevin's grandson (a nuclear physicist) eventually married Curie's granddaughter (also a nuclear physicist). Their son, perhaps not surprisingly, is an astrophysicist.

Langevin's remains, as well as those of Marie and Pierre Curie, are enshrined nearby in the Panthéon—Marie Curie being the first woman to enter these precincts on her own merits.

⌣

The **Panthéon**, a surprisingly uncrowded monument crowning the top of Montagne Sainte-Geneviève, has its own story, one that is linked with that of this remarkable fifth-century saint.

According to legend, Geneviève saved Paris from Attila the Hun. The barbarians from the east were hammering at the door, and Parisians were prepared to flee. But Geneviève persuaded them to resist, prophesying that

Paris would be saved. She was right. Miraculously, Attila reconsidered and moved on.

Years later, Parisians turned to Geneviève to save them from yet another onslaught, this time from the Franks. Never shying from direct action, Geneviève now brought in grain from Troyes during the Franks' siege of Paris. She also negotiated directly with the ruthless Frankish leader, Childeric, to save the lives of those prisoners he had taken. She prayed, and then she acted.

When Childeric's son, Clovis, conquered most of Gaul, including Paris, Geneviève adapted to the situation and persuaded this powerful ruler to become a defender of the faith. Under her influence, Clovis built a fine Christian basilica on top of the hill that would become known as Montagne Sainte-Geneviève—on the site of today's Panthéon. In time this basilica, and the influential abbey that grew up around it, would become dedicated to Sainte-Geneviève. Whenever the city faced danger, whether from invasion, famine, or epidemic, Sainte-Geneviève's reliquary (a casket of gold and gems containing her remains) was carried in an elaborate procession, accompanied by all the bells of Paris.

For more than a thousand years, Sainte-Geneviève received the appeals of Parisians, including royalty. In 1744, when Louis XV recovered from a serious illness after praying to her, he vowed to build a grand new church in her honor. The king soon forgot his vow, but the abbot of the abbey that bore her name kept after him until, at long last, the king laid the first stone for the new basilica—a grand edifice of monumental proportions to be built at the hill's peak.

Inspired by St. Paul's in London and St. Peter's in Rome, as well as by Rome's far-smaller Pantheon, the architect (Jacques-Germain Soufflot) gave his structure a façade reminiscent of an ancient temple, with a columned portico supporting a triangular pediment. Sainte-Geneviève's shrine was meant to rest at the center of the basilica, beneath the huge dome. But by this time, the Revolution had begun, and religion—as well as royalty—had severely fallen out of favor. Mobs of angry Parisians burned Sainte-Geneviève's remains and threw her ashes into the Seine. They then stripped her reliquary of its jewels and melted down the gold, leaving only a fragment of her stone sarcophagus. The Revolutionaries also suppressed the Abbey of Sainte-Geneviève and tore down its church. Only the church belfry, now known as the Tour de Clovis, remains.

After promptly closing down the new building, the Revolutionaries decided to turn it into the nation's Panthéon, a secular last resting place for France's great men (yes, men only). Up went the gold letters across the front pediment, declaring "*Aux Grands Hommes la Patrie Reconnaissante*" (To the Great Men, a Grateful Nation). Inside, the Revolutionaries removed all Christian references and walled up the huge windows, eliminating anything that might remind anyone of a church. Downstairs, in the crypt, they laid to rest the bodies of Mirabeau, Voltaire, Rousseau, and Marat (although Mirabeau and Marat encountered posthumous political riptides and were evicted).

The Panthéon soon encountered political riptides of its own as changing governments tossed it back and forth, from mausoleum to church and back again, and the inscription, "Aux Grands Hommes la Patrie Reconnaissante" was alternately put up or taken down. Only after the Second Empire came to its inglorious end in 1870 did the Third Republic at last reinstate the building's function as a Panthéon—a secular temple of fame and glory for the most illustrious of France's dead.

Victor Hugo provided the occasion for this final chapter in the Panthéon's story. Everyone agreed that the death (in 1885) of this revered literary and political giant called for a burial spot worthy of him. Only the Panthéon would do, and so he was given an extravaganza of a funeral, with his austere pauper's hearse (Hugo's own request) carrying the body through enormous crowds from the Arc de Triomphe to the Panthéon. There, Hugo was laid to rest in its huge crypt, which in time would honor other illustrious Frenchmen, including Emile Zola, Alexandre Dumas (père), and France's hero of the Resistance, Jean Moulin.

Of course, a most noteworthy addition to this celebrated group was the arrival of Marie Curie. Both she and her husband, Pierre, occupy tombs here, making the Panthéon's dedicatory words satisfyingly outdated. It took a while—Madame Curie died in 1934 and was not received into the Panthéon until 1995. But this two-time Nobel Prize–winner eventually cracked through the Panthéon's gender barrier, just as she cracked through professional gender barriers in life. Since that breakthrough, other women have joined the ranks of notables here—two heroes of the French Resistance, a champion for women's rights, and, most recently, Josephine Baker, an American-born French citizen and decorated hero of the Resistance. Baker's rise from the slums of St. Louis to fame in Paris, first as a headline-grabbing dancer, then as a glamorous singer, in turn was capped by her fight for civil rights in America (she was a prominent supporter of Martin Luther King Jr.) and her fight for her beloved France during World War II.

Not all of those granted residence here have arrived without controversy. Perhaps the most dramatic was the interment of novelist Emile Zola, who had capped his literary career with an ardent plea on behalf of Jewish captain

Alfred Dreyfus, who was wrongly convicted of treason, stripped of both rank and honor, and condemned to life imprisonment on Devil's Island. "J'Accuse!" (I Accuse), Zola's fiery denunciation of the military cover-up at the heart of the travesty, and his plea for a second trial, hit like a bombshell. Anti-Dreyfus mobs demonstrated in the streets, burning Zola in effigy and prompting him to flee to England until the death threats subsided. But his own death soon after was clouded in suspicious circumstances, and the transfer of his remains to the Panthéon in 1908 met with fierce resistance from royalists, ultranationalists, and anti-Semites, whose hatred of Zola—and Dreyfus—remained white hot.

All was well until the hearse and its escort crossed to the Left Bank and approached the Panthéon, where they encountered mobs that menacingly blocked the way. A last-minute arrival of soldiers and police managed to escort the bier into the Panthéon and continued to patrol outside throughout the night, while Zola's widow sat vigil inside. The ceremony the next day, which included Zola's family as well as a by-now exonerated Alfred Dreyfus, proceeded without incident until the close of the eulogy, when a shot rang out, then another.

Maurice Le Blond, who would soon marry Zola's daughter, was standing directly behind Dreyfus when he heard the first ominous click and wheeled about. Fortunately, Dreyfus heard the sound at the same time and threw up his arms, protecting himself from the bullets that followed. Le Blond tackled the would-be assassin (a military journalist), and Dreyfus was unhurt, with the exception of a flesh wound to his forearm. The ceremony proceeded, and Zola was at last peacefully interred in the Panthéon's crypt, across from his boyhood idol, Victor Hugo. But unfortunately, the vestiges of hate that had bubbled up around this solemn ceremony did not disappear and surfaced not many years later under France's Vichy government, during German Occupation.

This makes a recent addition to the crypt especially relevant—the installation of a plaque honoring Les Justes de France (The Righteous of France), commemorating the heroic actions of those French who saved Jews from persecution and the death camps during France's World War II German Occupation.

Enter the presence of greatness through a door to the left of the large sculpture at the Panthéon's far end, one that honors La Convention Nationale (The National Convention). En route, you will pass Foucault's Pendulum, swinging in its endless arc from the cupola. Or at least you could, until an unfortunate accident befell this simple but dramatic demonstration of earth's rotation, breaking the long wire and leaving the brass ball on the floor, looking like a bereft Christmas ornament. With the expectation that this is but a temporary glitch, you can leave Foucault and his eye-catching experiment behind and proceed to the Panthéon's starring attraction, the crypt.

A wide staircase leads to the entry area (the narrow winding staircase that I recall from earlier visits has now been repurposed, leading only to the toilets). Entering an area called the Vestibule, you will find that famous sculpture of Voltaire smiling his "smile of reason," as art historian Kenneth Clark once put it. Voltaire's tomb lies next to that of the Panthéon's architect, Jacques-Germain Soufflot, and across from that of Jean-Jacques Rousseau, whose last resting place bears a rather startling depiction of a hand emerging from the tomb, carrying a torch—perhaps the Torch of Liberty, or perhaps a symbol of the Enlightenment.

The crypt is not heavily visited, making this an eerie and empty last resting place for France's great men and women. The "greats" occupy a small portion of this vast space, leaving much of it clean and bare, much like the unfinished basement of a new house. Yet despite the emptiness, it is easy to become disoriented in these corridors, especially in the labyrinthine area around the central rotunda. At night, after everyone but the permanent residents go home, does a Minotaur of the Panthéon emerge from this thick-walled and mysterious place?

As for Sainte-Geneviève, there is not much of her in the Panthéon, although scenes from her life appear among the huge historical paintings across those vast walls where Soufflot's windows once stood. Those by Puvis de Chavannes, depicting her childhood and *Protection de Paris assiégée par les Huns* (*Protection of Paris besieged by the Huns*), are considered the best of the bunch.

As for the remaining fragment of Sainte-Geneviève's stone sarcophagus, it now resides in a shrine in the nearby church of **Saint-Etienne-du-Mont**, at the Panthéon's northeast corner. Jean Racine and Blaise Pascal are also buried here. Despite its rather austere exterior, this church is lovely inside.

Both Racine and Pascal, buried at Saint-Etienne-du-Mont, were dedicated Jansenists, a long-forgotten movement intent on reforming Roman Catholicism. Not far from their last resting place is the cloister of the famous **Abbey of Port-Royal**, now sheltered within the heart of the Baudelocque maternity hospital.

Dating from the early years of the seventeenth century, this convent's buildings—now in hospital use—are elegantly proportioned, with steeply pitched mansard roofs. These in turn enclose a formal French garden. The cloister itself is lovely, with the chapel on its northeast corner. Here is buried Mère Angélique, the remarkable woman who is responsible for this architectural treasure.

Mère Angelique was a mover and shaker, who in 1608 (in the midst of the many years of religious warfare between Catholics and Protestants) set to work to reform the old thirteenth-century Abbey of Port-Royal in the Chevreuse Valley, just outside of Paris. Her reforms drew so many new recruits that the number of nuns soon outgrew their ancient accommodations. Mère Angelique—who quite obviously was a powerhouse—now decided to move the community to Paris. Here the new convent, Port-Royal-de-Paris, became the center of the Catholic reform movement known as Jansenism, attracting some of the foremost intellects of the day, including Racine and Pascal. The women of Port-Royal lived in Paris, while the men made their home at Port-Royal's original site, which became known as Port-Royal-des-Champs.

Today, Jansenism is all but forgotten, but for well over a century it was a formidable force in French intellectual and religious life. Stressing rigorous piety and predestination (the limit of God's grace to the predestined few), Jansenists tended to be deeply suspicious of Jesuits as well as of the pope. Since the Jesuits enjoyed royal favor in France, it was not surprising that the Jansenists quickly ran afoul of both royal absolutism and papal authority. Had this movement been less dynamic and influential, it would not have drawn such white-hot opposition. But the power of its ideas, as well as the prominence of its supporters, made it dangerous to both church and state. After years of persecution, the nuns of Port-Royal-de-Paris were evicted, and their convent closed. As traumatic as this must have been, it was not nearly as dire a fate as that suffered by the original abbey, Port-Royal-des-Champs, which was razed to the ground.

But the convent buildings of Port-Royal-de-Paris most fortunately survived, serving as a prison and orphanage before becoming a maternity hospital. You may visit the tiny chapel where Mère Angelique is buried (open on Sunday mornings during Mass) and the convent's spacious cloister, which surrounds the formal French garden. Linger a while, enjoying the beauty and breathing in the tranquility. This was Mère Angelique's world, four centuries ago. But if you really want to catch a glimpse of this remarkable woman and the convent she headed, you will find both in her portrait, in the Louvre. Look carefully, for in the background is a wonderful contemporary view of Port-Royal—obviously a haven in a storm-swept world.

Almost four centuries have passed since that portrait was painted, and the convent of Port-Royal-de-Paris has long disappeared. But its beautiful cloister and chapel remain, a reminder that peace and serenity are possible, even in the midst of turbulent times.

Long ago, Paris—and especially this part of Paris—was dotted with religious houses like Port-Royal-de-Paris, many of them with extensive gardens and grounds. These monasteries and convents varied considerably in size and physical appearance, but all had cloisters—peaceful covered walkways that provided a tranquil setting for meditation as well as a sheltered passageway for hurrying feet. Usually constructed around a central courtyard, the cloister typically abutted its surrounding buildings and was open or arcaded on its courtyard side. This courtyard, in turn, could be a formal garden, much like the one at Port-Royal, or simply a grassy expanse.

Time and Revolutionary destruction have wiped out much of this part of Paris's history. But in addition to the extraordinary cloister of Port-Royal, there remain fragments of others, including one dating from the late thirteenth century. This **Convent of the Cordelières** was once a vast property of almost twenty acres, its ruins now meditating silently over the garden of Broca Hospital. When Marguerite de Provence (St. Louis's widow) founded this convent, Paris proper still was bounded by Philip Auguste's ancient walls, and the convent's lands lay beyond them in what then was the village of Saint-Marcel. Surrounded by fields and gardens, and richly endowed by royalty, this peaceful convent attracted its share of aristocratic sisters, daughters, and widows, who lived here in distinction and comfort.

The Revolution brought an abrupt end to this convent's many centuries of calm, seizing its lands and destroying its church. Tanneries and laundries from the nearby river Bièvre (now underground) soon moved into what was left. Finally someone had the bright idea of turning the former convent into a hospital. This worked well for more than a century, but when the new Broca Hospital went up, most of the remaining convent came down, leaving only remnants of its ancient cloister and Gothic refectory (dining hall).

Once it was easy to see the cloister's remaining columns from Rue de Julienne, and the refectory's soaring ruins from either there or Rue Pascal, but the hospital has recently planted a tall hedge around this treasure. Try to find a corner to see in, or do your best to see over. We can only hope that the hospital will soon realize its mistake and remove this barrier.

And now, let's return to the Latin Quarter, where scholars and lovers await.

Hôtel de Cluny (Musée national du Moyen Age). © J. McAuliffe

CHAPTER THREE

From Scholars to Lovers

Let's visit the scholars first, starting with the **Bibliothèque Sainte-Geneviève** (Sainte-Geneviève Library), located across from the Panthéon. This renowned library had its origins in the large collection of rare books and manuscripts saved by the monks of the nearby Abbey of Sainte-Geneviève when Revolutionaries destroyed the abbey—a center of learning for more than a millennium.

Now serving the many branches of the University of Paris system, this library's reading room is one of the glories of Paris's Beaux-Arts architecture, with a two-story double-arched ceiling that soars over an impressive space below. But although the architect, Henri Labrouste, embraced the prevailing Beaux-Arts style, at least in overall appearance, he broke with tradition by making use of exposed cast iron rather than stone for his arches, as well as in the columns over which these arches are suspended.

Architects love to view this early example of modernism, with its breathtaking open spaces, and it is a stunning place for anyone to visit—although few besides students and scholars seem aware of its existence. Brief afternoon visits are available, and if you would like something more in depth, lengthier morning visits can be arranged in advance.

This part of Paris has been a hub of learning for more than a millennium, dating from the earliest years of the three great abbeys (Sainte-Geneviève, Saint-Victor, and Saint-Germain) established on this side of the Seine.

These religious foundations survived the years of Viking raids and subsequent turmoil to become wealthy and powerful, exercising their influence in the political as well as the religious realms and fostering renowned schools on the Left Bank, even while the cathedral school on the Ile de la Cité also prospered.

The University of Paris, which emerged in 1200, eventually pulled together these disparate strands, despite early town-and-gown tensions. Fundamental to the emerging university was the monarch's decision to grant the students certain rights and protections. These relied heavily on enforcement by the Roman Catholic Church, under whose jurisdiction the students now came. This bothered few, as the concept of the separation of church and state was yet a long way off. Indeed, to be a student in those days was to be a cleric, albeit a lowly one. For years, this jumble of religiously affiliated but dismaying worldly students trooped through Paris, annoying their teachers and creating havoc in the local taverns. In the end, though, everyone usually managed to sort things out.

And then, in the mid-thirteenth century, members of the newly formed Dominican and Franciscan orders showed up. These newcomers, who had originated as mendicant, or begging, orders, had little in common either with those destined to become priests or those who would become members of monastic orders. The Dominican and Franciscan friars were teaching orders, and they brought with them some of the most brilliant teachers of the age, including young Thomas Aquinas. The friars' idealism (especially their vows of poverty) was attractive to many of the university's young and most idealistic students (as well as some of their teachers), and conflict soon erupted between the friars and the university's theology faculty (then located at Notre-Dame). The university attempted to expel the newcomers, and before long, the fracas reached the Vatican, leading to excommunication and a temporary shutdown of the university.

It was then that Robert de Sorbon began looking at real estate on the Left Bank. He purchased several properties, intent on turning them into endowed lodgings for poor students—specifically for those who were not Dominican or Franciscan friars. Sorbon, not coincidentally, was chaplain to King Louis IX (known to history as St. Louis), who strongly supported this project. After all, the Dominicans and Franciscans came under the direct authority of the pope, and despite his saintliness, Louis was no pushover when it came to protecting his royal prerogatives. Sorbon's project offered a way of quietly opposing the friars without direct confrontation.

Given the royal seal of approval, the **College de Sorbon**, or **Sorbonne**, prospered. Instead of competing with the university's theology faculty, it supported it by providing room and board for its poorest students. In time, Sorbon's college replaced the cloister of Notre-Dame as the official seat of the Faculty of Theology, and by the seventeenth century, the Sorbonne had become an established power in theological circles. It had also clearly outgrown its by-now shabby facilities, and Cardinal Richelieu—Louis XIII's powerful principal minister, who was also chancellor of the Sorbonne—replaced the Sorbonne's medieval structures with a far larger and grander arrangement, whose centerpiece was the impressive Baroque chapel that would eventually house Richelieu's own magnificent tomb.

Not surprisingly, the Sorbonne's theologians did not adapt well to the increasingly secular and scientific world of the Enlightenment, and by the time of the Revolution, its Faculty of Theology had earned a well-deserved reputation for flint-hard conservatism. This conservatism did not sit well with the Revolutionaries, who shut down the entire university, including the Sorbonne. They had only just begun to set up their own secular and scientifically oriented educational system when Bonaparte came to power—bringing the university under his own imperial supervision, kicking out all references to the Enlightenment, and restoring the Faculty of Theology. But this was not the same as restoring the Sorbonne, which for a time was occupied by a group of artists who had just been evicted from their residence in the Louvre.

Soon after returning to power, the Bourbon monarchs expelled these artists once again, and the Sorbonne now became the seat of the Faculties of Letters and Sciences as well as the Faculty of Theology. But the goal of the hidebound Bourbons was not simply to restore the Sorbonne, or even to expand its mission, but to bring the Faculties of Letters and Sciences under the influence of the Sorbonne's conservative Faculty of Theology.

Despite numerous obstacles during the years that followed, the liberal arts managed to survive within the Sorbonne, until the Franco-Prussian War and the Commune uprising shattered the Sorbonne's last remnant of religious conservatism. Society under the Third Republic was unmistakably secular, and it was not long before the Sorbonne's Faculty of Theology was suppressed. At the same time, work began on the complete physical reconstruction of the Sorbonne, which eradicated Richelieu's Sorbonne—with the sole exception of his now-secularized chapel. A republican and secular Sorbonne emerged.

This new Sorbonne's two remaining faculties—Letters and Sciences—quickly established their international preeminence with professors such as Pierre and Marie Curie (the university's first female professor) leading the way. Students (now including young women) poured in, and although most professors in traditional liberal arts courses continued to teach at the

Sorbonne proper, many of the Sorbonne's research facilities and specialized institutes had to be placed in outlying annexes, for lack of space.

Space was a problem for the students, too, who were jammed into the Sorbonne's lecture halls. This situation continued to worsen, and after France's liberation from German Occupation (which many of the Sorbonne's students and teachers actively resisted), the Sorbonne—and the university as a whole—returned to the pre-war problems of outdated curricula and unacceptably jammed classrooms.

By the 1950s, general student unrest had become fused with politics, especially opposition to the war in Algeria. The student protest movement drew additional fuel in the 1960s after a variety of educational reforms foundered, and after students in Paris joined with others throughout the world to protest the war in Vietnam. By 1968, the situation was already explosive when an ugly confrontation erupted between police and protestors in the courtyard of the Sorbonne. The uprising that followed shared many of the characteristics of Parisian uprisings of the past, in which university students had played a part, except now the students led the way. By the time the crisis of May 1968 was over, the entire nation had been shaken by events and was looking for a way to restore a measure of peace and stability.

Soon after, the university was split and regrouped into thirteen separate parts. Portions of these, as well as the university administration, currently share the Sorbonne's historic premises. The Sorbonne in turn has lent its name to Paris I (Panthéon-Sorbonne), Paris III (Sorbonne-Nouvelle), and Paris IV (Paris-Sorbonne), which between them have inherited the Sorbonne's academic traditions in the liberal arts. Recently, after some squabbles over the "Sorbonne" name, Paris IV and Paris VI merged to form Sorbonne University, while Paris V and Paris VII have merged, leaving the number in the university system at eleven.

The Sorbonne is now off-limits to tourists for security reasons, but you can view Richelieu's chapel from Boulevard St-Michel. And the lovely little park of **Place Paul-Painlevé** (named for a Sorbonne math professor and prime minister of France) provides a small haven from where you can gaze at the main entrance of the Sorbonne across the way.

Now turned into a garden with a medieval theme, this small park contains a surprising number of sculptures, including one of Romulus and Remus, given by the city of Rome to the city of Paris (commemorating Roman Lutetia), and one of Montaigne by Paul Landowski, installed on the four-hundredth anniversary of Montaigne's birth. Landowski depicts Montaigne casually seated, facing the Sorbonne, with Montaigne's tribute to Paris inscribed across the pedestal: "Paris has owned my heart since my childhood."

Before exams, Sorbonne students touch Montaigne's right foot for luck. It is well worn.

⌒

Behind Place Paul-Painlevé and across from the Sorbonne rises the Hôtel de Cluny, one of the oldest private residences in Paris and now home to the **Musée national du Moyen Age**.

It is gorgeous. Originally it was the town house of the Abbot of Cluny, a powerful monastic order that once controlled a network of abbeys across Western Europe. Dating from the late fifteenth century, this mansion is an especially sumptuous example of the Gothic style, unquestionably a residence meant to enhance the power and reputation of its owner—a high-ranking churchman who did not in the least object to luxury. Making it all the more interesting, this mansion was partially constructed on the massive remnants of Gallo-Roman baths, the Thermes de Cluny—most likely because the builder discovered that it would be prohibitively expensive to remove them.

This home with a history is now, most appropriately, the home of the Musée du Moyen Age, and you can quickly lose yourself in its collections, especially if you wander through on a rainy day, which seems to evoke a mood suitable to time traveling. This is a small museum, with treasures galore, but be sure to spend some time with the museum's prize, its set of six extraordinary tapestries, *The Lady and the Unicorn*. Take your time to properly enjoy them.

The Hôtel de Cluny's original chapel is another gem, and of course you should visit the enclosed frigidarium of the Thermes de Cluny, where you will find the *Pilier des Nautes*. I discover new treasures every time I visit.

In recent years, this has included a visit to Cluny's medieval garden, inspired by the museum's collections, especially *The Lady and the Unicorn* tapestries—many of whose plants and flowers have inspired the plantings here. A "forest of the unicorn" charmingly includes plants and footprints of those animals seen in the tapestries, while other garden beds more prosaically include a medieval kitchen garden (onions, cabbage, and garlic) and one featuring plants with medical uses (sage, hyssop, and rue). More unusual are the garden dedicated to the Virgin, with flowers symbolizing the virtues associated with the Virgin (daisies, violets, and white roses, symbolizing innocence, purity, and modesty), and the garden of Courtly Love, whose flowers waft delicate fragrances, suitable to romance.

Courtly love—which is beautifully illustrated in *The Lady and the Unicorn*—originated with the troubadours, and it had its most famous expression in Eleanor of Aquitaine's brilliant twelfth-century court in Poitiers. There,

Eleanor undertook to turn the scruffy, blood-soaked sons of the nobility into gentle knights in the service of love, beauty, and fair womanhood.

Key to courtly love was a new role envisioned for women, in which the suitor became his beloved's vassal in love, learning to please her in any way she chose—from nicer table manners and gentler speech to more sophisticated and refined methods of courtship. Rugged young knights, accustomed to rowdy camaraderie and the smell of the stables, could be persuaded to clean up and behave if such sacrifice promised something interesting in return. Under sufficiently enticing circumstances, their more courteous and chivalrous behavior might become long-term or even permanent.

Behind it all lay the assumption—reinforced by the typical marriages of the time—that marriage had little to do with love. Everyone knew that marriages were essentially political or economic mergers, moves on the great chessboard of life. From there it was but one step to the famous statement of Eleanor's daughter, Marie of Champagne, that love and marriage do not mix.

I recently discovered the role that the Hôtel de Cluny played in one such arranged marriage, one between a royal princess and a monarch almost twice her age. The young woman at the center of this story was Mary Tudor, daughter of England's Henry VII, who in 1514, at the age of eighteen, was married off (by her brother, Henry VIII) to France's Louis XII—a monarch who was thirty years her senior.

Mary was devastated by the prospect of this marriage and agreed to wed Louis only on condition that if she survived him, she could marry whomever she liked. This was an unusual demand at the time, even for a royal princess, but Mary was already in love with Charles Brandon, duke of Suffolk, and had hopes of eventually marrying him—a match that her brother and his advisors strongly opposed. Based on her agreement, Mary went through with the marriage to Louis, who was childless and desperately wanted an heir. Remember the Chambre Dorée, in the Palais de Justice, that Louis extravagantly ornamented for his wedding? Mary Tudor was his bride. One can only imagine her relief when, after only three months of marriage, Louis died.

Louis's successor, his cousin François I, promptly sent Mary into seclusion at the Hôtel de Cluny, to ensure that she was not pregnant with a posthumous son and rival. It was a dangerous time for the widowed queen, as François also wanted to keep her dowry in France and prevent Henry VIII from arranging another marriage for her, this time to one of France's enemies.

Caught in a swirl of international politics, Mary held firm, and when Charles, duke of Suffolk, arrived on the scene, François seems to have realized that Suffolk offered little danger to him and encouraged the match. Taking the great risk of angering the English king (who had no qualms about beheading those who offended him), Mary Tudor and Charles, duke of Suffolk, married in secret in the beautiful little chapel of the Hôtel de Cluny.

Henry VIII was predictably outraged at this marriage, but after a hefty fine, the couple escaped a worse fate and went on to live a quiet and happy life, complete with four children.

A happy—and unusual—love story to contemplate as you sit in the medieval garden of the Hôtel de Cluny, where it all happened.

Alpine Garden, Jardin des Plantes. © J. McAuliffe

~

CHAPTER FOUR

Along the Seine

East of the Latin Quarter, on the Left Bank of the Seine, is a garden that has entranced everyone from royalty to America's puritanical Founding Father, John Adams. In actuality, Adams was not so much of a prude as his detractors suggest, and he fell in love with Paris. When there, to negotiate with the French on behalf of the American colonies in their fight against Britain, he spent many pleasant hours exploring Paris with his eldest son, John Quincy, including the paths of what then was known as the Jardin du Roi.

On Adams's second stay in Paris, this time to negotiate peace with Britain, he continued his long walks, this time with both John Quincy and Quincy's nine-year-old brother, Charles, whom Adams introduced to Left Bank bookshops and the gardens of the Tuileries and the Palais Royal. Always, Adams returned to the Jardin du Roi.

Founded in the seventeenth century by Louis XIII, who had in mind a botanical garden for medicinal herbs, it was originally called the Jardin Royal des Plantes Médicinales and was used for teaching as well as healing purposes. From the outset, though, it was open to the public, even as it became an important center for research in the natural sciences, including botany. When the Revolution changed the garden's name to the **Jardin des Plantes**, its scientific establishment spun off to become the Muséum national d'Histoire naturelle (Museum of Natural History).

The garden is huge and includes large glass hothouses (Les Grandes Serres) and extensive study garden beds, as well as gardens devoted to roses, iris, and peonies. There is also a small zoo, whose first residents were refugees from the royal menagerie of Versailles. Another attraction is the Butte Coypeau, an artificial hill built on a medieval rubbish heap that rises abruptly in the garden's northwestern corner, encircled by a leafy labyrinth. At its summit is the Gloriette de Buffon, an antique iron gazebo (the oldest all-metal structure in Paris, dating from the 1780s), topped by a sundial with the inscription "Horas non numero nisi serenas," roughly meaning, "I count only the happy hours." Those on their daily runs (something that has recently caught on in Paris) frequently take in this climb as part of their regimen.

But my favorite spot in the entire place is the lovely Alpine rock garden, which is a bit difficult to find (via a sunken passage from the Botany School gardens)—making it all the more special to those who make their way there. Constructed some ten feet below the surface of the rest of the Jardin des Plantes, this little haven, protected from the extremes of wind and weather, provides a lovely setting of hills, rocks, water, and winding trails that is rarely crowded.

A twentieth-century extension of the Jardin des Plantes, the Alpine garden is too recent an addition for John Adams to have encountered—but undoubtedly he would have enjoyed it.

⌒

Adjacent to the Jardin des Plantes is the gorgeous **Grand Mosque (Grande Mosquée) of Paris**. This exotic addition to the Paris scene dates from the years following World War I (known in France as the Great War), when France substantially underwrote the project to honor the large number of Muslims from its North African and Middle Eastern colonies who had died fighting for France. The architecture and interior decoration are Moorish in style, and hundreds of North African craftsmen were brought in to work on the project. This culminated in a twentieth-century Muslim equivalent to France's ancient Gothic cathedrals, its minaret soaring into the Paris sky.

To reach its patio and garden, you need to take a tour, which allows one to absorb the beauty of the mosque's extraordinary mosaic-studded walls and floors, its exquisitely carved wooden doors and ceilings, and its wrought-iron chandeliers, as well as its rare Persian carpets. Gurgling fountains, pools of water, restful greenery, and stunning architecture provide the backdrop for this peaceful environment, and although the tearoom and dining areas are often crowded, it still is worthwhile to take the time to drink tea, eat pastries, and relax. And yes, there is the opportunity for a vigorous scrub down in the marble-paneled Turkish baths.

There is also the chance to contemplate the role this mosque played during the German Occupation of Paris, when it provided an essential place of refuge for Jews and Resistance fighters escaping Paris. Karen Ruelle has written a children's book about this moving story, which I recommend.

～

Centuries ago, when the second millennium was young and Paris was still recovering from the Vikings, a narrow pathway ran along the Left Bank, connecting the two great monasteries of Saint-Victor and Saint-Germain-des-Prés. The abbey of Saint-Victor no longer exists, although traces of this once-powerful center of learning remain in odd pockets around the University of Paris's Jussieu campus (now University of Paris VII), which occupies the site of Saint-Victor. Tiny Rue Saint-Victor, a sunken and obviously aged vestige of Old Paris, may be a piece of the ancient roadway leading to the old abbey.

But by the thirteenth century, learning was moving from the abbeys to the newly created universities, whether in Boulogne, Oxford, Cambridge, Heidelberg, or Paris. One stunning remnant of this change is located nearby, on Rue de Poissy—the refectory (dining area) of the **Collège des Bernardins**, founded in 1244 and named after the famed Cistercian monk Saint Bernard of Clairvaux. The college owed its origins to Stephen of Lexington, an English Cistercian monk and abbot of Clairvaux, who received authorization from Pope Innocent IV to send "honest and intelligent monks to follow courses in theology" in Paris. Much like Robert de Sorbon, Stephen was concerned about the inroads the Dominican and Franciscan friars were making among his flock, and his idea was to educate these young Cistercians at the then-new university, with this college, or residence, providing them a suitable—and safe—place to study and live. Safe, that is, not only from the usual temptations of the town, but from the friars, whose vows of poverty as well as their teaching (think Thomas Aquinas) were proving very attractive to young idealists.

Stephen bought up lands near Saint-Victor that until then were regularly flooded out by the mouth of the River Bièvre, which the monks of Saint-Victor had diverted to irrigate their expansive gardens and power a mill. The original buildings were extensive, occupying four levels, with courtyards, refectories, and dormitories. To prevent these from sinking in this marshy ground, the Cistercians built their foundations on oak piles.

Here in this college the young Cistercians studied theology from six in the morning to nine at night, with all classes conducted, of course, in Latin. The college prospered, and over the following centuries, thousands of young monks lived and studied here. One (Benoît XII) even became pope. But the Revolution put an end to all that. The Revolutionaries booted the monks out, and subsequently, the buildings were used as a prison, a fire station, and then as a school for police trainees. Meanwhile, the college's abandoned church was demolished to make way for Baron Haussmann's new Boulevard Saint-Germain. At length, early in the twenty-first century, the Catholic diocese of Paris bought the still-impressive but crumbling remnants of the Collège des Bernardins from the city of Paris. After extensive renovation, this remarkable piece of the past has been opened to the public but still remains off the beaten path in this otherwise heavily touristed area.

The refectory (called the nave) is enormous, and it originally housed classrooms as well as the dining area and kitchen. It now hosts meetings, conferences, and concerts, under the Académie Catholique de France. The refectory and small sacristy, as well as a small garden and café (La Table des Bernardins), are open to the public, and other areas, including its impressive medieval cellar, are open during guided tours.

What a find!

Long ago, the monks of Saint-Victor diverted the course of the River Bièvre to irrigate their lands and drive a mill. This mill was located at about where today's Rue de Bièvre joins the Seine, and anyone wishing to reach it had to cross a small bridge called the Poncel. Undoubtedly many along the busy lane connecting this mill with the Petit Pont repeatedly made this journey. This well-traveled road, now the Rue de la Bûcherie (formerly Boucherie), was for centuries a noisy thoroughfare crammed with students and trades-men. But today—along with its neighbors, the Rue de Bièvre and tiny Rue des Grands-Degrés—it has emerged from long years of overcrowding and neglect to become one of the most quietly evocative (and expensive) quarters of Paris.

The Rue de la Bûcherie leads to the Square René-Viviani (named for a politician who served briefly as premier of France during World War I) and then crosses Rue du Petit Pont, a heavily trafficked thoroughfare that quickly becomes Rue Saint-Jacques—once the main Roman road to Orléans. The Orléans road was a major dividing point between Left Bank traffic to the east, heading for Saint-Victor, and traffic making its way westward, toward the abbey and village of Saint-Germain-des-Prés. Underscoring this distinc-tion, the Rue de la Bûcherie long ago changed its name as it crossed this roadway, becoming the Rue de la Huchette on the other side.

Since medieval times, little Rue de la Huchette has been a boisterous place, lined with cookshops and taverns. For centuries it was also notorious for its cutpurses—the equivalent of pickpockets, who were busy slashing

Collège des Bernardins. © *M. McAuliffe*

and seizing money-purses long before pockets were invented. This narrow and colorful street has been considerably cleaned up, but the Mediterranean kebab joints that now proliferate here are a gaudy reminder of an indecorous past.

Almost immediately on your left, at no. 5, is the **Caveau de la Huchette**, a legendary bar and jazz club, where dancers and onlookers crowd into the basement *caveau*, part of the extensive system of ancient and long-deserted quarries that lie beneath Paris's Left Bank. Elliot Paul, the American writer who lived on Rue de la Huchette during the 1920s and 1930s and authored *The Last Time I Saw Paris*, writes that it was in the Caveau de la Huchette that he "found Paris—and France." He describes his descent down a spiral stone stairway "that smelled of antiquity" into a cool stone cellar that led to yet another stairway. In the end, after traversing a narrow corridor and passing what looked like a medieval dungeon cell, in which wine was stored, he found unexpected camaraderie and a meal behind a heavy oak door, in a subterranean vault. "The place appeared less likely to produce a sandwich than any I had seen in my life," he wrote, but he indeed found interesting new acquaintances and a hearty ragout plus a substantial chunk of bread and a carafe of red wine.[1]

The jazz and swing parties would come later, after the war, with the influx of American G.I.s into Paris. The jazz and the dancing have continued, with great enthusiasm, to the present day.

This is perhaps a good place to introduce the subject of **Underground Paris**, which fascinates many. Paris's Left Bank is networked underground with worked-out limestone quarries dating from the twelfth century (earlier Gallo-Roman quarries were open rather than underground quarries). The blocks of limestone that were hauled into place on the great cathedral of Notre-Dame (Lutetian limestone, also known as Paris stone) came from these nearby quarries, and as the years passed, new galleries were dug farther and farther out and beyond the city's periphery.

In the meantime, houses and other buildings went up over the abandoned quarries, leading to occasional cave-ins. In addition, there was the 1804 discovery of the skeleton of one Philibert Aspairt, who had gotten lost in the featureless labyrinth in 1793. This led to a royal edict calling upon the services of Charles-Axel Guillaumot, one of the king's architects, to map the underground quarries and stabilize the ground above them by erecting pillars. This job turned out to be so huge that an entire department was created to inspect and stabilize the quarries that stretched beneath the city (a Quarry Inspection Unit still exists today, under the name "Inspection Générale des Carrières"). The outcome was that each street located above an old quarry was doubled by a phantom street below, with each gallery propped up by pillars and given the name of the street above. In time, the Quarry Inspection Unit mapped between 250 and 280 linear kilometers of these underground passages.

The best way to view this arrangement, dating from before the Revolution, is to descend into the **Carrière Médiévale des Capucins**, located beneath Hôpital Cochin on Faubourg St-Jacques (14th). Tours of small groups are given at irregular intervals by SEADACC (Société d'Etudes et d'Amenagement des Anciennes Carrières des Capucins), the association in charge of studying and maintaining the quarries. More easily accessible are the nearby **Catacombes de Paris**, which in the late eighteenth century famously received the bones from the overflowing cemeteries of central Paris, especially from the Saints-Innocents Cemetery and its nearby charnel houses. The stench from rotting cadavers had become unbearable, and the hazards this posed became even greater when basement walls began to collapse under the weight of bodies stacked in mass graves nearby.

The outcome was that, beginning in 1786, the cemetery of Saints-Innocents and other cemeteries were closed and their bodies and bones removed by night, in black-draped funerary carts, to a new underground cemetery—the Catacombs Ossuary in the quarries underlying the Montsouris Plain. It took fifteen months to empty the cemetery of Saints-Innocents of some two million bodies, followed by the contents of sixteen other cemeteries. In all, the project took place over more than thirty years, and visitors to the Catacombs now take spooky delight in the walls of bones artistically stacked in its extensive Ossuary.

The lines into the Catacombs are usually long, but right across the street, in the matching tollgate from the infamous Farmers-General Wall that once encircled Paris, is a less well-known way to dive into the past. The **Musée de la Libération de Paris—Musée du Général Leclerc—Musée Jean Moulin** has recently been moved from its site above the Gare Montparnasse to encompass the shelter used as command headquarters for Col. Henri Rol-Tanguy in the 1944 liberation of Paris from German Occupation.

Jean Moulin is celebrated as leader of the Resistance, in which he perished, and General Leclerc is renowned for his leadership in in the Free French cause, especially for his role in leading the Second Armored Division in the battle of Normandy and the liberation of Paris. The museum has creatively arranged photos, documents, videos, and archival materials illustrating the paths each man took in freeing France. But the most dramatic of all are the hundred steps downward into the former air-raid shelter that served as Colonel Rol-Tanguy's command post during the city's liberation.

Telephones operated here as well as a ventilation system, and bicycles generated electricity, but the primitiveness and grimness are unmistakable. One can only imagine what these people (including Rol-Tanguy's wife, who served as secretary) thought as they descended those stairs and swung the heavy door shut behind them. They must have wondered whether they would survive to see daylight again.

⌣

Returning to daylight and the Rue de la Huchette, let us pause partway down the street on the left, where there is a tiny theater, the **Théâtre de la Huchette**. Since 1957, it has continuously presented Eugène Ionesco's delicious and disturbing duo, La Cantatrice Chauve (The Bald Soprano) and La Leçon (The Lesson), in French. The humor (and the insanity) begin immediately, when a narrator informs the audience that we are viewing a middle-class English interior on an English evening, with an Englishman (Mr. Smith) seated in an English armchair, smoking an English pipe and reading an English newspaper. His wife (Mrs. Smith) is seated beside him, darning some English socks. At this point, members of the audience begin to giggle, but they are all waiting for the clock to strike. Which it does—three times in this production, seventeen in others. But no matter. Mrs. Smith immediately follows this with, "There, it's nine o'clock." And we are off, plummeted into a mad tea party of non sequiturs, in which even the most mundane facts collide and spin, merrily annihilating one another.[2]

Ionesco took his inspiration for this madcap classic from his frustrating experience in learning English from a conversation manual. Instead of seeing language as a connection, he saw in this phrasebook a series of meaningless clichés and the breakdown of communication. Words, he realized, do not mean what we think they do, and in fact, may mean nothing at all. This somber underpinning of La Cantatrice Chauve becomes darker yet in La Leçon, the second one-act Ionesco play in the Théâtre de la Huchette's double bill. Here the nonsense turns chilling when authoritarianism emerges and violence follows.

A Romanian by birth, with an authoritarian and violent father, Ionesco eventually broke with his father and moved to France, where he became a French citizen and acclaimed avant-garde playwright (his works include the frequently performed Rhinoceros, in which a man watches his friends turn one by one into rhinoceroses as they capitulate to the forces of conformity). Ionesco lived long enough (until 1994) to see the breakup of the Soviet Union and the fall of dictatorship in his native Romania, but he was not cheered by the world's prospects. Having seen at close hand the rise of both Nazism and Communism, he viewed twentieth-century life as a cross between the tragic and the ridiculous.

So go and have a good chuckle at *La Cantatrice Chauve* and *La Leçon*. But as you giggle, remember that Ionesco did not create this hour of nonsense just for laughs. And if you feel just a bit uneasy at the plays' end, he will have accomplished his purpose.

⌢

This entire quarter, including the equally ancient Rue Xavier-Privas and Rue de la Harpe, almost succumbed to Baron Haussmann's wrecking ball, but it was saved by events. Haussmann lost his job when Parisians wearied of his ever-larger plans for digging up and rebuilding the city, which brought ever-mounting cost overruns. This put a stop to his myriad works in progress, including a plan for gutting this old quarter. Intent on street-widening, Haussmann did succeed in destroying significant portions of the Latin Quarter, especially in the path of his new Boulevard Saint-Germain. But fortunately, many of its remarkable old streets and alleys (now considerably cleaned up and gentrified) remain.

Place Saint-Michel, a creation of Baron Haussmann, lies ahead, but more of our ancient roadway continues beyond.

Garden of Musée Delacroix. © J. McAuliffe

CHAPTER FIVE

~

Ancient Byways

Crossing Place Saint-Michel, our ancient roadway continues along Rue Saint-André-des-Arts—originally called the Rue de Laas, because it passed through the Clos de Laas, an extensive tract of land belonging to the Abbey of Saint-Germain-des-Prés, where cows once grazed. Adjacent to this, and bordering the river across from the king's palace on the Ile de la Cité, was a large field known as the Pré-aux-Clercs ("pré" meaning meadow). This was a place of recreation and a constant source of tension between the abbey and the students, who used the field for games and other hijinks and frequently were more rowdy than the good monks were willing to tolerate.

Just off the Rue Saint-André-des-Arts is a lovely enclave of three tiny courtyards called the Cour de Rohan. A charming and now exclusive pocket of the past, including a piece of Paris's twelfth-century wall (in the third and last courtyard), the residents have lately wearied of tourists and blocked off these courtyards to all but themselves. Try to peer inside, though—these little courtyards are beautiful.

Around the corner is a more welcoming spot for tourists, who flock here regularly—the **Cour du Commerce Saint-André**, where an entire tower from that twelfth-century wall spectacularly survives at no. 4, thanks to the efforts of successive occupants. This picturesque eighteenth-century passage runs parallel to the storied Rue de l'Ancienne-Comédie, home (at no. 14) of Molière's company of actors, or players (called "comédiens"), who in time would become known as the Comédie-Française. Across the street, and undoubtedly benefiting from the location, is the Café Procope—quite

possibly the oldest café in Paris, or at least the oldest in continuous operation. Like anything in this vicinity, come early to avoid the crowds.

From Rue Saint-André-des-Arts, the age-old roadway continues into
another that curves into Boulevard Saint-Germain and the site of the abbey's
former entrance. Many centuries ago, this was a formidable place, with stone
ramparts and a drawbridge. Haussmann destroyed much of this neighborhood when he blasted the boulevard through, but many tiny streets remain
in this now-expensive quarter, many of them now housing art galleries and
boutiques. Perhaps the loveliest of these quiet streets is the Rue de Furstemberg and the equally small and delightful Place de Furstemberg. The painter
Eugène Delacroix moved here in 1857, to be closer to Saint-Sulpice and its
Chapel of the Holy Angels, which he had been commissioned to paint.

By the time of his move, Delacroix was ailing, and the lovely house and
garden at 6 Rue de Furstemberg was his last home and studio. The **Musée
Delacroix** was created to preserve his last residence from demolition. Today,
although now officially part of the Louvre, it is rarely crowded, and a visit
to his studio and, especially, his small garden, is a delight. It was the peace
and privacy of this garden that convinced Delacroix to move here from his
far larger studio on the Right Bank, and he lived and worked in this oasis of
calm until his death. One can appreciate the comment that he made in his
diary, soon after moving in: "The view of my little garden and the cheerful
appearance of my studio always make me happy."

Nearby, at the corner of Passage de la Petite Boucherie and the Rue de
l'Abbaye stands the sixteenth-century abbey palace of the Abbey of Saint-
Germain-des-Prés, a remarkable brick-and-stone edifice that has recently
been restored. The abbey church itself, the **Church of Saint-Germain-des-
Prés,** is the abbey's most important survivor—its one remaining tower dating
from the turn of the first millennium, and its Romanesque nave being only
slightly younger. Small marble columns from the church's sixth-century predecessor decorate the upper level of the choir. And if you look closely inside
the Chapelle de Saint-Symphorien, to the right of the entry, you can see
vestiges of that sixth-century basilica.

But my favorite spot is just outside the church, in the small **Square
Laurent-Prache,** which most people overlook. Here, among a variety of
memorials (one, by Picasso, of his mistress, Dora Maar, presented to the Ville
de Paris in tribute to his long-dead friend, the poet Guillaume Apollinaire)
stand several haunting remnants of the abbey's thirteenth-century Chapel of
the Virgin, as well as fragments of the abbey's vanished cloister.

The Picasso sculpture has been stolen and recovered, with a copy now in the place of the original. Given the value of Picasso's work, this may disappear as well. But the remnants of the ancient Abbey of Saint-Germain-des-Prés attract little interest and remain as a treasure for those who know their secret.

Among the many cafés that Picasso frequented during the course of his long life, one of his favorites was the **Café de Flore**, located only a few steps from its rival, the **Café Les Deux Magots**, both located right across the busy square from Saint-Germain-des-Prés.

The Deux Magots, patronized by the surrealists and writers such as André Gide and André Malraux—and, eventually, Jean-Paul Sartre, Albert Camus, and Simone de Beauvoir—had its origins in the early 1800s, when it began as a dress shop. It transformed into a café but kept its name, which it may have owed to a popular play called *Les Deux Magots de la Chine*—a "magot" being a Chinese mandarin. Somewhere along the way it acquired the two large figurines of mandarins that still gaze placidly from their perch on the room's central pillar.

The Flore, located close by, dates only from 1870 and was a café from the start. Existing for many years in the Deux Magots' shadow, the Flore began to emerge into its own in the 1930s, although it still labored under the stigma of Charles Maurras—a notorious anti-Semite and leading thinker of the monarchist, ultranationalist, and far-right Catholic organization Action Française—who famously held court there during the height of the Dreyfus Affair. Maurras lived to join the Académie française, just before World War II and the German Occupation of France. After his arrest as a collaborationist following the liberation of France, and subsequent sentence to life imprisonment, as well as dismissal from the Académie française, he remained adamant to the end, proclaiming that his conviction was Dreyfus's revenge.

The Deux Magots suffered its own stigma during World War II, when it became popular with Paris's German occupiers. But after the war, both the Deux Magots and the Flore moved on. The postwar years brought a wave of famous writers and thinkers to both cafés, including Picasso, who seemed to show up with the in-crowd wherever it migrated.

Both cafés are famous, both are crowded and expensive, but if you want to have an espresso or hot chocolate to sip while people-watching, go ahead. A local friend insists that the Deux Magots has the best hot chocolate in town. I feel this is debatable, but by all means, give it a try.

Saint-Sulpice, the church that prompted Delacroix's move to the Left Bank, is only a short walk from the painter's house and studio. The second-largest church in Paris after Notre-Dame, Saint-Sulpice dates from the seventeenth century and, like Notre-Dame, suffered recently from fire—although thankfully the damage was not as extensive.

This landmark is noted for its massive mismatched twin towers and its grand interior, including a great organ and a gnomon (yes, the one featured by Dan Brown in *The Da Vinci Code*) that helps determine the time of the equinoxes and, most importantly, the date for Easter. Look for the meridian line of brass inlaid across the floor that meets with and climbs a marble obelisk topped by a small cross. According to witnesses, a ray of light shining through an opening in the south transept window will touch this line on the obelisk at noon on December 21 (winter solstice), while on March 21 and September 21 (the equinoxes), the shaft of light reaches a copper oval on the floor near the altar.

Join all the other sightseers as they try to figure all this out, but be aware that most of Brown's version is fiction, much to the irritation of those who love Saint-Sulpice. The church's caretakers have in fact posted a disclaimer notice. So don't spend a lot of time on the gnomon, and focus instead on the dome and sculpture of the Virgin in the beautiful Lady Chapel, or the murals that Delacroix painted in the last years of his life in the Chapel of the Holy Angels (first side-chapel on the right).

On one side you have *Jacob Wrestling with the Angel,* and on the other, *Heliodorus Driven from the Temple* (Heliodorus was sent to take the treasure from the Temple in Jerusalem to pay the Romans). On the chapel's ceiling is yet another masterwork by Delacroix, *Saint Michael Vanquishing the Demon.* Huge and filled with color and action, these three murals make a fitting ending to Delacroix's career as the leading Romantic painter of his day and are some of the greatest treasures of this magnificent church.

⁓

Delacroix, although coolly aristocratic in temperament and birth, was the bad boy of nineteenth-century painting. Officially he was the son of Charles-François Delacroix, a high-ranking government official, but unofficially he was rumored (with good reason) to be the illegitimate offspring of the diplomatic powerhouse Charles Maurice de Talleyrand. After all, many thought that Delacroix resembled Talleyrand, who treated—and protected—him as a son.

Whatever his origins, Delacroix moved imperturbably and aristocratically through the artistic storms he created as he broke with the prevailing neoclassical style of the period, creating a sensation as he went. His most influential painting, *Liberty Leading the People* (1830), quickly became an icon of the romantic spirit of liberty, but although the French government of King Louis-Philippe bought the painting, it considered it inflammatory and a threat to the monarchy and removed it from public view. The painting did not appear in public until after the Revolution of 1848 sent Louis-Philippe packing.

At the heart of the agitation over Delacroix was the rivalry dividing French artists, especially between Delacroix and Jean-Auguste-Dominique Ingres, leader of the neoclassical school. While Ingres painted the coolly classical ideal, proclaiming the superiority of line over color, Delacroix portrayed the heroic, with a fervor for action and color. Neither had much respect for the other, and the Ecole des Beaux-Arts, where Ingres and his followers reigned, snubbed Delacroix for years.

At long last, in 1857—on his eighth attempt—the Académie des Beaux-Arts in the Institut de France received Delacroix as a member. This considerable honor allowed him to serve on the prestigious Salon jury, but Delacroix was dismissive of the honor. He merely commented that he flattered himself that he could be of use there, "because I shall be nearly alone in my opinion."[1]

He proved this two years later, when young Edouard Manet submitted his first painting to the Salon—*The Absinthe Drinker*, a study of one of the Parisian characters Manet had met in the course of his strolls around the city. The Salon emphatically rejected Manet's effort, on the grounds that its subject matter was vulgar. Manet was furious, but he was partially consoled by the information that Delacroix had liked it. Delacroix's opinion mattered to Manet: "I don't care for his technique," Manet wrote a friend, "but he knows what he wants and gets it."[2]

The **Ecole des Beaux-Arts,** whose members Delacroix so regularly infuriated, has its roots in the reign of Louis XIV. After being suppressed during the Revolution, it was revived in the early 1800s under state supervision, with the mandate of promoting the fine arts at the highest levels. Under the watchful eye of successive monarchist governments, it is not surprising that the school's administration and teachers (and their students) followed a conservative course, and over the years, numerous artists besides Delacroix found it hidebound (Viollet-le-Duc flatly refused to attend). But the institution did at length embrace reforms, however slowly.

Today's school (formally L'Ecole Nationale Supérieure des Beaux-Arts de Paris, and informally known as BAP, or Beaux-Arts de Paris) occupies a considerable chunk of land along the Seine and has absorbed several earlier structures, most notably the seventeenth-century chapel and cloister from the former convent of the Petits-Augustins. Their founder was Marguerite de Valois—daughter of Henri II and wife of Henri IV—whose colorful career intersected with the bloody religious wars devastating France (it was her wedding with then-Protestant Henri that prompted the Saint Bartholomew's Day massacre). In the early 1600s, now divorced from Henri, she retired to a palace that she built along the Seine, complete with extensive gardens on what had been the medieval playing field, the Pré-aux-Clercs. Here she provided shelter for the Order of the Petits-Augustins, whose chapel and portions of its cloister remain.

All of this might have disappeared had it not been for the efforts of Alexandre Lenoir, a self-taught archaeologist, who took it upon himself to save whatever he could of France's historic monuments and sculptures from the hands of the Revolutionaries. He was not able to prevent much of their vandalism, but he did manage to preserve some significant sculptures and architectural features, largely from châteaux and churches, which he gathered in Marguerite's convent of the Petits-Augustins—and which in turn was saved.

Lenoir's efforts gave birth (in 1795) to the Musée des Monuments Français, which he administered for many years. It now comprises one part of the Cité de L'Architecture and du Patrimoine in the Right Bank's Palais de Chaillot.[3]

Enter the vast Cour d'Honneur, which faces the grand Palais des Etudes. On your right is the Baroque Chapel of the Petits-Augustins, and ahead, if you can get inside, is the Palais des Etudes with its central Cour Vitrée, a magnificent glassed-over courtyard in opulent classical style. And then head around the corner to the **Cour du Mûrier**, a lovely surprise in the center of this vast architectural spread. This gracious courtyard is surrounded by the chapel of the Petits-Augustins and the convent's cloister, whose arcades are now artistically filled with some of the classical sculptures and fragments that Lenoir rescued.

But the courtyard itself is the star. Named after the ancient mulberry trees at its center, the Cour du Mûrier is a gem, where plantings and the trickling water from a Baroque fountain provide peace and quiet beauty. It is a lovely place of refuge in the midst of the overwhelming architecture that surrounds it.

⌣

Cour du Mûrier, Ecole Nationale Supérieure des Beaux-Arts de Paris. © M. McAuliffe

Nearby is the surprising **Hôtel des Monnaies,** "the last factory in Paris"—a beautiful eighteenth-century structure that is the historic site of the Paris Mint. This institution has roots going back more than a millennium, with its official founding in 864 A.D.—making it France's most ancient institution and, according to its claims, the oldest enterprise in the world.

Since the 1970s, a regional plant in Pessac does the heavy-duty minting of circulating coins, making all Euro coins used in France as well as those used in several other small countries in the Euro zone. The Pessac plant also mints the coins of a number of other countries. But here in Paris, the Hôtel des Monnaies no longer mints everyday coinage and tends to the artistic side of things, producing works of artistic craftsmanship in its still-going artisan workshops.

These can be visited, as can treasures in the Monnaies de Paris's recently opened collections. But do not miss the opulent grand salon and palatial double staircase in the building's Seine-facing frontage. Michelin-starred chef Guy Savoy has moved to the first-floor rooms of the west wing, over-looking the Seine, and there also is a less-pricey café below. But you can come and gawk for free at the salon and staircase, and eventually we will be able to walk through a garden planned for the Hôtel des Monnaies' Mansart Wing, originally the Petit Hôtel de Conti.

After being closed to the public for centuries, the Hôtel des Monnaies is no longer a huge building to avoid en route to someplace else, but one to explore.

Henri IV celebrated the birth of his heir, the Dauphin (who in time became Louis XIII), with a plethora of place-names: Place Dauphine, at the western end of the Ile de la Cité; Rue Dauphine, which continues the route of the Pont Neuf onto the Left Bank; and **Passage Dauphine,** a tiny cobblestoned byway that can take one back to the seventeenth century. The last is a small gem in the midst of one of the most loved parts of Paris, leading to other small byways, such as Rue Christine, where Gertrude Stein made her last Paris home—moving from her famous 27 Rue de Fleurus address to 5 Rue Christine, right around the corner from the Rue des Grands-Augustins studio of Stein's longtime friend and sparring partner, Pablo Picasso.

It is near here that Philip Augustus built his wall encircling the Left Bank of what then was Paris. This twelfth-century wonder consisted of stone ram-parts ten feet wide and thirty feet high, punctuated by a battery of towers and reinforced with a deep ditch. His Left Bank encirclement began with a tower (the Tour de Nesle) on the approximate site of the present Institut de France and continued along present Rue Mazarine to Rue de l'Ancienne-Comédie and Rue Monsieur-le-Prince. A remnant of one of Philip's towers stands in the Cour du Commerce Saint-André, and a piece of his massive wall rises near the Panthéon, on Rue Clovis, while place-names such as the Place de la Contrescarpe and Rue des Fossés Saint-Bernard trace the wall's semicircular route (the Place de la Contrescarpe marked the southern point of the counterscarp, or sloping outer side of the deep ditch surrounding the wall, while *fossé* means moat or ditch). Rue Mazarine, by the way, was once called Rue des Fossés-de-Nesle, while Rue Monsieur-le-Prince was once Rue des Fossés-Monsieur-le-Prince.

But the anchor of this massive fortification lay on the Right Bank, in a fortress that Philip built that soon became known as the **Louvre**.

Saint-Germain l'Auxerrois, from La Samaritaine. © M. McAuliffe

CHAPTER SIX

~

Dangerous Times

The **Louvre**, or Palais du Louvre, began life as a fortress, a defense against the king of England. Philip II, later called Philip Augustus, responded vigorously to the fact that the current English monarch, the famed Richard Lionheart, was also—thanks to William the Conqueror, Henry II, and Eleanor of Aquitaine—duke of Normandy and ruler of half of France besides. Ever since William the Conqueror captured the English crown, the English monarchs had outclassed their French counterparts in everything that mattered, and the two crowns had been sparring meaningfully along the frontiers of their holdings for more than a century. By Philip's time, it was not difficult to imagine the legendary warrior, Lionheart, crossing the bloody Vexin borderlands and leading an army the mere fifty miles from his Norman holdings to Paris. In response to this nightmare, Philip erected the original Louvre, a bristling castle keep surrounded by a moat.

The current Louvre, now the abode of one of the richest collections of art and antiquities in the world, has little to do with the Louvre of the past. In the centuries since Philip Augustus, Henri IV extended the Louvre's long waterside Galerie du Bord de l'Eau (the Grande Galerie), while Bonaparte and his nephew, Napoleon III, built the parallel northern (now Richelieu) wing. In the meantime, Louis XIV erected the grand Colonnade that faces east. The Louvre of today is no longer either a fortress or a palace but a museum toured by millions, all of them intent on having seen the *Mona Lisa* and a few other wildly popular works.

I would not argue with the thrill that one gets from glimpsing the *Winged Victory* from the bottom of the Daru staircase—the staircase that Audrey Hepburn so memorably floated down in *Funny Face*, her red chiffon gown wafting behind her in glorious imitation of the marble Victory above. Nor would I object to those whose lists include the *Venus de Milo*, although the crowds milling around (selfies anyone?) can dissipate the proper mood. Still, it is possible. I recall catching a memorable glimpse of Venus one evening when the Louvre was closing and the guards had begun their sweep. The lights had gone off, leaving Venus backlit at the end of a long corridor—an unforgettable vision.

Not surprisingly, waiting in long lines to see the *Mona Lisa*, only to be hustled through her presence, can be disappointing. But these same crowds tramp unseeingly past two of Leonardo's most extraordinary creations, *The Virgin and Child with Saint Anne* and *The Virgin of the Rocks*. Ignore the throngs surging past. You have found treasure.

Nearby, in the company of other nineteenth-century French paintings, is Delacroix's *Liberty Leading the People*, an understandably popular destination for Louvre-goers, with its now-familiar but still dramatic scene from the bar-ricades of France's 1830 Revolution. The French claim it for their own, but everyone else can respond just as easily to its color and drama.

A friend once advised me to limit each of my visits to the Louvre to a handful of items, and this advice has proved wise—anything more can be overwhelming, like eating too much ice cream. For newcomers, it's probably best to include the major attractions, but others may want to pick a theme, whether an artist, a period, or even a type of historical object. Recently, I focused on the museum's ceilings. Ceilings? But of course! There are many glorious ones in this former palace, especially as you wander from the Denon Wing to the Richelieu, not forgetting to look up as you go. As you leave the masses lined up to see the *Mona Lisa* in the Salle des Etats, check out the magnificent ceiling of the Salon Denon, followed by the ceiling of the glittering Apollo Gallery. Be careful to watch your step crossing the Escalier Mollien (Mollien Staircase), which distracts with its own ceiling paintings, and then make your way down the connecting corridor between the Denon and Richelieu Wings, which forms the western side of the Sully Wing sur-rounding the Louvre's Cour Carrée—an open square of Renaissance gran-deur, whose southwest corner is built on the foundations of the medieval Louvre.

The famous portrait of the Sun King, Louis XIV, will greet you as you pass, and then pause at the Salle Henri II, where Henri II (mid-1500s) actually lived and climbed into his royal robes. The ceiling painting here is a surprise, a 1953 contribution by Georges Braque, called *Birds*. Braque, after all, is more usually found in the Pompidou's Musée National d'Art Moderne. From there, turn left into the Richelieu Wing, where with some luck, you'll find yourself in the glittering Napoleon III rooms, with their own magnificent ceilings. Also in this much-quieter Richelieu Wing, Vermeer's *Lacemaker* offers a stillness that transcends the centuries.

As for Philip's **medieval fortress**, you can still see portions of its base, including its impressive donjon, as well as the Salle Saint-Louis—a hall built around 1200 and given its ribbed vaults and sculptures a few decades later. These reside in the depths of the Sully Wing and were discovered only recently in the course of archaeological digs. Dimly lit and rarely visited, these extraordinary remnants provide a powerful glimpse of the past.

Philip's fortification was never put to the test—Lionheart and his troops never appeared on the horizon, and subsequently, the Louvre served as an arsenal and repository for the royal treasury. But royalty never considered it a suitable residence until Charles V hastily decamped from the Palais de la Cité—the royal palace built, like its Gallo-Roman and Merovingian predecessors, at the western tip of the Ile de la Cité. Charles evacuated this palace for good in 1357, following a bloody confrontation with Etienne Marcel and a Paris mob.

Charles moved into a new palace, the Hôtel Saint-Pol, or Saint-Paul, in the shadow of his Right Bank fortress, the Bastille. He also took up residence in the Louvre, which he transformed into a comfortable residence, complete with library. The Louvre had lost its defensive function long before Charles moved in. Still, his new palace retained much of its old look, and in 1546, François I gave the order to demolish much of the outdated structure and replace it with a lavish new one. He did not live to complete the job, but his son, Henri II, carried on, transforming the medieval great hall located above the Salle Saint-Louis into the magnificent **Salle des Caryatides**—one of my favorite destinations in the Louvre.

Jean Goujon, the sculptor responsible for carving the pillars in the shape of draped women (caryatides) that gave the hall its name, also contributed the rich carvings above the massive Escalier Henri II outside. These easy-to-miss but superb carvings extend for two full staircases, and if you are sharp you will find numerous references there to Henri's beloved mistress, Diane de Poitiers. These include Henri's "H" entwined with Diane's "D," as well as crescent moons and hunting themes, all symbols of the goddess Diana.

Henri was madly in love with Diane but was married to Catherine de Medici, who completed the unhappy triangle by being deeply in love with him. Although primarily residing at the Louvre, the royal couple also held court at the nearby Hôtel des Tournelles, located just north of today's Place des Vosges, which occupies the former Tournelles gardens. When a freak accident in a festive tournament at the Hôtel des Tournelles led to Henri's death, his distraught queen had the whole place razed to the ground. She tried living at the Louvre but didn't like it, and so she built her own residence nearby. And this is how the Palais des Tuileries came to be.

Not many years later, Catherine's son-in-law, Henri IV, began to reconstruct much of Paris, including the Louvre, to which he added the massive riverside gallery stretching all the way to Catherine's Palais des Tuileries. This ambitious project certainly was not meant to facilitate visits from his formidable mother-in-law, who had been instrumental in the Saint Bartholomew's Day massacre that had narrowly missed killing him. Probably to Henri's relief, Catherine had died by the time he became king and embarked on his grandiose plans—many of which remained incomplete at the time of his own death.

Henri's son, Louis XIII, lived in the Louvre and reportedly enjoyed it, although he found it a bit cramped and kept on with the work of enlarging it. But Henri's grandson, Louis XIV, had unhappy memories of both the Louvre and of Paris. As a child, he had been forced by angry mobs to abandon the Louvre for the nearby Palais Royal. There, the boy king and his mother lived in the midst of civil war and danger.

Once safely on the throne, Louis (soon to be known as the Sun King) returned to live in the Louvre. But although investing in huge building projects there (such as the Apollo Gallery, the Cour Carrée, and the great Colonnade), he never really liked the place—nor Paris. Eventually he abandoned both for Versailles, leaving the Louvre to fall into ruin. It was not until the nineteenth century that two Napoleons, I and III, restored and completed the massive edifice, creating the Louvre whose outlines we know today.

But neither of the Napoleons (Bonaparte or his nephew) actually lived in the Louvre, which Bonaparte turned into an enormous museum for his plunder. Instead, both preferred the **Palais des Tuileries**, the palace built by Catherine de Medici and which, by Napoleon III's day, stretched from one tip to the other of the Louvre's extended northern and southern wings, with its palace gardens beyond and to the west. Although dating from the sixteenth century, the Palais des Tuileries never really came into its own as a royal—or imperial—abode until the nineteenth century. Even its builder, the superstitious Catherine de Medici, departed after a few years, prompted by a horoscope that seemed to predict her death if she remained there.

The Tuileries' return to notice as a royal residence was not an auspicious one—at least, not so far as royalty was concerned. The Paris mob forcibly brought Louis XVI and his family here from Versailles in 1789, the better to keep an eye on them. Louis, Marie Antoinette, and their children lived here as virtual prisoners for almost three years, until a mob stormed the place. Prison and the guillotine ultimately followed.

But this was not enough to discourage Napoleon Bonaparte, who only a few years later turned the Tuileries into the most imperial of palaces. This lasted throughout his reign, but after Waterloo, the Bourbons—Louis XVI's younger brothers—returned to power. Although determined to eradicate all memories of the years of empire and revolution, both of these monarchs (Louis XVIII, followed by the even more hidebound Charles X) were quick to adopt the Tuileries rather than Versailles as their primary residence. By the time the 1830 Revolution booted out Charles X, making way for Louis-Philippe (of the royal Orléans line), Paris and the Tuileries seemed to be unquestionably the place for French royalty to live.

But it was Napoleon Bonaparte's nephew, Emperor Napoleon III, who brought the Palais des Tuileries into its greatest glory. Guided by his beautiful Spanish empress, Eugénie, Napoleon III created at the Tuileries a lifestyle that was the envy of Europe. The gilded **Napoleon III Rooms** in the Louvre's Richelieu Wing give a taste for the sumptuousness in which he indulged.

After two decades of imperial rule, France went to war with Prussia, with disastrous results. Napoleon III was captured, and Paris underwent a four-month winter siege of brutal hardship followed by a widespread uprising of Paris's battered poor. During this bloody uprising, known as the Paris Commune of 1871, thousands of Parisians died at the hands of other Parisians, and much of Paris, including the Palais des Tuileries, went up in flames.[1] The Tuileries' sad and somber hulk remained until 1883, when it was razed, leaving the view of the Tuileries Gardens and beyond that today's visitors to the Louvre so enjoy.

Fortunately, the Louvre escaped burning (by a hair), as did the Palais de l'Elysée—formerly the Paris abode of Louis XV's favorite, Madame de Pompadour, and since 1873 (and the birth of the Third Republic) the official residence of the president of France. Just as off-limits to today's hoi polloi as the royal palaces of centuries past, the Palais de l'Elysée looks sumptuous, and evidently is. Charles de Gaulle, in fact, complained about it—he preferred something simpler.

⌒

One remnant of the Tuileries' glory days is Bonaparte's **Arc de Triomphe du Carrousel**, the lesser-known sibling of Bonaparte's grand (and twice as large) Arc de Triomphe de l'Etoile to the west. Still, this is an impressive monument, and Bonaparte erected it as a suitably grand entrance to the Palais des Tuileries, which then stretched from one side of the Louvre to the other (picture the entire eastern end of the Tuileries Gardens filled by it). Bonaparte capped it with the glorious bronze *Horses of Saint Mark*, a Byzantine treasure from the loggia of Saint Mark's Basilica, which he brought back after capturing Venice. Following Waterloo, these went back to Venice, and a copy took their place.

After the Palais des Tuileries burned during the Communard uprising of 1871, the Third Republic dithered over whether or not to replace the palace but then decided to clear out the blackened ruins that remained. Nowadays crowds stream through this arch without realizing what it once was, or what it signified. It remains as a rather lonely link to Bonaparte and to all the French monarchs who resided in a palace that no longer exists.

Arc de Triomphe du Carrousel. © J. McAuliffe

On the Louvre's eastern side, the church of **Saint-Germain l'Auxerrois** has a dramatic history. Located right across the street from the oldest portion of the Louvre, this church dates from the twelfth century and was the parish church of royalty.

It is best known for its role in the bloody events of Saint Bartholomew's Day, 1572, when its bell tower rang out the signal for the massacre of thousands of Huguenots (French Protestants), who were in town for the wedding of their king, Henri of Navarre, to Marguerite of Valois, sister of the French king. The wedding was supposed to mark a truce during the bloody Wars of Religion, but now all bets were off, especially as the massacres spread throughout France.

Despite the odds, Henri survived and eventually put an end to the warfare and became king of France (as Henri IV) by converting to Catholicism. He established peace, good government, and prosperity and undertook an extraordinary building plan for Paris, including that vast waterside (or Denon) wing of the Louvre, the Pont Neuf, and much more.

Marguerite, for her part, went on to a colorful career, while her mother, Catherine de Medici, ruthlessly exercised power as queen-mother during the consecutive reigns of her young sons, following the death of her husband, Henri II. History has held Catherine accountable for the Saint Bartholomew's Day massacre, and although some have excused her from this particular atrocity, it would have been entirely in character. As was the possibility that, as a young bride, she was responsible for poisoning her husband's older brother, making her husband heir to the throne.

These were brutal times, and Catherine was a survivor. But many she encountered were not so lucky.

After spending the morning at the Louvre, you may want a place to sit and catch your breath, preferably someplace that's quiet. The renowned writer Colette was looking for just such a quiet place in the heart of town when she moved to tiny Rue de Beaujolais, on the far side of the **Palais Royal**. This palace, a near neighbor of the Louvre, was originally the sumptuous residence of Cardinal Richelieu, Louis XIII's powerful chief minister of *Three Musketeers* fame (or infamy, take your pick). Upon his death, the palace became the property of the crown, acquiring the name of the Palais Royal, and it housed a series of royal exiles, including the very young Louis XIV.

By the late 1600s it had become the property of the duke of Orléans, the younger brother of the king, and it remained in the Orléans line until the Revolution. By then its current owner, Philippe d'Orléans, had significantly augmented his income by erecting colonnades around the palace gardens and filling them with elegant cafés and purveyors of luxury goods, where it became the height of fashion to shop and socialize. As Revolution approached, the cafés of the Palais Royal became a favorite with political activists, while gamblers and prostitutes frequented the arcades by night, providing a more raucous atmosphere to this otherwise refined garden of delights.

Philippe, who had capped a life of dissolution by shrewdly reinventing himself as a revolutionary champion of the common man, changed his name during the Revolution to Philippe-Egalité to symbolize his sympathies. But scarcely a year after casting his vote for his cousin Louis XVI's execution, he followed his king to the guillotine. In time, Philippe's son would become king of France (Louis-Philippe, the so-called Bourgeois King), but the Palais Royal remained a popular shopping destination. Frederick Chopin, a dandy and elegant dresser, enjoyed shopping there in the 1830s and 1840s.

There still are expensive shops and a famed restaurant in the gardens of the Palais Royal, but it is a far quieter place than it once was, and famous writers, including Jean Cocteau and Colette, lived here—Cocteau at 36 Rue de Montpensier, and Colette at 9 Rue de Beaujolais, a place she adored.

The gardens of the Palais Royal are especially lovely in the spring, but happily, the roses continue into autumn.

Just a skip and a jump from the Palais Royal—up some stairs and across Rue des Petits-Champs—is the Galerie Vivienne, one of the many **Passages of Paris**. These are networks of glass-covered walkways lined with shops and cafés that wind through and between buildings, many connecting the streets around the ever-popular Grands Boulevards. Dating from the early 1800s, these could be called the first shopping malls, and they were immediately popular with customers who enjoyed browsing while keeping warm and dry. These passages also remain popular with those who want to cut through from one street to another.

Some, like the Galerie Vivienne, are glamorous, while others range from charmingly funky to downright tacky, but they are a trip back to the past, to the early years of the nineteenth century. They can lead you on a merry chase, with a certain amount of puzzlement as to where you will come out. Galerie Vivienne (built in 1823) extends parallel to Galerie Colbert, also gorgeous but no longer lined with shops. The nearby Passage des Panoramas (built in 1799) is a regular rabbit warren that leads (across Boulevard Mont-martre) to the Passage Jouffroy. This in turn connects with the Passage Verdeau, a less elegant but still charming member of this evocative group.

Once there were many more of these covered passages, creating an even more widespread network. But those that remain are a great treat to wander through, a pleasant way to soak up the atmosphere of nineteenth-century Paris.

Tour Jean-sans-Peur. © J. McAuliffe

CHAPTER SEVEN

~

Walls and Wars

Passages and walls—all are curious and relatively unknown mementoes of Paris's past. The walls of Paris are especially intriguing because, for centuries, Paris was a walled city, surrounded by real, working walls—walls meant to keep out an enemy. And although it may seem strange to think of the City of Light enveloped by bristling defenses, this has been exactly the case for much of its history.

In fact, Paris has had many walls, each encircling the city like so many rings on a tree. Just as rings tell the story of a tree's growth, these walls tell the story of this city's growth. For Paris's walls, or series of walls, have given the city its distinctive shape—not only the outwardly spiraling outline of its arrondissements, but the arch of its Grands Boulevards, the curvature of its No. 2 and No. 6 Métro lines (circling Paris from the Arc de Triomphe in the west to the Place de la Nation in the east), and the familiar path of its beltway, the Périphérique.

The earliest of this long string of fortifications dates from the third century A.D., when the Romans erected sturdy walls around the Ile de la Cité and their nearby forum to protect Gallo-Roman Paris (Lutetia) from barbarian attacks. Centuries later, when Paris was struggling with yet another onslaught—this time from the Norse—Eudes, count of Paris, built fortifications at the entrance to both bridges linking Right and Left Banks to the Ile de la Cité. In time, a wooden stockade may have encircled a portion of the Right Bank. Its eastern gate, Porte Baudoyer, may have bestowed its name on Place Baudoyer.

Wooden defenses and the crumbling remains of Roman walls seem to have done the job for a while, but by the late twelfth century, the threat from the English monarch, Richard Lionheart, set the French to building a far sturdier set of fortifications. Philip Augustus surrounded the Paris of his day with stone ramparts and towers, anchored by his formidable riverside castle, the Louvre.

One portion of this grand enterprise encircled a substantial portion of the Left Bank, while the other—starting from the Louvre fortification itself—enclosed an area that extended as far north as the remarkable Tour Jean-sans-Peur and ended at the river, near a surviving tower-to-tower stretch along Rue des Jardins-Saint-Paul (4th).

The **Tour Jean-sans-Peur** (20 Rue Etienne-Marcel, 2nd), which stands close to the wall's northernmost point, is a stunning relic of the fifteenth century, not the twelfth, but it incorporates a piece of Philip's wall, including the base of one of its many towers. According to legend, Jean-sans-Peur, duc de Bourgogne (Burgundy), built the tower (between 1409–1411) as a place of refuge following his assassination of Louis d'Orléans, brother of the French king (one of many violent episodes during the Hundred Years' War). It is just as likely that the fearless duke erected it as a highly visible and impressive symbol of his power. After all, civil war between the Burgundians and the House of Orléans had erupted following the assassination, and the duke had just returned to Paris in triumph after defeating supporters of the House of Orléans. This left Jean-sans-Peur and his followers in charge of Paris.

What a showpiece he built! Soaring high above his Parisian quarters at the now-defunct Hôtel de Bourgogne, and muscled right up against Philip's twelfth-century wall, Duke Jean's tower bristled with rugged stonework. Its spiral staircase and open stories effectively islanded its topmost floors, where legend tells us that Jean hid out.

Ironically, this formidable tower never had to prove its military worth, for Jean's enemies never dared attack him inside Paris. Instead, in a perfectly executed act of vengeance, they assassinated him outside the city. After that, the tower fell into decline until the nineteenth century, when enthusiasts rediscovered its romantic ruins. Still, little was done to save it until recent years, when a trained archaeologist from the neighborhood decided to restore it and open it to the public. This includes exhibits giving visitors historical context as well as glimpses into fifteenth-century life.

The Tour Jean-sans-Peur is the only medieval fortified structure in Paris to have survived intact, and it is a beauty. Its spiral staircase is dramatic, and its carved vaulting (entwined branches and leaves of oak, hawthorn, and hop vine) is unequaled in France. Supported largely by admission fees as well as private efforts and funds, it welcomes all visitors.

It's a rare glimpse into a vanished world.

Philip Auguste's twelfth-century wall remained the city's only defense for two centuries, when hostilities once again broke out between France and England. By this time, the burgeoning city had grown into a cramped metropolis that was pushing hard against the confines of Philip's outdated wall. Given England's crushing victories on French soil, France's king Charles V determined to do something about the antiquated ramparts that so indifferently defended—and grievously constrained—his people.

His solution was to build a new wall, encircling a far larger area. But unlike Philip, he chose to place this bristling new fortification around only the commercial Right Bank, which by this time had far outstripped the university-centered Left Bank in growth and prosperity. Leaving the Left Bank to whatever protection Philip's antiquated ramparts could still provide, Charles flung his bulwarks in a wide arc from approximately the site of the present Place du Carrousel (in the midst of today's Louvre) in the west to his formidable new fortress, the Bastille, in the east.

Moving the old city gates outward along such major thoroughfares as Rue Saint-Denis and Rue Saint-Martin to the north, and Rue Saint-Antoine and Rue Saint-Honoré to the east and west, he in effect created a new and larger shell for the prospering Right Bank city within. He also provided protection for the new royal palace at the Hôtel Saint-Paul (the site now bounded by Rue Saint-Paul, Rue Saint-Antoine, and Rue du Petit-Musc, near the Bastille) and the Louvre, which—now inside the city walls and denied all defensive pretense—he converted into a royal residence.

Some two centuries later, as religious and civil warfare engulfed France, yet another Charles (Charles IX) and a Louis (Louis XIII) extended this wall in an arc from the Saint-Denis gate westward, to encompass the city's growing Right Bank. The wall now stretched in a rough semicircle from the Bastille in the east to a point ending between the present-day Place de la Concord and the Tuileries Gardens in the west.

Remnants of this wall unexpectedly came to light during recent renovations of the Musée de l'Orangerie (Place de la Concorde), where a lengthy section has now been preserved. The Bastille of course was demolished, but you can find vestiges of its counterscarp in the Bastille station of the No. 5 Métro line. You can also find the remains of one of its eight towers, the Tour de la Liberté, in the nearby **Square Henri-Galli**, on the banks of the

Seine, where it was carted stone by stone. Most importantly, though, you can still trace the course of Louis XIII's wall as you stroll down the **Grands Boulevards**, from the Place de la Madeleine in the west all the way to the Place de la Bastille in the east, for the Sun King himself, Louis XIV, laid out these most Parisian of all promenades along the course of his father's defensive wall, which he pulled down in the wake of satisfying victories over all his enemies.

The word "boulevard" itself, historians remind us, derives from an old German word for "bulwark."

⌒

Charles IX, the sixteenth-century monarch who extended his predecessor's Right Bank wall, was a young man in a lot of trouble. The son of Catherine de Medici, he came to the throne in 1560 at the age of ten, upon the death of his older brother, Francis II (who had been married to Mary, Queen of Scots, the Catholic rival to England's Protestant Queen Elizabeth).

Wars between the Catholics and the Protestants (Huguenots) were raging in France as elsewhere following Martin Luther's bold proclamation of his Ninety-Five Theses in 1517. In France, after several attempts at peace between the warring sides, the by-now twenty-two-year-old Charles ordered his sister, Marguerite, to marry the Huguenot leader Henri of Navarre. Facing an uprising of those who opposed this attempt at peace, Charles did nothing to stop the Saint Bartholomew's Day massacre that his mother, Catherine de Medici, is usually blamed for instigating.

Catherine was by this time a widow, and a deeply embittered one. The first ten years of her marriage to Henri II had produced no children, and by then the pressure was on to produce a male heir. At last, a son was born, followed in rapid order by nine siblings, the last of which, twins, almost killed Catherine. But this diminutive lady was a survivor, possibly helping her husband to the throne through poisoning his older brother, and most likely prompting the massacre of all those Huguenot leaders who were threatening the French crown.

But Catherine's cup was a bitter one. Having done all this for her husband, whom she seems to have dearly loved, he returned the favor by turning his attentions elsewhere, to the beautiful Diane de Poitiers. Intelligent, well-educated, and supremely capable, this sixteenth-century aristocrat could have run a twenty-first-century corporation; instead, Diane de Poitiers virtually ran France. The king adored this beautiful and confident older woman, whom he had worshipped since the age of twelve, when he charmed onlookers at a royal tournament by requesting to wear her colors (famously, black and white). Diane de Poitiers had been thirty-one at the time—nineteen years Henri's senior, in an era when women were considered over-the-hill at thirty.

But this remarkable widow, with children of her own, was an exception to just about every rule. Maintaining an impressive regimen of skin care and exercise, she retained her slim figure and beauty well into her sixties. Diane dazzled young Henri. And what everyone assumed was a platonic friendship eventually developed into something far more serious. By the time Henri was eighteen (and possibly earlier), the two were lovers. Diane insisted on discretion, and she never openly assumed the role of royal mistress. But over the course of their more than twenty-year relationship, Henri ran his kingdom with Diane's advice, entrusted her with the crown jewels, gifted her with the extraordinary Château de Chenonceau, and entwined their initials into a single monogram that he lovingly inscribed just about everywhere.

Henri died in a freak accident during a festive tournament at the Hôtel des Tournelles, when a lance thrust by a royal favorite, the Count de Montgomery, accidentally pierced the king's eye. On his deathbed, the king absolved Montgomery, who nonetheless wisely fled from Paris. Many were deeply grieved at the king's death, and the royal widow, Catherine, was furious. She seems to have taken out her anger on the Hôtel des Tournelles, which she had never much liked anyway, and had it razed. She also took the opportunity, at long last, to banish Diane de Poitiers from court.

Several decades of unsettled royal politics and religious warfare followed, but after a notable conversion to Catholicism, Henri of Navarre became King Henri IV. Among the many building projects with which he gifted the city of Paris, he built what now is known as the Place des Vosges, on the site of the garden of the Hôtel des Tournelles.

This was only a portion of Henri's plan for this part of Paris. Having already constructed a magnificent entry to Paris on the west, he set out to build an equally splendid gateway from the east, with broad avenues named after French provinces spreading out in a semicircular pattern from a monumental Place de France. Unfortunately, Henri's assassination put an abrupt end to this project, leaving only a few of the "spokes" of this gateway (Rue de Normandie, Rue de Bretagne, and Rue de Poitou), linked by the semicircular Rue Debelleyme.

But Henri was more fortunate in his breathtaking **Place des Vosges** (originally the Place Royale). Henri spotted the huge empty space that the Hôtel des Tournelles left in its wake and, determined to make his mark here, much as he had elsewhere in Paris, he set his architects to creating a harmonious and symmetrical square rimmed by thirty-six adjoining houses. These were

Place des Vosges. © J. McAuliffe

crowned by the splendid Pavillon du Roi to the south and a slightly smaller Pavillon de la Reine to the north. Built of brick and stone, with steep slate roofs, much like those in the Place Dauphine, these arcaded houses—nine to a side—still comprise one of the most elegant settings in Paris.

Inaugurated with the double wedding of young Louis XIII and his sister to Austrian and Spanish royalty, the square, then known as the Place Royale, became the most fashionable address in town. This reputation continued even after Louis XIV established Versailles as *the* place to be, although in time the aristocrats moved out and the neighborhood changed. When Victor Hugo lived here in gloomy Gothic splendor in the 1830s and 1840s, the square existed as a kind of island in the midst of a working-class sea. (Hugo's house, now a museum, is at no. 6.) By this time it had shed its royalist name and become the Place des Vosges—in honor of the department of the Vosges, which in 1800 stood first in line to pay its taxes to the new Republic.

Now this magnificent square is once again home to wealth and splendor, conveyed—in characteristic Henri IV fashion—with elegant restraint. By late afternoon this square of fountain-dotted lawns can become filled with students lounging on the grass, mothers and nannies supervising their charges (there are two large in-demand sandboxes), and a mix of locals who come here regularly and tourists who just happened to wander in.

My favorite entrance to this urban oasis is through the **Hôtel de Sully**, a mansion built in the early 1600s and acquired by the Duke de Sully, Henri IV's all-powerful minister of finance. This, like other private mansions of its era, is built between courtyard and garden, with its garden in the rear. Enter the courtyard from Rue Saint-Antoine. After some steps and a visit to the intriguing bookshop run by the Centre des Monuments Nationaux, cross into the mansion's formal garden, which is a delight on a warm day. There you will find one of the most photographed whatsits in Paris, an ancient-looking carved stone wheel. Tourists regularly whip out their cameras, photographing Junior peering through, but this is no museum piece. Turns out it's a relatively recent student project for artisans learning their trade. Unexpectedly, it was such a success that the powers that be decided to keep it, much to the delight of those now passing by.

But the best is yet to come. Go through that small doorway in the garden's far right-hand corner and you will find yourself under the arcade that surrounds the Place des Vosges. There, linger a while beneath the well-clipped trees, listening to the fountains and watching the children. This may be a high-rent district, but all the quiet park benches are free.

Word of the Place des Vosges' charms has been spreading, but few still seem to know about its virtual twin, just north of the Place de la République. Here, with typical concern for his city's well-being, Henri IV built a hospital for plague victims just outside the city walls (a necessary consideration, given the contagious nature of the disease). Like the Place des Vosges, and much like the Place Dauphine, the original portion of the **Hôpital Saint-Louis** consists of a brick-and-stone quadrangle surrounding a tree-filled courtyard. The similarities have prompted speculation that the architect of the Place des Vosges created this beauty as well. This rarely crowded courtyard is open to visitors on weekdays and may be entered through the original gate on Place du Docteur-Alfred-Fournier.

Beyond the walled complex lie other original buildings, including a lovely little chapel, whose exterior has recently been restored. There is also the Pavillon Gabrielle, where Henri is rumored to have frolicked with his favorite mistress, Gabrielle d'Estrées. Henri had always been an unapologetic womanizer, and golden-haired Gabrielle did not change his ways. Still, she mesmerized him sufficiently that it was rumored he would wed her, once the annulment of his current (and childless) marriage to Queen Marguerite came through. This news created consternation at court, for although Gabrielle was nobly born, her enemies (most notably, the Medici clan) did not want to see her son by Henri become heir to the throne. At the age of twenty-six, Gabrielle had already borne Henri three children, and she now was pregnant with a fourth.

It was Gabrielle d'Estrées whose nude portrait in the tub, with her sister, I mentioned earlier. It is a curious painting. Both women are shown nude from the waist up, and the sister is pinching Gabrielle's nipple. Odd? Certainly. But art historians believe that this pose, and the ring that Gabrielle flaunts, may allude to her pregnancy by and anticipated marriage to the king.

Gabrielle may have been beautiful and intelligent, but she does not seem to have been sufficiently prudent. Instead of maintaining a discreet silence about her prospects, she boasted of them. Subsequently, in the midst of dinner, she suddenly went into convulsions, gave birth to a stillborn son, and died. Poison? Many thought so, although there never was any proof. But it was enough to give pause to those royal mistresses who followed.

～

While Henri was frolicking with Gabrielle, what was happening to his queen, Marguerite de Valois? They had begun wedded life under the shadow of the Saint Bartholomew's Day massacre and the resumption of France's wars of religion, and had gone on from there. Henry was the leader of the

Huguenots, and Marguerite, a Catholic, was burdened with a family that was remarkably adversarial, even for royals of the time. Making her position even more difficult, she did not produce an heir—or any children at all.

Was she a beautiful, intelligent, and cultured woman of great refinement, who bravely attempted to bring peace between her warring (and frequently villainous) relations? Or was she a scheming nymphomaniac who committed incest with her brother and deserted her husband? Political pamphleteers of the time popularized the latter, but Alexandre Dumas drew upon the more attractive version in his historical novel, *La Reine Margot*. In any case, the disparity between the two Marguerites is perhaps best illustrated by her two après-exile residences in Paris—her palace on the Left Bank and her temporary residence on the Right Bank, the Hôtel de Sens.

Remember that by the time Marguerite returned to Paris, after eighteen years of exile, she was divorced. Henry, after all, had wanted an heir and, soon after the annulment of his marriage with Marguerite, he married Marie de Medici, who promptly gave him a son (the future Louis XIII). If Marguerite was going to live in Paris, where she had previously reigned as queen, she wanted a suitable palace—which she proceeded to build along the Seine, complete with extensive gardens and its own convent, the Petits-Augustins (possibly meant as a sign of her religious devotion). This of course took time to build, and while it was under construction, Marguerite accepted the invitation of the archbishop of Sens to stay in his Paris residence (the archbishops of Sens then claimed the diocese of Paris as an ecclesiastical dependency).

Completed in 1519, the **Hôtel de Sens**, located on the Right Bank near the river, was widely regarded as one of the most beautiful residences in Paris, concocted in the Flamboyant Gothic style and arrayed with fierce corner turrets—as befitted a feudal dwelling in still-dangerous times. Yet since its inception, it had remained virtually vacant, making it an ideal residence for a divorced queen. Marguerite, now pudgy and with a blonde wig, arrived there in 1605 and immediately set the place swinging. Soon two of her lovers were at each other's throats, and before long one had killed the other at the mansion's door. Infuriated by the loss of her current favorite, Marguerite did not hesitate. The next day, the luckless survivor went to his own death—on the very doorstep where he had dispatched his rival. Not the fainting kind, Marguerite grimly watched his execution.

It was without question the most newsworthy event ever to come out of the staid Hôtel de Sens. It was rivaled only by Marguerite's memorable encounter with a large fig tree near the front door, which gave offense by blocking her carriage. The tree lost the contest, but the street still is known as the Rue du Figuier.

Hôtel de Sens. © J. McAuliffe

Fortunately for us, the Hôtel de Sens has remained virtually unchanged since that time, as no one took serious interest in renovating it. But benign neglect turned less benign after 1622, when Paris finally got its own archbishop, and subsequent archbishops of Sens began to rent the place out. The once-elegant mansion now languished, first as an office for the Lyon stagecoach and eventually—reflecting the decline of the entire Marais quarter—as a jam factory and glassworks. When the city of Paris came to the building's rescue, it had a huge renovation job on its hands, but one with a happy ending. Today's Hôtel de Sens is once more a highlight of Paris's Right Bank, complete with a formal French garden to the rear—a welcome oasis of meticulously kept shrubbery, easily accessible and open to the public.

One little-known feature of today's Hôtel de Sens is the Bibliothèque Forney, located upstairs. Here you will find a wealth of reference materials on the decorative arts, including slides, posters, and drawings as well as an impressive array of fabric and wallpaper samples, some centuries old. If this is not of interest, then browse around the library itself—a magnificent room of carved stone and beamed ceilings. Off to the left, duck into the tower and explore the spiral staircase, which leads to other nooks and corners.

A great destination for a rainy day, the Hôtel de Sens is also remarkable after dark, either with or without a moon (it's almost magical on a misty night). Now one of the oldest surviving examples of domestic architecture in Paris, it effortlessly evokes the beauty and violence of a dangerous queen and a now-distant past.

Medici Fountain, Luxembourg Gardens. © J. McAuliffe

CHAPTER EIGHT

~

An Imperious Queen

Marie de Medici, Henri IV's second wife (following Marguerite de Valois), brought two essential gifts to her new husband: an heir (little Louis XIII, born just nine months after his parents' marriage) and money, lots of it. After all, Marie (much like Marguerite's mother, Catherine) was a member of the fabulously wealthy Medici banking family of Florence, and arrangements for her dowry included cancellation of the huge debts that Henri owed to Marie's father, Francesco de Medici. Henri had racked up enormous bills in beautifying Paris, and in addition had never managed to pay off the debts he incurred for the many years of warfare he conducted en route to the French throne.

Marie produced five more children during the course of their marriage, but she and her royal husband were continually at loggerheads. Henri's insistence on giving his mistresses prominent positions at court was a constant humiliation for Marie, who at length took to extending the hand of friendship to Henri's former wife, Marguerite. Marguerite's return to Paris, after years of exile, was in large part due to the efforts of Henri's second queen.

Money was another source of bickering between the royal pair, as Henri refused to give Marie the money she felt necessary (and due her) to establish and retain her position. Raised in great wealth, but from a family of commoners (as French nobility regarded bankers), Marie was intent upon establishing her position as queen by an over-the-top display of wealth. Her arrival in Paris, accompanied by a retinue of two thousand, was only the beginning.

But perhaps the most galling of all to Henri's second wife was his refusal to officially crown her queen of France. It took her almost ten years, but at length, as Henri was about to depart for battle, Marie was officially crowned queen—the idea being to give her, and her son, greater legitimacy during the king's absence. Astonishingly, the day after her coronation, Henri IV was assassinated.

Of course talk of conspiracy spread, despite the fact that Henri had been the target of other assassination attempts, and despite evidence that his assassin, François Ravaillac, was a religious fanatic with no connection whatever to Marie. Ravaillac, who was subject to visions, claimed that he was destined to save France from the Protestants, and that Henri's upcoming war in Flanders was a war against the pope, which Ravaillac personally had to prevent. He denied under torture (boiling oil, molten lead) that he had any accomplices and went to his dreadful death—pulled apart by four horses—alone.

Henri IV's reign, which he had filled with peace and rebuilding, was soon regarded by the French as a golden age, while Marie's regency was a different matter entirely. She immediately became regent on behalf of her young son, now Louis XIII, and even while under a cloud of suspicion for Henri's death, she surrounded herself with Italian Catholic advisors and royal favorites, whom the French despised. Despite the Italian Catholic influence, Marie did maintain her dead husband's policy of religious tolerance toward French Protestants, reconfirming his remarkable Edict of Nantes. But overall, she now was able to do much as she pleased. This of course meant that the moneybags were opened.

Marie had already made her mark with an extensive Right Bank riverside promenade, the Cours-la-Reine, and now aimed to make a splash on the Left Bank. Her eye fell on the Hôtel du Petit-Luxembourg, home of François de Luxembourg, whom she persuaded to sell. After adding several more adjoining properties, she set to work to build a palace worthy of a queen—a palace, moreover, that would remind her of her Florentine childhood home, the Pitti Palace. The result may be more French than Italian, but it is unequivocally grand, and the queen commissioned Peter Paul Rubens to paint a series of twenty-four huge narrative paintings of her life for the palace's first floor (they are now located in the Louvre's Richelieu Wing). Rubens loved to depict well-padded women, and Marie—still blonde and unquestionably plump—qualified as an ideal Rubens subject. Although her life was hardly heroic, Rubens managed to change the subject to one of gods and goddesses and Greek mythology.

Rubens never completed the second cycle of paintings, which were to illustrate Henri IV's life, but by then, Marie was not in a position to complain. Her son, Louis XIII, had come of age and, resenting his mother's interference in just about everything, organized a coup that assassinated one of Marie's most hated favorites and sent Marie into exile. She returned the favor by fomenting a rebellion against her son. Louis eventually was persuaded to accept his mother's return to Paris, where she once again engaged in plots but—thankfully—kept herself busy with the construction of her Luxembourg Palace and gardens.

Marie was especially engaged in creating her extensive garden, today's **Jardin du Luxembourg** (Luxembourg Gardens). Here she planted some two thousand elm trees and directed an army of gardeners to create a park in the style of the gardens she had known and loved as a child in Italy. Although neglected during the years following Marie's second (and final) exile, a variety of efforts, especially during the Second Empire, reestablished the garden in all its glory. Spreading southward from the Palais du Luxembourg, which now houses the Senate, the garden is now a major destination for those seeking rest and calm in central Paris. Everyone has a favorite spot to hang out here, whether on the terraces overlooking the fountain and basin or in one of the many smaller and more intimate gardens throughout.

A favorite for many is a spot near the Grand Bassin, where youngsters sail rented boats or proudly bring their own. A little more off the beaten track is the **Medici Fountain** (la Fontaine de Médicis), a fountain commissioned by Marie herself. With its grotto and long basin, it provides a spot that is lovely, cool, and dark, a place of mystery and enchantment that many overlook.

Fountains, especially large ones, were greatly in fashion when Marie was building her garden here, but much as at Versailles, the available water pressure was not up to the job. This had always been the case: apart from the Seine, there simply was not enough water in Paris—especially not on the Left Bank (the Right Bank's water table was nearer the surface, making it more available but also more prone to pollution). This situation of course grew infinitely worse during the summer, when the river—then much wider and shallower than today—sank into marshes and mud, leaving many Parisians quite literally high and dry.

The Romans first recognized the problem and addressed it with their customary decisiveness. Having settled the slopes of the Left Bank rather than the boggy marshes along the river, they soon realized that if they were going to supply their thermal baths and homes with enough water, they were going to have to do something besides lug the stuff up the hill from the river. Not having the means to lift it from the Seine, they looked for another solution. Soon they discovered it to the south, in the Rungis area, where they found spring water that they could bring in by gravity, letting it flow gently into their city through a narrow covered channel. It was a major undertaking, approximately ten miles from source to destination, and required a dramatic aqueduct-bridge en route over the Bièvre river valley at what today is Arcueil. (Vestiges of this remarkable structure still remain in Arcueil, and you can admire fragments in the Musée Carnavalet.)

The Gallo-Romans seemed to take this sophisticated system well in stride—at least until the surge of barbarian attacks in the late third century sent them flying to their fortified island in the Seine (now the Ile de la Cité). Without regular maintenance, their extraordinary aqueduct slowly deteriorated until it all but disappeared.

This was the situation when Marie de Medici imperiously decided to build the extraordinary Luxembourg Palace for herself, complete with extensive gardens and fountains. Since water was not available in the quantities she required, she sent engineers scurrying to look for new sources. Bits and pieces of the old Gallo-Roman aqueduct had already surfaced, attracting the attention of her late husband, Henri IV. His assassination interrupted plans to reconstruct the aqueduct, but now Marie took up the huge enterprise.

Work began in 1612 and continued for years, following the approximate course of the old Gallo-Roman watercourse. At last, in 1623, spring water from Rungis traveled the eight-mile underground channel, crossing the Bièvre at almost the same point where the Gallo-Romans had positioned their aqueduct-bridge all those centuries before, and arriving in Paris just · south of the Luxembourg Gardens. En route, the water passed through twenty-seven regards—small buildings with steps down to the water level, whose job was to collect the water, protect it from pollution (primarily from animals) and thieves (mostly the two-legged variety), and send it along its way. The last of these, and the grandest, the Maison du Fontainier, rises behind a wall at 42 Avenue de l'Observatoire, at the tip of the Luxembourg Gardens. This was where the waters from Rungis were divided between Marie de Medici's grand new Luxembourg Palace, several public fountains, and a number of religious communities in the vicinity. The waters from Rungis fed the Medici Fountain in the Luxembourg Gardens until 1904, and today some still flow into Parc Montsouris' peaceful lake.

The Medici Fountain was moved during the Second Empire, thanks to Baron Haussmann, who was determined to send his Boulevard Saint-Michel unimpeded on its southward journey, right through a corner of the Luxembourg Gardens. This caused an uproar, not from those devoted to the fountain, but from those Senate officers whose outbuildings, stables, and service buildings would have been affected. After much haggling, a compromise was reached: one official's stables and another's house were rebuilt elsewhere, and the Medici Fountain was moved a bit and turned to face the gardens—a solution that appealed to all.

∿

You are now in the heart of *The Three Musketeers* country, where Alexandre Dumas set his swashbuckling novel. Cardinal Richelieu, who serves as villain for the piece, was not someone to cross, as Marie de Medici learned, to her sorrow. In a face-off with the cardinal, Marie lost badly, was deprived of her status (and pensions) as queen-mother, and spent the rest of her days in ragtag exile. Her son, the wimpy Louis XIII, did not seem to mind.

The moral of this story, which Dumas was quick to grasp, was that Richelieu was a larger-than-life powerhouse, an antagonist who would serve Dumas' four intrepid heroes well. As for these heroes, the foremost of them, **d'Artagnan**, was based on a real person—Charles de Batz-Castelmore d'Artagnan—who was Capitaine-Lieutenant of Louis XIV's Musketeers. Until his death at the siege of Maastricht in 1673, the real d'Artagnan lived near the Seine, at what now is **1 Rue du Bac**. Several years after his demise, a certain Gatien de Courtilz de Sandras published a largely fictionized version of d'Artagnan's life, in the form of memoirs, which drew Dumas' attention. It is possible that Dumas may already have known about d'Artagnan, since the novelist once lived on Rue de l'Université at the corner of Rue du Bac—not far from where d'Artagnan once hung his plumed hat.

Dumas was also quick to use settings that he knew. Much of the Paris portion of *The Three Musketeers*, for example, unfolds in an area close to Dumas' Rue de l'Université lodgings. In this area, between the Luxembourg Palace and Saint-Sulpice, Dumas gave d'Artagnan an attic room on ancient Rue des Fossoyeurs (Gravediggers), a street now more happily named Rue Servandoni, after a French theatrical designer. Dumas placed Athos practically next door, on Rue Férou, while Aramis resided nearby, on Rue de Vaugirard. Porthos lived immediately to the west of Saint-Sulpice, on Rue du Vieux-Colombier—not far from the home of Tréville, which served as headquarters for the Musketeers.

One of the most famous scenes in *The Three Musketeers* takes place in the shadow of a Carmelite monastery, where d'Artagnan has brashly arranged to duel with Athos as well as Porthos and Aramis, one after the other. Instead, he joins forces with all three Musketeers in an impromptu battle against Richelieu's guards. This was a quiet spot where duels—which had been banned—could be fought without much notice. The Carmelite monastery is long gone, but its church (the **Church of Saint-Joseph-des-Carmes**) and some of the monastery's original structures still remain, now serving as the heart of the Institut Catholique de Paris. The monastery's beautiful garden, the **Jardin des Carmes**, also has survived and is open to the public during Paris's annual Fête des Jardins in September. From the outside, you can see that portion of its ancient wall where the three Musketeers and their new colleague first joined forces.

Dumas of course did not limit himself to settings from this particular portion of Paris. Throughout his long life, he lived at many different Paris addresses and was familiar with the Rue aux Ours, home of the lawyer's wife who was Porthos' mistress, and he also knew the mansion on the Avenue des Champs-Elysées where the Count of Monte Cristo planned the well-deserved ruin of his enemies. Best of all, Dumas was quite familiar with the Place des Vosges (or Place Royale in d'Artagnan's time). Here, at no. 6, Dumas placed that extraordinary villainess, Lady de Winter—in the home of Dumas' friend and literary colleague, Victor Hugo.

Whether or not Hugo enjoyed the joke, we do not know. He and Dumas certainly had a lot in common, including their epic womanizing. Of the two, though, Dumas was the more unreservedly adventurous, with a gargantuan appetite for life. This meant many mistresses, several illegitimate children (one of whom, Alexandre Dumas *fils*, became a successful author and playwright in his own right), numerous escapades, and steadily mounting debts. No matter how much Dumas earned (and it was a lot), he always managed to outspend his income. Kindly and good-natured, he spent freely, was an easy target for loans, and supported not only his current mistresses but also those who had come before.

He came from flamboyant stock. His father—the son of a minor French nobleman and a Haitian slave—was a Napoleonic general who had risen fast and plunged faster, falling out of favor with Bonaparte, dying young, and leaving his family destitute. Dumas' mother brought little in the way of financial assistance to the marriage, being the daughter of a failed French innkeeper. But despite these unpromising beginnings, Alexandre Dumas managed to rise from abject poverty into fame and wealth as one of the nineteenth century's most successful playwrights and novelists.

And which of his many books did he like the best? Toward the end of his life, when asked for his judgment on *The Three Musketeers*, Dumas replied, "It is good." What, then, did he think of *The Count of Monte-Cristo*? He thought a bit. "It is not as good as *Les Mousquetaires*," he finally replied.[1]

⌣

The church and garden of **Saint-Joseph-des-Carmes** played a role in yet another story, this one taking place during the brutal Terror of the French Revolution. Here, Josephine de Tascher de La Pagerie, eventually known as **Josephine Bonaparte,** was imprisoned and came close to death.

She was born on the Caribbean island of Martinique, where she and a cousin once sought out a fortune teller, who (as fortune tellers so often do) foresaw lives of adventure for them both. According to the fortune teller, the cousin was destined for abduction by pirates and life in a Turkish harem, where she would give birth to a future sultan. Josephine, in turn, would endure many hardships but would at last become greater than a queen.

Oddly enough, both predictions came true. According to legend, Josephine's cousin indeed was abducted on the high seas and ended up in a harem, where she became the sultan's favorite and gave birth to Sultan Mahmud II. And Josephine, this pleasant and easygoing young woman from Martinique, did eventually become consort to Napoleon Bonaparte and empress over his far-flung empire.

But it was the most unlikely of fates. Disinterested in politics or power, all Josephine ever really wanted was fine clothing, beautiful surroundings, and men who adored her. Instead, she soon encountered hardship. After leaving Martinique for Paris, she entered into an arranged marriage with Alexandre de Beauharnais, a handsome but dissolute young nobleman. Unfortunately, the naïve and provincial Josephine was neither sufficiently beautiful nor sophisticated to interest him. After she bore him two children (Eugène and Hortense), Alexandre finally washed his hands of her, decreeing that she return home or enter a convent. Despairing, she left her house for the Abbaye de Penthemont (now the Ministère des Anciens Combattants).

Ironically, it was at this retreat—bolstered by a supportive group of widows, spinsters, and abandoned wives—that Josephine came into her own, establishing friendships and learning the art of being a stylish Parisian. Emerging from her convent experience with newfound confidence and allure, as well as with a financial settlement from her husband that allowed her to live comfortably, she moved during the early years of the Revolution to a domicile of her own.

She had by now successfully entered the Parisian social whirl, easily attracting important male companions even as the Revolution turned increasingly violent. But danger was everywhere, and Alexandre's arrest exposed her to suspicion. Soon she, too, was arrested and sent to the former Carmelite convent of St-Joseph-des-Carmes, which had been used as a prison since 1792, when its prisoners were massacred. (Pikes, swords, and other weapons used to kill the victims in the garden remain in the crypt today.)

Scheduled for the guillotine, Josephine narrowly escaped death only because Robespierre himself died, a victim of his own guillotine, thus ending the Terror. But Alexandre did not survive, which meant that now, in the Terror's aftermath, Josephine was free from both prison and husband. She was also desperate for financial support, which she soon found from the wealthy new president of the National Assembly.

It was as his mistress that she first met young Napoleon Bonaparte. Josephine, who was six years older than Bonaparte, was by then light-years beyond him in experience and sophistication, having become one of the most celebrated—and notorious—women in Paris. Napoleon was impressed with the company she kept as well as with her aristocratic connections. But more to the point, Napoleon became obsessed with Josephine herself—not with her beauty or intelligence, which were unremarkable, but with her enticing figure and languid sensuality.

She would not, however, hold the upper hand for long.

～

Not far from the memories of heroism and bloodshed at Saint-Joseph-des-Carmes is a rugged monument on the site of the **Cherche-Midi Prison** (Boulevard Cherche-Midi at Boulevard Raspail), a military prison where heroes of the French Resistance were interred and tortured before being shot. Decades before, Capt. Alfred Dreyfus was also held here—in solitary confinement throughout his first trial.

Many today have never heard of **Capt. Alfred Dreyfus**, but there was a time (in the 1890s) when the so-called Dreyfus Affair almost tore France apart. The man himself was blameless, an innocent victim, but for too long too many people believed that he had committed treason by spying for Germany, when he had done no such thing, Yet despite his French birth, his love for his country, and his devotion to the military that he served, Dreyfus was a convenient scapegoat because he was Jewish, regarded by too many as fundamentally "foreign" and therefore a prime suspect for wrongdoing—even though the real suspect had been discovered (and fled the country). After conviction for treason and more than four hellish years of imprisonment on Devil's Island, which—to his enemies' surprise—he survived, Dreyfus eventually received full exoneration.

Despite the treatment he had received from the military and from his fellow countrymen, and although still suffering infirmities from his imprisonment, Dreyfus stepped right up at the age of fifty-five to serve his country in World War I, requesting assignment to the combat zone. He would serve for fourteen months as a squadron chief of an artillery group on the Chemin des Dames sector, one of the hundreds of thousands of men who took part in this doomed offensive. By the war's end, he at last received his long-overdue promotion to lieutenant colonel.

The entire Dreyfus family was just as patriotic: Dreyfus's son, Pierre, an engineer, served at the front during World War I (at Mulhouse, the Marne, Verdun, and the Somme), for which he received citations and the Croix de

Guerre. As for Alfred Dreyfus, he survived the war and lived long enough to see the rise of Hitler, but not the German occupation of France, during which his grandchildren worked for the Resistance. His granddaughter died in Auschwitz.

A remarkable **Dreyfus memorial** stands nearby, on Boulevard Raspail. This sculpture, by Louis Mitelberg (TIM), dramatically depicts Dreyfus standing erect, with his sword ceremonially broken—an act that took place during his military degradation, to the jeers of the crowd.

Just behind the Palais du Luxembourg, on Place de l'Odéon, is the venerable **Théâtre de l'Odéon** (now the Odéon-Théâtre de l'Europe), where Sarah Bernhardt had her great breakthrough—after having washed out at the Comédie-Française. She would in time return, triumphantly, to the Comédie-Française, but she then went on to have her own theaters, including the elegant little Théâtre de la Renaissance, near Porte St-Martin, and her last theater, the Théâtre de la Ville in the Place du Châtelet, which she renamed the Théâtre Sarah Bernhardt.

Bernhardt was a Parisian through and through, born on the Left Bank in the imposing mansion at 5 Rue de l'Ecole-de-Médecine. Her mother was a Dutch courtesan who had climbed out of poverty via the bedposts, while her father remains unknown to history. Thanks to her mother's influential lovers, Bernhardt entered the Paris Conservatory and then, with additional push from one of the most influential, she gained admission to the Comédie-Française, where her hot temper as well as stage fright (from which she suffered throughout her career) led to expulsion. She eventually found her way to the Théâtre de l'Odéon, which marked the real beginning of her meteoric career, primarily as a tragedian. Dramatic death scenes were her specialty.

Bernhardt was beautiful and knew how to attract publicity as well as men, charming a never-ending series of lovers and famously posing in a satin-lined coffin, where she claimed to sleep. Ignoring her critics, she lived fully and well, gutsy to the end—entertaining the troops at the front during World War I, despite her age and the fact that by then she had a wooden leg.

There is a square in Paris named after her, in the twentieth arrondissement, and a memorial statue of her, in her famous role as Phèdre, in Place du Général Catroux (17th). But it was here, at the Odéon, that she first found fame—and discovered her lifelong love of the theater. "Oh, that Odéon Theater!" she later enthused. "It is the theater I have loved most. . . . We thought of nothing but putting on plays, and we rehearsed morning, afternoon, and all hours, and I liked that very much." Even her Spartan surroundings could not dampen her enthusiasm. "I always ran up the cold, cracked steps of the theater with veritable joy," she wrote, "and rushed up to my dressing-room."

But it was the stage that delighted her the most—"to be once more in that infinite darkness with only a poor light." For her, there was "nothing more brilliant than that darkness."[2]

∼

During the course of her long career, Sarah Bernhardt played the role of queen (most memorably as the queen of Spain in Victor Hugo's *Ruy Blas*). But a century after Josephine, and two centuries after Marie de Medici, another woman—who lived quite near the Théâtre de l'Odéon—held court much like a queen. Her address, **27 Rue de Fleurus**, became famous, as did the woman—the American writer, art collector, and prickly salon hostess, **Gertrude Stein**.

She arrived in Paris with her brother, Leo, in 1903, and settled on Rue de Fleurus, which then had little to recommend it save its low rents and proximity to the Luxembourg Gardens. Situated unpromisingly between the Latin Quarter and Montparnasse, which itself still remained in the artistic shadow of Montmartre, the Steins nevertheless quickly made themselves at home, enjoying the cultural vibrancy of Paris and forming connections throughout its avant-garde artistic milieu.

Gertrude Stein, or Miss Stein, as she preferred to be called, was a native of Oakland, California, just across the bay from San Francisco. The pampered youngest of five surviving children, she grew up in the happy assurance that those around her existed to care for and indulge her. As it happened, her supreme confidence and ability to charm usually got her what she wanted.

She was brilliant, charming when she bothered, and lazy. The story of her leaving an exam room during her college days because she did not feel like taking an exam that day may be apocryphal, but it sounds like her. Similarly, she left after two years at Johns Hopkins Medical School after flunking a critical exam, because she had no intention of making up the work in summer school. Europe with brother Leo was more fun, and they traveled in Italy and England before deciding to stay in Paris, convinced by Leo's friend, the young Pablo Casals, that this was the place to be.

Bankrolled by their elder brother, Michael, who took over family finances after the death of their parents, she and Leo were reasonably well off, especially in such economical quarters. This allowed them to begin collecting art, and their first acquisition was a Cézanne. "It was lovely," Gertrude later wrote, "it did not cost much and they bought it"—a transaction that left Leo feeling like he was "a Columbus setting sail for the world beyond the world."[3]

Soon brother Michael and his wife, Sarah, joined them, enticed by Leo and Gertrude's enthusiastic letters, and set up house nearby, at 58 Rue Madame. They began to collect as well, discovering the works of Henri Matisse, while Leo and Gertrude began to buy early Picassos. Thus it was that Leo and Gertrude found their way to Pablo Picasso's studio in the Bateau-Lavoir, where they both were sufficiently impressed with the young Spaniard that, soon after their first introduction, Picasso and his latest love, Fernande Olivier, dined with the Steins at 27 Rue de Fleurus—the first of many such visits to come.

Picasso was as fascinated with Gertrude Stein as she was with him, and soon after this first dinner he asked to paint her portrait. An enormous number of sittings followed (Gertrude claims some ninety of them), for which she regularly crossed Paris by horse-drawn omnibus to Place Blanche and the Moulin Rouge, where she got off and climbed up steep Rue Lepic to Place Ravignan (now Place Emile-Goudeau) and the Bateau-Lavoir. There, in what would soon become (in Max Jacob's words) "the Acropolis of cubism," she sat in a broken chair by a red-hot stove while Picasso perched on a kitchen chair and leaned close to his easel while he painted from a very small palette of a uniform brown gray color.

By this time Picasso would have seen Henri Matisse's extraordinary *Woman in a Hat*, which now hung at 27 Rue de Fleurus. Keenly aware that his portrait of Gertrude Stein would hang in the same room as Matisse's own glorious breakthrough, every competitive bone in Picasso's body would have compelled him to come up with a portrait that would overshadow Matisse's. And so, at the end of the afternoon, when Leo and others came to look at what Picasso had done and exclaim in praise, the artist shook his head and said, *non*, it would not do.

After many months of this, Gertrude and Leo brought Matisse and his daughter, Marguerite (then eleven years old), to visit Picasso's squalid Bateau-Lavoir studio, thus first bringing together Matisse and Picasso, two giants of this or any age. Picasso seems to have said little during this encounter; he still spoke little French, and as he later told Leo, "Matisse talks and talks. I can't talk, so I just said *oui oui oui*. But it's damned nonsense all the same."[4]

Matisse was more generous in his dealings with Picasso, but unquestionably the two were well aware of the competition each represented to the other. As Gertrude Stein noted, "They had . . . to be enthusiastic about each other, but not to like each other very well."[5] Despite—or perhaps because of—their rivalry, Picasso's famous observation from his later years is especially trenchant: "No one," he said, "has ever looked at Matisse's painting more carefully than I; and no one has looked at mine more carefully than he."[6]

Soon after this meeting, Picasso spent the summer high in the Pyrenees at Gósol, where a twelfth-century church Madonna with widely staring eyes riveted his attention and subsequently found its way into his work. Matisse spent the same time journeying to North Africa, where he became entranced with boldly patterned carpets and the bowls of goldfish the carpet merchants stationed beside them. Soon after his return, he bought a little Congolese figurine and brought it to the Steins, where he showed it to Picasso. Picasso became completely engrossed with the figurine and subsequently drew it compulsively.

It was around this time that Picasso completed Gertrude Stein's portrait, whose face he had blanked out after all those sittings, saying irritably, "I can't see you any longer when I look." Now he quickly painted her face, this time with masklike features perhaps inspired by that medieval Madonna and perhaps by Matisse's African figurine. Under these influences, Picasso captured Stein's essence, and even her appearance as she aged.

"When she saw it he and she were content," Gertrude Stein said afterward.[7]

Not far from 27 Rue de Fleurus, at 12 Rue de l'Odéon, another queen—but not an imperious one—presided during the interwar years over her small but essential bookshop and literary hub, **Shakespeare and Company**. This modest literary queen was Sylvia Beach, the bookshop's American owner, who early in her career had famously published James Joyce's *Ulysses* when no other press would touch it.

The daughter of a prominent Presbyterian minister, Beach had lived in Paris during her father's ministry at the American Church there and had returned during the years of the first world war. Given Beach's passion for France and for books, a Paris bookstore was a logical if not financially obvious solution to her need to make her own way. Shakespeare and Company began on a small side street, where Beach lived on a daybed in the back room. It soon moved to its famous location at 12 Rue de l'Odéon.

Ever since its establishment in 1919, Beach's bookstore served as an essential hub for the Left Bank's English-speaking expats, where they could keep up with the latest gossip as well as the latest publications. Shakespeare and Company operated as a lending library as well as a bookstore, but Beach also cheerfully served as an informal (and free) post office, where members of the community regularly left her with messages as well as forwarding addresses for one another. She also lent money to her tribe of frequently broke patrons, leading her to observe that she "used to call the shop 'The Left Bank.'"[8] Her friends were legion, but among the staunchest was Ernest Hemingway, who returned to see her whenever he returned to Paris, after his second marriage permanently took him away from the City of Light.

The 1930s and Depression years were hard on Beach and Shakespeare and Company. Americans and British left Paris, and book sales sagged, even as rent and taxes rose. Beach cut all unnecessary expenses, dismissed her assistant, sold her car, and canceled vacations as the economic crisis deepened. Then came war and German occupation of Paris in 1940, which doomed Shakespeare and Company, but Beach still refused to leave. The streets remained peaceful, but she was painfully aware of the changes that had occurred as the Nazis marched in—changes that especially impacted Paris's Jewish population. Beach briefly hid one Jewish friend from the Gestapo and shared with another "some of the special restrictions on Jews"—although not the large yellow Star of David that her friend had to wear. "We could not enter public places such as theatres, movies, cafés, concert halls, or sit down on park benches," Beach later recalled.[9]

Shakespeare and Company was already struggling for survival when the Germans banned the sale of English literature published after 1870. But the end of Beach's beloved bookstore came with the entry of the United States into the war. "My nationality, added to my Jewish affiliations, finished Shakespeare and Company in Nazi eyes" she later wrote.[10] One day in December 1941, soon after Pearl Harbor, a high-ranking German officer stopped by to look at a copy of James Joyce's *Finnegans Wake*, which Beach had put in the window. It was her last as well as her own personal copy, and she told him that it was not for sale. He was enraged and left. Two weeks later he reappeared to announce that they were coming to confiscate all her books.

Beach promptly located her concierge, who opened unoccupied rooms over Beach's own upstairs apartment. Beach then rallied friends, who loyally carried upstairs the shop's remaining books and photographs, in clothes baskets, and removed every piece of furniture—even the light fixtures. She persuaded a carpenter to quickly remove the bookshelves, and within a short space, there was nothing left of Shakespeare and Company. A housepainter even painted out the name on the front of 12 Rue de l'Odéon.

The Germans seem not to have returned to witness the now-barren room, although in August 1942 they did come to arrest Beach, sending her to an internment camp. Beach was released from internment after six months, thanks to the efforts of a friend in Vichy headquarters who had been one of her earliest customers. But warned by German military authorities that she could be taken back any time they chose, she promptly went into hiding on the top floor of a friend's youth hostel, where she remained for the rest of the war.

The liberation of Paris in August 1944 brought Ernest Hemingway to the Rue de l'Odéon. Hemingway had joined up as a journalist in the wake of the Normandy landing, and then he attached himself to the Twenty-Second Regiment of the Fourth American Infantry Division before establishing himself as leader of a small patrol of Free French fighters outside Paris (despite Geneva Convention prohibitions banning journalists from bearing arms). His exploits were not exactly legitimate, and certainly not quite as glorious as he afterward made them. Most certainly, he was not the first into Paris, nor did he "liberate" his favorite bar at the Ritz. But nonetheless, he seems to have performed capably and courageously, and afterward he won a Bronze Star for bravery.

On August 25, 1944, Hemingway appeared on the Rue de l'Odéon. Sylvia flew downstairs, where they met with a crash. And then he picked her up and swung her around and kissed her, while people on the street and in the windows cheered.

Gertrude Stein's war was not so worthy of mention. She and Sylvia Beach had never been close, although it was Stein who maintained the distance. Beach had become famous, at least as well known in their mutual literary circles as Gertrude Stein—an affront that Gertrude Stein did not take lightly. Worse yet, Beach had achieved her fame by publishing James Joyce's *Ulysses*, and Gertrude Stein emphatically did not care for James Joyce or *Ulysses*. "It was like mentioning one general favorably to another general," Hemingway later remarked. "You learned not to do it the first time you made the mistake." After *Ulysses* appeared, Stein even came with her partner, Alice B. Toklas, to announce that, as a consequence, they had transferred their membership from Shakespeare and Company to the American Library (then located across the Seine). Beach seems to have recovered nicely from the blow: "In Rue de l'Odéon, I must admit, we kept low company," she added with a twinkle, after recounting the event.[11]

But the size of the divide between Stein and Beach became increasingly apparent during the 1930s, as Gertrude Stein leaned increasingly and unapologetically toward Hitler and Hitler's Germany. Stein in 1934 even shocked one of her salon's guests by speaking of Hitler as a great man. "I was stunned," the guest later recalled. "Hitler's persecution of the Jews was well publicized in France by that time."[12] And of course, although her guest did not say it, Stein was Jewish. Yet her praise of Hitler was not an anomaly: that

May, she told an interviewer with the *New York Times Magazine* that "Hitler should have received the Nobel Peace Prize . . . because he is removing all elements of contest and struggle from Germany. By driving out the Jews and democratic and left elements, he is driving out everything that conduces to activity. That means peace."[13]

Unquestionably, Gertrude Stein enjoyed shocking people, and these pronouncements have been defended as examples of her irony and dark humor. But there was a disturbing continuity and insistence in her praise of Hitler throughout the decade, culminating in her work for Gen. Philippe Pétain and the collaborationist Vichy government during the war by translating Pétain's speeches into English—apparently as part of a Vichy government propaganda attempt to persuade the American public that France's Vichy government was one they could trust. She continued to work on the project until after the United States entered the war, and after the Germans had occupied all of France.

During the dangerous war years, Gertrude and Alice remained safe, despite the fact that they both were Jewish. They spent much of the war at their country home in Bilignin, where they managed well despite wartime austerity, enjoying the protection of their friend Bernard Faÿ, who under the Pétain regime had become general administrator of the Bibliothèque nationale de France and director of the regime's anti-Masonic purge (an effort that sent almost one thousand Freemasons to concentration camps, of whom more than half were killed). Pétain—and Faÿ—were convinced that Jews and Masons were to blame for France's troubles during the interwar years, but Faÿ nonetheless had no hesitation in using his good offices to protect Stein and Toklas, who were fervent Pétain supporters.

Once the war was over, when Faÿ was imprisoned as a Nazi collaborator, Alice B. Toklas seems to have aided him financially to escape to Switzerland. By this time, Gertrude Stein had died—but not before having renewed her celebrity and prestige in postwar America.

⌢

After the war, Sylvia Beach never attempted to revive Shakespeare and Company, and she spent the last years of her life writing her memoirs. Other bookshops have taken the name of Shakespeare and Company, but whether they are attempts at tribute or efforts to benefit from the name, they have no connection with the original, which was unique.

Today, there is nothing left of Shakespeare and Company, except for a plaque on 12 Rue de l'Odéon (now a clothing shop) and memories of an era, in which Sylvia Beach and her bookshop played such a vital role.

Rue Cortot, Montmartre. © J. McAuliffe

CHAPTER NINE

~

Montmartre

When Picasso arrived there in 1900, Montmartre still was "a real village, almost unknown to the uninitiated," as the poet J. P. Contamine de Latour later recalled. Several decades later, the poet reminisced that "this was the real bohemian life, with its uncertainties and expedients, but free and happy."[1]

Montmartre had remained outside the Paris orbit until the middle of the nineteenth century, when Baron Georges Haussmann, in his capacity as prefect of the Seine (and Napoleon III's right-hand man), undertook to reshape and modernize the City of Light. Haussmann created wide and spacious boulevards, uniform and gracious housing, and an array of expansive parks—all at the expense of the undulating terrain, winding streets, and ancient but shabby neighborhoods of Old Paris. Hammering his vision into reality, Haussmann in 1860 removed one of the last walls that still enveloped Paris—the Farmers-General Wall. This was a customs barrier erected around the city in the 1780s, ringing Paris with more than fifty tollhouses linked by a wall ten feet high and more than fifteen miles in circumference.

The purpose of the Farmers-General Wall was not defense, for the walls of Paris had always served the king in another capacity—that of foiling smugglers intent on evading the traditionally steep royal tariffs on incoming goods. The disappearance of Louis XIII's wall under the command of his son, Louis XIV, had left the royal tax collectors in the lurch, giving resourceful Parisians a major assist in bypassing the tollgates. The new Farmers-General

Wall ("farmers" referring to tax collectors or tax farmers, as they were known) went up just before the Revolution, and it managed to survive the Revolution and those regimes that followed because the income it collected was substantial and useful. Not until 1860 did the government at last take it down, leaving only the boulevards that had run beside it and, eventually, the No. 2 and No. 6 Métro lines to mark its course.

The Butte of Montmartre rose on the far northern side of this wall, and until the wall's removal it had been predominantly rural, although poverty-stricken urbanization—the detritus of industrialization—was beginning to crowd in at its foot. The anything-goes atmosphere of the brothel-filled neighborhoods of lower Montmartre also fostered an array of nightlife that drew bourgeois pleasure-seekers northward from their more sedate quarters in the heart of the city. Cabarets proliferated, the most famous being Le Chat Noir and the Mirliton, while dance halls such the Moulin de la Galette and the Moulin Rouge featured rowdy cancan girls and other delights.

The quarries that once tunneled deep into the steep hillside of the Butte for gypsum, or plaster of Paris, had closed years before, leaving place-names such as Place Blanche (recalling the white of gypsum) along with a treacherous network of quarries that destabilized much of the Butte's southern face. Builders of the dazzling white **Sacré-Coeur** found it necessary to sink more than eighty massive stone pillars almost one hundred feet to bedrock in order to support the basilica's bulk and weight. They succeeded in their daunting project, but the portion of Montmartre's southern face directly below the basilica would remain scarred and desolate until the city undertook to change this desert into the steeply pitched garden one sees today—the recently renamed **Square Louise-Michel**, after the extraordinary woman who came to Paris to teach the poor children of Montmartre and became a leader of the 1871 Commune uprising.

Michel mobilized women in support of the Commune, served as an ambulance worker, and organized day care for children in the besieged areas. But most memorably, she fought on the barricades, fighting in battles from Issy and Neuilly to Les Batignolles and Place Blanche, from Montmartre cemetery to the barricades at Clignancourt. After the last of the Communard resistance was shot down, she was arrested and brought to trial. There she defiantly dared the court to kill her. Instead of granting her wish, the court sentenced her to what it probably believed was a slower form of death—deportation to the harsh penal colony in France's South Pacific islands of New Caledonia.

There Michel remained, defiantly surviving, until she was released on general amnesty almost ten years later. She returned to Paris, where she continued to fight for causes in which she deeply believed, especially those affecting workers and the poor. Her death, in 1905, prompted an enormous turnout of mourners along the funeral route to her burial plot in Levallois-Perret, just outside Paris, where she was buried with her mother. The funeral route wound its way through the heart of Communard territory: from the Gare de Lyon, where the casket arrived from Marseilles (where she had died), through the Place de la Nation and past Père-Lachaise Cemetery, where government troops had gunned down the last of the Communards in 1871—a date still raw in the memories of many of the people paying tribute that day. The hearse, preceded by a wagon laden high with wreaths, continued through militant Belleville, where much of the male population of a certain age was missing, martyred to the Communard cause. It slowly continued past Sacré-Coeur, where someone cried out, "Down with the priests!" And finally, it reached its destination in Levallois-Perret.

It was the largest crowd of mourners that Paris had seen since the massive turnout for Victor Hugo's funeral twenty years earlier.

The Basilica of **Sacré-Coeur** itself was not welcomed by the Butte's residents, who were largely impious bohemians or staunch supporters of the bloody and failed 1871 Commune uprising, who had heartily opposed the basilica's construction from the outset.

After all, the site chosen for the basilica was the very place where the first confrontation between government troops and the people of Montmartre had occurred—the place, in fact, where the Commune was born.[2] Not surprisingly, many Parisians, especially residents of Montmartre and Belleville, were angered by what they viewed as a blatant attempt to wipe out all memory of the Commune by building over and obliterating this site. Worse yet, from their viewpoint, the offending edifice would be dedicated to the Sacred Heart, a potent symbol of royalist and counterrevolutionary sympathies.

Not only had the Commune suffered a bloody defeat, but its most stalwart supporters would henceforth live their lives in the shadow of a huge monument built to assert, in solid stone, the convictions of the counterrevolution.

⌒

Whatever one's sympathies, the crowds around Sacré-Coeur are usually daunting. Still, there are usually far fewer willing to climb to the basilica's rooftop to see the spectacular view of Paris. And if yet another climb sounds onerous, the small park next door, **Square Nadar**—dedicated to the great nineteenth-century photographer—offers quite a pleasant alternative, with benches overlooking the city.

Nadar (born Félix Tournachon) has a real claim to this spot on Montmartre. Drawn to ballooning by the possibilities of aerial photography as well as by the adventure and romance of air travel, he had already flown giant balloons (equipped for gracious living and dining by twenty people) when he decided to make use of his balloons in wartime. During the Franco-Prussian War in 1870, when the Prussians under Bismarck were closing their siege around a defiant Paris, Nadar proposed that he and two companions make tethered ascents from Montmartre to provide reconnaissance for the military. Without waiting for official sanction, he and his colleagues established a base on top of Montmartre and began their first tethered ascents. After the encirclement was complete, Nadar proposed that the balloons be untethered and float sacks of correspondence over the Prussian army and toward the provisional government, which had escaped to Tours.

His idea was accepted, and on September 23, 1870, Nadar's balloon, *Le Neptune*, took off from Montmartre with more than two hundred and fifty pounds of mail and dispatches, in what amounted to the world's first airmail. But the flight was risky—the balloons were fragile, and the Prussians could easily use them for target practice. In addition, the question of how to get news and letters back remained. It was impossible to steer a balloon accurately enough to make a pinpoint landing in a besieged city.

The answer was homing pigeons. *Le Neptune* and the balloons that followed carried caged birds that flew back to the capital. But how to manage the weight of mail they must carry? An unidentified engineer approached Nadar with the answer—a proposal to gather the Paris-bound correspondence and photograph it, shrinking it and sending the film (an early version of microfilm) by pigeon. Microfilm had in fact been invented a decade before, and its inventor was willing to fly to Tours by balloon with the requisite equipment. Film rolled into goose-quill tubes then was tied by silk thread to the homing pigeons.

In all, sixty-six balloons (not all by Nadar) flew out of Paris during the siege, and nearly one hundred thousand messages made the return trips. Hundreds of pigeons gallantly served.

⌣

Most people view Sacré-Coeur from the front, either from below or from afar, but another fine view of the basilica is from the back, in the steeply pitched **Square Marcel Bleustein-Blanchet**, formerly known as Parc de la Turlure. Few people find their way here, which is a blessing. Afterward, skirting the madhouse of the tourist-crammed Place du Tertre, you may then want to head for lovely Rue Cortot on the Butte's northern slope.

Life in Montmartre at the turn of the last century was undeniably gritty for the poets and artists who increasingly congregated here, drawn by its cheap rents and a growing community of like-minded bohemians. Yet it also retained some of the bucolic aura of its past. As Contamine de Latour recalled, "Once you'd climbed its rough steps, you felt as though you were hundreds of miles away from the capital. . . . Everything about it was rustic and peaceful. Streams ran down the middle of streets, . . . and birds twittered in the luxuriant greenery that covered the old, ruined walls."[3]

The oldest of these walls belonged to the mansion that now houses the **Musée de Montmartre**. Located on Rue Cortot, this splendid old building had by the turn of the last century become a run-down haven for impecunious artists. Pierre-Auguste Renoir lived here during the early years of his career, when he painted his *Dance at the Moulin de la Galette*. He later recalled that his only belongings at the time were "a mattress (which was put on the floor), a table, a commode, and a stove—to keep the model warm."[4]

It was also here that Renoir painted Suzanne Valadon, the free-spirited former circus performer who (most agree) modeled for his famous *Dance at Bougival*. Valadon went on to become a respected artist in her own right, breaking hearts along the way—especially that of composer Erik Satie, who never offered his heart to another woman. Valadon had affairs with Renoir and others, and after one of these gave birth to a son, Maurice Utrillo, whose paternity she never acknowledged, but whose paintings of Montmartre would in turn bring him fame—enough to pay for his alcohol, to which he was sadly addicted.

The museum has recently expanded, acquiring the garden and next-door building containing the rooms where Valadon lived as well as a replica of the atelier of painter and designer Raoul Dufy, whose original atelier was located nearby. In the room of Valadon's son, Utrillo, a worn teddy bear first catches one's eye, then a wine bottle. This building now houses an extensive exhibition of Dufy's work and, in fine weather, serves tea in the garden. A replica of *The Swing*, where Renoir painted his young lady in conversation with a clearly enchanted young man, hangs at the top of a pathway leading down alongside the tiny vineyard for which Montmartre is famous ("the most expensive bad wine in Paris," as someone has called it). This opens to visitors during the Grape Harvest Festival in mid-October, in which the miniscule harvest is enthusiastically celebrated. Along the way, you can peer into the **Jardin Sauvage Saint-Vincent,** a small wilderness that is infrequently open to the public from Rue Saint-Vincent (currently the first Sunday of the month at 10:30 a.m.).

Returning through gardens to the museum's original building, you will find mementoes from Montmartre's lively past, including **Le Lapin Agile** and **Le Chat Noir,** most notably the sets of elaborate zinc cutouts from Le Chat Noir's famed Shadow Theater. The figures appeared as silhouettes as they moved back and forth on runners positioned at different distances behind a white fabric screen and in front of the highly sophisticated scenery. The political cartoonist and satirist Caran d'Ache, as well as other artists, journalists, and writers, joined with Henri Rivière to create the many sketches and design the figures, sets, and program covers. The themes were usually biblical, classical, or historical, with hundreds of cleverly designed silhouettes, including those of current notables. One of my favorites, to be found in the collection of the Musée d'Orsay, is that of an amusingly bear-like Zola, as well as that of Le Chat Noir's founder, the painter and caricaturist Rodolphe Salis.

Despite the cabaret's location in the heart of the Pigalle quarter and its poster image, created by Théophile Steinlen, of a lecherous-looking tomcat perched on a wall, this was not some sort of bordello experience. Le Chat Noir's clientele were looking for good times, to be sure, but their idea of a good time was a convivial (and well-lubricated) evening based on shared intellectual and cultural interests, a happy combination of the serious and the flippant. The place was typically jammed with poets, painters, and musicians, including Erik Satie, who for a time played the cabaret's piano, and Claude Debussy, who occasionally played there as well.

Le Chat Noir thrived for almost two decades at the foot of Montmartre (first on Blvd de Clichy and then at 12 Rue de Laval, now Rue Victor-Massé) until its closure in 1896, shortly before Salis's death. Look for any remains and all you will find is a plaque on the wall of the Rue Victor-Massé address telling passersby that this edifice, once the home of the famous cabaret, the Chat Noir, "was consecrated to the muses and to joy."

In the meantime, further up the steep slope of the Butte, another cabaret was about to become a legend. Its roots went back to 1860, when Paris incorporated Montmartre as part of the new eighteenth arrondissement, after the hated tax walls came down. Industrialization had already begun to chew up the nineteenth and twentieth arrondissements, but the higher portions of Montmartre remained relatively bucolic (with the exception of those areas around the gypsum quarries, which had only recently closed).

A small tavern opened at the corner of Rue Saint-Vincent and Rue des Saules, right below the mansion that now houses the Musée de Montmartre. Over the next few years this tavern took several different names, until the painter André Gill created a memorable sign for it, featuring a laughing rabbit with a bottle of wine leaping out of a saucepan. Soon locals were calling the tavern the Lapin à Gill, or Gill's rabbit—a pun on Gill's abbreviated name. From there, it was only a step to the Lapin Agile, or nimble rabbit. Thus, the **Lapin Agile** was born.

In 1903, the cabaret singer and owner Aristide Bruant (memorably depicted in red scarf and black hat by Henri de Toulouse-Lautrec) bought the Lapin Agile and leased it to Frédéric Gérard, who soon turned the Lapin Agile into a hub of bohemian nightlife. By this time Montmartre's free-wheeling atmosphere and cheap rents had attracted a virtual colony of starving poets and artists, most of whom (including Picasso, Modigliani, Utrillo, Braque, Apollinaire, and Max Jacob) eventually found their way to the Lapin Agile. When they had no money (which was often), they paid for their meals and drinks with paintings, and they regularly joined in literary evenings or in raucous song accompanied by Frédé and his guitar.

Generally, evenings at the Lapin Agile were cozy and jolly affairs. Such as the time when Frédé and friends tied a paintbrush to the tail of his pet donkey and submitted the resulting canvas to the 1910 Salon des Indépendants as a work of abstract art. Frédé and his accomplices got away with the ruse for a while, and the donkey even managed to collect some respectable reviews.

But not everything was always light and joy at the Lapin Agile. Picasso's masterpiece, *Au Lapin Agile*, is a somber one, depicting him as a grim Harlequin figure averting his gaze from the beautiful woman at the bar beside him. She is Germaine Pichot, the woman responsible for his best friend's suicide. Picasso paid his bar tab at the Lapin Agile with this remarkable painting, which Frédé put on his wall but eventually sold for a pittance. Several years ago it sold for forty million dollars and now is on view at New York's Metropolitan Museum of Art.

Montmartre has changed dramatically since those days when Picasso lived and worked here, but the pink cottage-like Lapin Agile still occupies its corner, and still is in business. This is a quieter and less touristed part of the Butte, and although the Chat Noir may no longer exist, the Agile Rabbit (albeit a copy) still jumps out of his saucepan at the Lapin Agile, ready for a good time.

Picasso regularly carried a gun, a Browning revolver that had once belonged to the legendary poet and playwright Alfred Jarry, the bizarre and outrageous creator of the bizarre and outrageous *Ubu Roi*. Picasso and Jarry probably never met—Jarry was dying at the time Picasso was establishing himself in Paris. But Picasso and Jarry shared many friends, and either Max Jacob or Apollinaire may have nabbed the revolver or arranged for it as a gift at the end of Jarry's life.

However it came into his possession, Picasso regularly carried this rusty old revolver. He claimed (in Jarryesque fashion) to use it to ward off bores and morons as well as anyone who spoke ill of Cézanne, and he is credited with having fired off several shots at the Lapin Agile in exasperation with several Germans intent on extracting aesthetic theories from him.

Despite the bucolic memories of former residents, a revolver could be a useful accessory in Montmartre, especially by night. Artists generally did not encounter trouble, largely because they were too poor to attract attention. Yet even Picasso's favored cabaret, the Lapin Agile, encountered occasional violence—especially one memorable night, when a thug shot Frédé's son-in-law dead at the counter. The police ignored the fracas—the son-in-law had apparently encroached on the territory of another small-time criminal—and life, such as it was, went on.

Just past the lovely little cemetery of Saint-Vincent (and down some steps, as so frequently happens in Montmartre) is a monument dedicated to Le Chat Noir's Théophile Steinlen, a lovely sculpture of a man and woman in the small park where Steinlen liked to sit. This little park is now called the **Square Joël Le Tac** and, like so many of the city's small islands of greenery, has in recent years gained in gravel and playground equipment at the expense of its gardens. Still, the sculpture is exquisite, of a man and woman tenderly in love, and is a beautiful tribute to Steinlen—in quite a different mode from the Chat Noir tomcat he is best known for.

Back up the stairs again and past the lovely **Château des Brouillards** (Château of the Mists), a mansion hidden in the trees, and the adjacent

Allée des Brouillards, where Renoir once lived and worked at number 6. The mansion dates from the eighteenth century and underwent considerable decay before it was saved from complete deterioration in the early years of the twentieth century by the composer and violinist Marius Casadesus, of the musical Casadesus family. This is the family commemorated just a few steps beyond, in **Place Casadesus.**

Never heard of them? Well, you should. Originally the family was Catalonian. Then one of the sons, Luis, moved to Paris and, in 1870, became a French citizen. Forbidden by his father to become a musician, Louis made his living as a cashier in a biscuit company, but on weekends he satisfied his musical dreams by directing small dance-hall orchestras on Montmartre. Loving music as he did, he made his home a musical haven and encouraged his own children to become musicians. Remarkably, almost all of his large brood attended the Paris Conservatory, and all but one became classical musicians.

The oldest, Francis—a composer—served as director of the American Conservatory in Fontainebleau, where the illustrious Nadia Boulanger taught many promising American composers, including Aaron Copland, Philip Glass, and Elliott Carter. Henri (a viola player) founded the Société des Instruments Anciens and played in the celebrated Capet Quartet, while his sister Régina played harpsichord with his ensemble. Rosette became an accomplished pianist, and Marcel, who died in World War I, was a promising cellist.

One son, however, strayed from the musical realm to become an actor, under the name of Robert Casa. As a young man, Casa—who eventually became director of the Théâtre Français in New York—fathered an illegitimate son. This son, born in 1899 and also named Robert, eventually became the most famous member of the family.

Little Robert's mother, a young music student who was anxious to keep this shameful birth a secret, was unwilling to keep the child. But his father's family warmly embraced him. Raised by his grandmother and aunt, "le petit Robert" thrived, showing remarkable musical aptitude, especially on the piano. Soon young Robert entered the Paris Conservatory (then located on Rue du Conservatoire, near the family home on Rue de Rochechouart). Here he quickly attracted the attention of many notables, including composer Gabriel Fauré, who at that time was the conservatory's director. Here as well, Robert met the talented young pianist Gabrielle L'Hôte, who—in a sweet love story that she records in her memoirs—eventually became his wife.

Still, there were obstacles. When the two decided to wed, Gaby's father—fearing for their future—opposed the marriage. "You are two pianists," he warned his daughter. "One will be better than the other. If it is him, this will be fine, but your career will be finished. If it is you, it will go worse."[5] But they went ahead and married, and for the record, the marriage thrived, with the two eventually celebrating their golden wedding anniversary together.

Robert first caught the public eye in a storybook turn of events, when the Paris Opera called upon him at the last minute to substitute for an ailing soloist. From then on his career skyrocketed, and for the next half-century he concertized everywhere, playing a repertoire ranging from Mozart and Beethoven to the contemporary and (at first) controversial Ravel, who admired Casadesus greatly and became a good friend.

In the ensuing years, Robert and Gaby played together as well as solo, and Gaby, a fine pianist in her own right, carved out a satisfying career of her own. But of the two, it was Robert who had the more brilliant career. And what an extraordinary pianist he was! Many years ago I was privileged to attend a concert where I heard (and saw) him play Ravel's daunting and lushly beautiful Piano Concerto for the Left Hand. Bowled over, I immediately went out and bought several Casadesus recordings, including a Mozart concerto for three pianos performed by Robert and Gaby with their oldest son, Jean—a talented pianist in his own right, who tragically died young, in an automobile accident.

Now, when I pass through the small square that bears the family's name, I think of this famous French family of musicians, including one of the greatest French pianists of the twentieth century and his equally remarkable wife. Together they made beautiful music—at the keyboard and in life.

Just beyond Place Casadesus is the terraced **Square Suzanne Buisson**, a quiet haven off the beaten track from the usual Montmartre tourist buzz. The square pays tribute to a leader of the French Resistance during German Occupation who died at Auschwitz, but a side fountain and statue pays tribute to yet another local martyr—**Saint Denis**, the first bishop of Paris.

Saint Denis figures prominently among those saints who flank the north portal of Notre-Dame, and rightly so, because just as Sainte-Geneviève became the patron saint of Paris, Saint Denis became the patron saint of all of France. Denis suffered an especially dramatic martyrdom around the year 273 A.D. at the hands of the Romans, who already had their hands full in fighting off barbarian hordes when this charismatic Christian arrived on the scene. According to legend, Roman soldiers tortured Denis near the present site of Notre-Dame and then decapitated him on the slopes of Montmartre, near where this small statue now presides.

But this was not the end of the story, for according to legend, the martyred saint proceeded to astonish one and all by picking up his head and walking northward until he at last collapsed on the site now marked by the remarkable basilica (now basilica-cathedral) that bears his name.

As the Empire crumbled and Roman influence waned, an abbey dedicated to the memory of Saint Denis grew up on the place where he so dramatically died. There, in the eighth century, an abbot of distant memory built a fine church, and by the time the visionary Abbot Suger took charge of the Abbey of Saint-Denis, the abbey had acquired a unique and powerful place in the affairs of Paris as well as all of France. Royalty had been buried here ever since King Dagobert, making this church the royal mausoleum. King Louis VI not only deposited the coronation regalia here, but carried into battle the oriflamme, the military standard of the nearby lands over which the abbey held sway. For nearly three centuries thereafter the French would go into battle bellowing their famous war cry, "Monjoie Saint-Denis!" and carrying before them this flame-colored banner, which became the royal standard of France—even as Saint Denis was emerging as the national saint.

What the saint himself would have made of all this is anyone's guess, but as you sit here, remember that this statue of a bishop holding his mitered head is a link to a distant past, one where stories evolved into legends, and where even the most unlikely legends evolved into treasured fact.

～

Just around the corner, in tiny **Place Marcel-Aymé** at the end of Impasse Girardon, is one of the oddest sculptures you could ever hope to find. It is actually a portion of a sculpture—a man's head, upper torso, and right leg—mounted on a stone wall, and looking for all the world as if the man was emerging from the wall.

Well, that is exactly the idea, for the sculpture is a portrait of the writer Marcel Aymé in the guise of one of his most beloved characters, *Le Passe-Muraille*, or *The Man Who Passed Through Walls* (a short story written in 1943).

Unlike most other successful French writers, Marcel Aymé was not born into a family where intellect and education were especially valued. The son of a blacksmith, Aymé went through a number of disappointing careers before most fortunately discovering that he could write. Leaving behind his native Franche-Comté for Paris, he happily settled in Montmartre, where he soon was making a living with his satirical yet enchantingly surreal novels and short stories, of which *Le Passe-Muraille* is perhaps the most famous.

Le Passe-Muraille's hero, a mousy bureaucrat named Dutilleul, lives his dull life in a corner of Montmartre. Until one evening, when he discovers quite by accident that he has acquired the power to pass unhindered through walls. Unsettled by this discovery, he goes to see a doctor, who gives him some strange powder. Dutilleul promptly places the stuff in a drawer and forgets about it.

But his new powers transform his life. Badgered mercilessly by his boss, the previously timid Dutilleul repeatedly sticks his head through the office wall and terrifies the fellow—who soon is carted off to a mental institution.

Delivered from this office tyrant, Dutilleul now realizes that he seeks adventure, and soon he is launched on a life of crime, leading the Paris police on a merry chase. Under a pseudonym, he becomes an overnight celebrity, the hero of Paris.

And then he meets a beautiful young woman—one who is married to a jealous tyrant who keeps her locked up at night (while he makes his own nocturnal rounds). You can guess the rest. Dutilleul and the young woman fall in love and carry on their affair behind locked doors and thick walls, which Dutilleul has no trouble in negotiating. Until one fateful night, when he accidentally takes the long-forgotten powder, in the mistaken belief that he is downing some aspirin.

The results are devastating. The powder begins to work just as Dutilleul is exiting his true love's abode, and he is caught there, frozen forever inside the thick wall. Some nights, says Aymé, you can hear him, a muffled voice that seems to come from beyond the grave. Those who pass think that it is just the wind, but it is Dutilleul, lamenting the end of his glorious career and regretting his all-too-brief love affair.

Adding to this oh-so-French ending, Aymé has Dutilleul's artist friend come to the wall on certain nights, to console the poor prisoner with a song. These notes, Aymé says, "penetrate to the very heart of the stone, like drops of moonlight."[6]

Well, no wonder the French love the story. Aymé wrote many others during the course of his long and successful career, but this is the one that was turned into a hit French musical, courtesy of composer Michel Legrand (the show, renamed *Amour*, also ran briefly on Broadway). And it is in the guise of Dutilleul that Aymé—himself a modest and unpretentious man—appears in Place Marcel-Aymé, in the heart of his beloved Montmartre.

Long ago, Montmartre was dotted with windmills, as many as twelve of them, but now only two remain—**Le Moulin Blute-Fin** and **Le Moulin Radet**, dating from the early seventeenth century (the famed Moulin Rouge, despite its windmill shape, was never a real mill). During the late nineteenth century Le Moulin Blute-Fin was renamed **Le Moulin de la Galette**, due to the flat little cakes, called galettes, made from the mill's flour, which the owners now sold with a glass of wine. The Moulin de la Galette became a popular *guinguette*, or dance hall, inspiring Renoir's *Ball du Moulin de la Galette* as well as paintings by Toulouse-Lautrec and Van Gogh. Saved from destruction in the early years of the twentieth century, it has been restored and moved to its present location, where it is now evocative-looking but off-limits, being private property.

The second remaining windmill, Le Moulin Radet, is perched just around the corner and now is the entrance to a restaurant—also confusingly named Le Moulin de la Galette, in an obvious effort to cash in on the local legend.

Further down the hillside is small Place Emile-Goudeau, home of the legendary **Bateau-Lavoir**. This ramshackle place, essentially a wooden hillside tenement, had been inhabited by anarchists and impoverished bohemians since the late 1880s. It was seedy, but it was cheap, and Picasso gratefully moved in after his permanent return to Paris in 1904. His old friend Max Jacob may have been responsible for the name, as the ungainly building (which spills down the hillside from what then was called Place Ravignan) did faintly resemble a laundry boat. But however dismal the accommodations, its years of glory began when Picasso arrived, attracting a coterie of other artists and writers.

Squalor and camaraderie were mixed in equal portions in the Bateau-Lavoir of the Picasso years. Max Jacob moved there, as did André Derain, Maurice de Vlaminck, Kees van Dongen, and—for a brief while—Amedeo Modigliani. Picasso painted Gertrude Stein here, and it was here that Picasso met his first great love, Fernande Olivier.

Olivier was beautiful, had survived a brutal adolescence, and was living with a sculptor at the Bateau-Lavoir when she first met Picasso. One memorable late summer afternoon, as a thunderstorm broke, she dashed for shelter and found Picasso laughingly blocking her way while holding out a kitten to her. She wrote in her journal that she couldn't resist the magnetism of "his huge deep eyes," and thus the affair between Olivier and Picasso began.[7]

Olivier left her sculptor to move in with Picasso, but they managed on a pittance until Gertrude and Leo Stein entered their lives. Fernande noted that "they're rich and intelligent enough not to worry about looking ridiculous" (Gertrude regularly appeared in loose, flowing robes, and both she and Leo had taken to wearing sandals).[8] The Steins (as well as Picasso's art dealer, Ambroise Vollard) provided sufficient income for Picasso to work unhindered, and it was at the Bateau-Lavoir in 1907 that Picasso, inspired by a recent exhibit of Gauguin's Tahitian-inspired sculptures as well as by African tribal art and early Iberian sculpture, began work on *Les Demoiselles d'Avignon*—a work that he fervently believed would challenge the centuries-long traditions of European art and place him at the forefront of the modern art movement.

He was right, but initial reaction was not reassuring. Gertrude and Leo Stein were shocked by the painting, and Leo even burst into laughter, calling it "a horrible mess." Georges Braque was reported to have said that it made him feel as if Picasso was "trying to make us drink petrol to spit fire," while André Derain predicted an unhappy end for the painting's unfortunate creator.[9] But from then on, Gertrude would be a strong Picasso supporter, while André Derain would transfer his allegiance from Matisse to Picasso. Soon Braque would abandon the Fauvist movement and gravitate into Picasso's orbit, beginning a competitive partnership as the two developed Cubism together.

Picasso would not show *Les Demoiselles* until 1916, and it would remain in his studio until 1924, when he sold it to the fashion designer Jacques Doucet. After Doucet's death, *Demoiselles* made its way to New York and to the Museum of Modern Art, where it has remained. But even before this, its influence had well begun.

Instead of participating in the official salons in Paris, Picasso relied on his principal dealers (soon to become Ambroise Vollard and Daniel-Henry Kahnweiler) and on exhibitions they arranged for him in other major cities. In addition, he relied on collectors such as the Steins and the Russian collector Sergei Shchukin. By 1909, Picasso had become sufficiently well-off that he could move from the Bateau-Lavoir to a remarkably bourgeois apartment at the foot of Montmartre—11 Boulevard de Clichy, complete with maid.

Yet despite the Bateau-Lavoir's bohemian squalor, Picasso departed with reluctance. He soon would leave Montmartre as well.

Parc Montsouris. © J. McAuliffe

CHAPTER TEN

~

Montparnasse

Unlike Montmartre, Montparnasse has never been a distinctly defined quarter with its own picturesque charm. Instead, when Picasso moved there in 1912, it was a hodgepodge of shacks housing down-at-the-heels artists and poets, interspersed with new buildings of more comfort but no distinct character for those who—like Picasso—could afford something better.

Students from the Latin Quarter had long before named the area Mont-Parnasse, or Mount Parnassus, after the hilly slag heap left by the quarries below. They and others came to drink and dance here, at *guinguettes* and cafés such as the **Closerie des Lilas,** which benefited from its location at the intersection of Boulevard du Montparnasse and Boulevard Saint-Michel, connecting Montparnasse with the Latin Quarter and the Right Bank.

A longtime favorite with artists and students, the Closerie became a focus of weekly poetry readings that by 1905 attracted Picasso and his crowd, including André Salmon and Apollinaire. Fernande Olivier recalled walking with Picasso and Salmon clear across Paris from Montmartre to join in these drunken evenings at the Closerie, which ended only when the owner closed up and threw them out.

Legends abound on the subject of the Closerie, including one about the painter Fernand Léger. He was sitting on the terrace of the Closerie one day, enjoying drinks and camaraderie, when he noticed a beautiful young bride riding a bicycle, her veil streaming in the wind. Even for Montparnasse, where the unusual was commonplace, this had the earmarks of adventure. Jumping to his feet, Léger hailed the young woman, who came to a breathless stop. It was her wedding day—she was about to marry a notary's son—but one of the wedding gifts had been this bicycle. How could she resist a short ride? In any case she hadn't been gone long—or, had she?

Rapidly consulting the clock, it turned out that she had sadly underestimated the length of her ride. But Léger, a handsome and gentle man, soon persuaded her that all was not lost. And indeed, it wasn't, for not long after, the beautiful bicyclist became *his* wife.

Stories like this have put the Closerie on the map for more than a century. But things change, and by the 1920s, when Ernest Hemingway discovered it, most of the Closerie's celebrities had drifted off to other Montparnasse cafés. Pleased by the quiet, Hemingway found himself a secluded table on the terrace and wrote.

Hemingway, who gave the Closerie some priceless publicity in *A Moveable Feast*, is almost single-handedly responsible for its continued fame. Recognizing this, current management has given him star billing, with an upstairs banquet room called the Salon Ernest Hemingway. Downstairs, in the elegant dark and mirrored bar, small nameplates recall other luminaries who have passed their time here, including Jean-Paul Sartre, Samuel Beckett, André Gide, and Simone de Beauvoir. Even Lenin seems to have been enough of a regular in the old days to earn a plaque. But Hemingway's nameplate stands alone, on the bar itself—a fitting location, by all accounts.

The Closerie's turn-of-the-century décor continues from bar to brasserie, while restaurant and terrace are more garden-like, with the terrace actually under the trees. No longer a magnet for down-at-the-heels artists and poets, the Closerie has become a meeting place for the well-heeled and trendy, a clubhouse for celebrities who come to see and be seen.

And what about the lilacs? It turns out that the Closerie never had any. They belonged to a rival establishment, and the Closerie—mindful of the appeal—simply adopted the name.

One did not find painters painting street scenes in Montparnasse, such as Utrillo in Montmartre. Montparnasse never was picturesque, and even in 1912, when Picasso arrived, it had not yet become fashionable, as it would between the wars. By itself it never did offer inspiration—even if the people who inhabited it did.

Drawn by camaraderie and well-lubricated wit, Picasso joined friends at the Closerie or at either of the two newer cafés at the intersection of Boulevard du Montparnasse and Boulevard Raspail (then called Carrefour Vavin, now Place Pablo-Picasso). These were the **Café du Dôme** and the **Café de**

la Rotonde, which were located within minutes of the Closerie on Boulevard du Montparnasse. The completion of the Nord-Sud line of the Métro (Line 12, finished by 1910 for most of the distance from Gare Montparnasse to Montmartre), together with the long-awaited cut-through of Boulevard Raspail to Boulevard du Montparnasse, suddenly made the Carrefour Vavin a hot spot, and both the Dôme and the Rotonde benefited. **Le Select** and **La Coupole** (by far the largest of the bunch) soon followed. This intersection suddenly became the quarter's focal point, where artists and their comrades could meet, drink, and talk.

The more well-to-do Americans, British, Scandinavians, and—before the war—Germans hung out at the Dôme, while just about everyone else gravitated to the Rotonde. In general, impoverished artists and writers could enjoy warmth and good company for hours at any of these cafés while nursing a mere *café crème*. "Innocent beverage!" rhapsodized André Salmon of the *café crème*, in his memoirs of Montparnasse, "ordered as a way of paying for the right to remain, for permission to reside a certain time, the most time possible, seated in front of a small table of this Bourse of the new artistic values, this temple of living Art!"[1]

Victor Libion was the Rotonde's owner, and Kiki—artists' model and reigning queen of Montparnasse during its 1920s glory days—proclaimed in her memoirs that "Père Libion is the best of men, and he loves them, his ragtag bunch of artists!" She fondly recalled how the huge loaves of bread delivered daily to the Rotonde were placed in a willow basket near the bar, with ends of the loaves sticking out above the top—at least, until Père Libion turned his back, when the tops of all the loaves promptly disappeared. After which, day after day, everyone sauntered out with a piece of bread in his pocket.

One night, to celebrate Amedeo Modigliani's sale of a work, he and his friends decided to throw a big dinner. Père Libion was invited with the rest of the crowd, but at the sight of him, Modigliani became edgy. The problem was that the chairs, the knives, the glasses, the plates, and even the tables had all come from the Rotonde, and Père Libion clearly realized this. Soon, he got up and left, and Modigliani berated his friends for bringing him. "I love him as much as you do," he told them, "but if I did not invite him, it is because of all these dishes which I have taken from him." The party fell silent, when suddenly the door opened and Père Libion returned, his arms filled with bottles. "Only the wine wasn't from me," he told them, "so I went to get it. Let's go to table. I am as hungry as a wolf."[2]

〜

Picasso's departure from the Bateau-Lavoir signaled the beginning of the end of that establishment's position as center of the avant-garde universe, and Montmartre with it. It was around this time that a new center began to emerge in a far corner of Montparnasse, focused around an odd building on Passage Dantzig called **La Ruche.**

La Ruche dated from 1900, when a successful society sculptor and committed philanthropist by the name of Alfred Boucher bought land at the southern edge of Paris, just inside the last and most inclusive of Paris's walls (the 1840s Thiers fortifications), where he created an artists' colony. Cleverly recycling the octagonal wine rotunda from the recently closed Paris exposition, he divided it into numerous small trapezoidal studios, each with its own source of natural light, and opened these to a passel of struggling artists. Boucher charged next to nothing for these accommodations (when he even bothered to request rent), which was about what the traffic could bear. Grandly inaugurated as the Villa Médicis, the place quickly became known as La Ruche, or the Beehive.

Buzzing with activity (as well as the usual array of vermin), La Ruche became home to the most starving of starving artists, many of whom (including Marc Chagall, Ossip Zadkine, Chaim Soutine, Alexander Archipenko, and Jacques Lipchitz) had made their way to Paris from Russia and Eastern Europe, to escape crushing poverty and anti-Semitic persecution. Here they lived in freedom—the freedom to create—and create they did, becoming part of a generation of painters and sculptors soon known as the Paris School. But before fame came poverty, and although La Ruche looked fine enough from the outside, with its imposing doorway flanked by carved female figures, or caryatids, the interior studios were cramped, squalid, and without heat. Worse yet, Boucher's land was located downwind of a major slaughterhouse and surrounded by a notorious wasteland known as La Zone. Freezing in winter, broiling in summer, it required grit simply to survive at La Ruche.

Chagall later recalled being holed up in one of the tiny rooms on La Ruche's second floor. "While in the Russian ateliers," he later wrote, "an offended model sobbed; from the Italians' came the sound of songs and the twanging of a guitar, and from the Jews debates and arguments, I sat alone in my studio before my kerosene lamp." Nearby, amid the breaking dawn, "they are slaughtering cattle, the cows low and I paint them. . . . My lamp burned, and I with it."[3]

As a twelve-year-old, Alice Prin (soon to be known as Kiki) moved from her grandmother's household, where she was raised with a swarm of other illegitimate cousins, to join her mother in wartime Paris. There, she learned to make her way in a tough world. Meals, when available, consisted largely of beans, and so when she met up with some painters who asked her to pose in the nude for them, she readily accepted. Money, however little, was money. And as she put it, "if you want to know, I had a figure that you'd have a hard time passing up anywhere."[4]

Her mother's apartment was located near the Gare Montparnasse, a quarter that had rapidly become a center for artists and bohemians. Kiki soon made the acquaintance of Chaim Soutine, who occupied a studio in a cluster of ramshackle buildings called the Cité Falguière, just to the west of the train station. Amedeo Modigliani, another artist well acquainted with poverty, had moved there first, and others followed. These flimsy shacks were hot in the summer and freezing in the winter—so cold that, as Kiki remembered, Soutine "spent the night burning up everything in his place to keep us warm."[5]

Soutine shared his rugged atelier, off and on, with his good friend Modigliani, and an acquaintance who once visited the two late at night recalled seeing them lying on the floor surrounded by a water-filled trench to ward off bedbugs. Each held a candle, by which Modigliani was reading Dante.

One evening in 1921, Man Ray noticed an attractive woman at the Rotonde. Man Ray, an American, recently from Brooklyn, was an aspiring artist drawn to Dada and surrealism who was on the cusp of fame as both a photographer and painter. As for his name, that really was his. Man Ray's father had arrived at Ellis Island as Melach Radnitsky, and Emmanuel, Max's oldest son, informally shortened the family name to Ray. Emmanuel, already known as Manny, began to sign his works as "Man," and Man Ray thus emerged.

The woman that Man Ray noticed was with a friend, and the waiter had pointedly refused to serve them because they were not wearing hats. The prettier of the two became irate and shouted that a café was not a church, and besides, "all the American bitches came in without hats." The manager then arrived and tried to reason with her, telling her that since they were French, the fact that both were *sans chapeau* might lead some to mistake them for whores. This made the woman furious, but Man Ray's companion knew her and promptly invited her to join them. The waiter was all apologies—he did not realize that they were Man Ray's friends.[6]

And that was how Man Ray met Kiki. Kiki agreed to pose for him, and they became lovers soon after that. She had already become a popular model in Montparnasse, as much for her jaunty good humor as for her beauty, but now that she was with Man Ray, she no longer posed for other artists. Instead, she sang bawdy songs at the Jockey Club—the first nightclub and cabaret in Montparnasse—and worked with Man Ray in numerous photographic sessions over the coming years. Many of these took place in a combined studio and living space that Man Ray moved into at **31 bis Rue Campagne-Première**, in the heart of Montparnasse. This space was small, but the building was and still is a treasure, covered with colored ceramic tile and a wealth of detail. Man Ray was pleased with it, especially as he soon was sharing it with Kiki.

Their eight-year love affair and professional collaboration became a byword for 1920s Montparnasse.

Kiki was undisputed queen of the Jockey Club, where every night she delighted patrons with her cheerful vulgarity and sheer joy. This famed nightspot, now defunct, owed its name, so they say, to the retired jockey who wandered into the place when it was still a simple zinc bar, liked it, and took it over. An American artist then decorated it with large painted figures à la Wild West, in haphazard imitation of a Western saloon, and music and entertainment followed—as did the crowds. Late each night, after the theater, long lines of limousines let out patrons at the Jockey's door, where they came to drink, talk, and revel in the ongoing party, to the accompaniment of American jazz and blues.

The Jockey continued to draw late-night crowds throughout *les Années folles*, but soon a new nightclub, the **Bal Nègre**, offered competition. Originating as a local dance hall for West Indians, it quickly captivated an A-list of Parisians and Americans. Soon it began to draw crowds to its run-down quarters on the far side of Montparnasse, at 33 Rue Blomet—where it has recently been restored as the **Bal Blomet**.

What many consider the last major Montparnasse fling of *les Années folles* took place here during the spring of 1929, some months before the great financial crash. The occasion was a raucous costume ball given by Madeleine Anspach, mistress of André Derain, the colorful and by-now wealthy painter who adored race cars and who was fully capable of tearing up any bar he was in when sufficiently drunk. Anspach chose the theme of Ubu, the character from Alfred Jarry's bizarre and outrageous turn-of-the-century play, *Ubu Roi*, and partygoers came dressed appropriately (Anspach came as Mère Ubu, and the painter Foujita as a whore). Soon the festivities settled into an all-night orgy, with Kiki obligingly doing a semi-topless cancan to the insistent beat of the jazz band, while another woman danced naked on a crate of champagne.

Before it was over, one especially sozzled female was dragged screaming from the dance floor, where she had been conducting a frenzied attempt to seduce any or all of the players in the band.

Six weeks later, Madeleine Anspach was dead, a suicide—whether from drugs or depression, it is not known.

Other artists came and went from this quarter, although one—Antoine Bourdelle—came and stayed, even after achieving success. The son of a cabinetmaker in southern France, Bourdelle made his way to the Ecole Nationale des Beaux-Arts in Paris, where he arrived, full of hope, in 1884. There he entered the studio of Alexandre Falguière, an acclaimed sculptor, who in time gave his name to this quarter of Montparnasse.

Bourdelle continued to show promise, but he chafed under the rigidity of Falguière's teaching and finally left—a move that threatened to end all prospects for his long-dreamed-for career as a sculptor. Struggling to find himself—as well as to survive—he settled into a ramshackle studio at 16 Impasse du Maine (now Rue Antoine-Bourdelle). Here and in adjacent buildings that he acquired over time, he would live for more than thirty years.

While plugging away in his uphill struggle to discover his identity as an artist, Bourdelle encountered Auguste Rodin, who had traveled much the same road. Rodin took notice of Bourdelle and hired him as an assistant or *praticien*, to help carve his growing output of marble sculptures. Bourdelle remained with Rodin for fifteen years, during which time Bourdelle's own sculptures began to reflect Rodin's influence. But in the end, Bourdelle broke away from Rodin's powerful and easily identifiable style. This became quite clear with Bourdelle's remarkable *Tête d'Apollon* (*Head of Apollo*), which prompted Rodin to say, "Ah, Bourdelle. You are leaving me."

Rodin meant this metaphorically, of course, and Bourdelle stayed with Rodin but continued to develop as an artist in his own right, mounting exhibitions of his work, including his striking *Héraklès archer* (*Heracles the Archer*). He then began a lengthy teaching career. Realizing how difficult but essential it was for each one to express oneself, Bourdelle told his students, "Do not copy me. Sing your own song." Over the years he would teach a remarkable group of students, including the young Swiss sculptor Alberto Giacometti—each one learning to express their own song.

Today, Bourdelle's former atelier, living quarters, and garden are encompassed in the **Musée Bourdelle**, a modern structure on Rue Antoine-Bourdelle. Bourdelle's atelier, a soaring two-story space with glass wall overlooking the garden, offers a fascinating look into the life and work of this artist, as does his apartment, which contains his furniture and pieces from his personal art collection. The garden, where Bourdelle liked to stroll, is a particular delight, a leafy, intimate sculpture garden shaded by trees and overflowing with flowers and ivy.

Perhaps the most interesting sculptures here are Bourdelle's bas-reliefs for the then-new Théâtre des Champs-Elysées (on Avenue Montaigne). It was here that Stravinsky's *Rite of Spring* had its tumultuous opening and where (twelve years later) Josephine Baker made her spectacular Paris debut— both of them setting off cultural fireworks to the accompaniment of primal rhythms. The theater's appearance had already created controversy, being a startlingly clean-lined structure made of reinforced concrete.

Bourdelle's decorative friezes for the theater's exterior include one celebrating a dance between Isadora Duncan and Nijinsky that had occurred only in the sculptor's imagination. He had seen Duncan dance and never forgot the experience: "Each movement, each pose of this great artiste remained like flashes of lightning in my memory," he wrote. As for Nijinsky, Bourdelle conceived of him as "wrenching himself free of the marble with a savage movement, . . . but the marble block restrains this man who carries within himself the winged genius of birds!"[7]

Another hidden garden in Montparnasse belonged to yet another sculptor, Ossip Zadkine, and now is the entrance to what once was his house and atelier, forming the **Musée Zadkine**.

One of a flood of artists from Russia and Central Europe who arrived in Paris during the heady years before World War I, Zadkine at first washed up—along with so many of his colleagues in what became known as the Paris School—at the fabled La Ruche. He should have fit in well here with compatriots such as Chagall, Soutine, and Lipchitz, but he hated La Ruche, finding nothing either pleasant or romantic about its living conditions or even its legendary bonhomie.

Fortunately, Zadkine did not have to stay long. Yet after escaping first to one address then another, he found nothing that truly pleased him until, in 1928, he bought a rustic house and garden at the end of a small lane behind Rue d'Assas (100 bis, Rue d'Assas), a remarkably secluded spot in the heart of Montparnasse. "Come see my pleasure house," he wrote a friend, "and you'll understand how much a man's life can be changed by a dovecote, by a tree."

As it happened, these idyllic surroundings did not inspire Zadkine to celebrate either beauty or nature—at least, not in any traditional sense. In fact, having survived a fraught Jewish boyhood under the Russian Empire, as well as frontline service during World War I, where he served as a stretcher-bearer, Zadkine retained a dark vision of the world around him. Still, he found in this tranquil setting the inspiration and freedom he needed to channel his anguish over the human condition into ever more powerful and dramatic forms. These include the huge bronze figure that Zadkine created for the city of Rotterdam not long after World War II. Its arms are outstretched in torment, its torso pierced with a jagged hole—much as Rotterdam itself had suffered after Germany bombed its heart out.

Having found a measure of peace in his Paris studio and garden, Zadkine remained there until his death in 1967, evolving during the course of a long career from Primitivism and Cubism to the highly individual and abstract style of his later years. Only during the German Occupation did he temporarily escape to New York, returning immediately after the war to Rue d'Assas, where he produced some of his finest sculptures, including his famous Rotterdam memorial, which many consider his masterpiece. A small model of this, along with several other of his most famous sculptures, dot the diminutive garden—a tranquil spot where an artist struggling with the world's darkness found a degree of peace.

Wealthy American collectors made the fortunes of earlier French painters, such as Claude Monet, and later collectors, such as the Steins, would bolster the early years of Picasso and Matisse. But it was an especially unlikely collector, Dr Albert C. Barnes from Philadelphia, who discovered Chaim Soutine. Dr. Barnes, a forceful and often alienating personality, had made his millions by inventing and marketing an antiseptic that treated gonorrhea. Raised in a working family with little time or money for anything but getting by, Barnes developed a surprising interest in art through a high school friend who became an artist. Soon after Barnes became a millionaire, he sent this friend to Paris to buy art for him (including works by Cézanne, Renoir, Degas, Van Gogh, Monet, Gauguin, and Matisse), which became the core of the fabled Barnes Collection in Philadelphia.

But it was when Barnes visited Paris in person, in the early 1920s, that he first spotted a painting by Soutine. He then paid Soutine what seemed to the painter to be an astronomical sum for Soutine's total available output. According to stories that circulated soon after, Soutine celebrated this event by rushing into the street and hailing a taxi. "Where to?" the driver asked. "Why not the Riviera?" Soutine retorted. The driver was dubious, but Soutine flashed his wad of cash, and the taxi took off. Fortunately, in the end the ride cost him only a fraction of the money he had received from Barnes.

Not surprisingly, word soon spread following the Barnes purchase, and Soutine's career took off. His paintings rose in price, and he quickly abandoned his desolate shack near the railroad station for better quarters. Soon, like other successful artists in Montparnasse, he moved to the lovely area of tiny streets just west of Parc Montsouris, where he rented an apartment on Rue du Parc-de-Montsouris. Here he was near his friends, including Foujita, André Derain, and Georges Braque. As an ultimate sign of success, the street where Georges Braque lived now is named **Rue Georges-Braque**. He lived at number 6.

Nearby is the **Villa Seurat**, another haven for artists and writers such as Henry Miller, who lived in comfort (skylight, balcony, private bath, and kitchen) at number 18 on this up-to-date cul-de-sac created for painters and sculptors. His lover, Anaïs Nin, paid the rent and helped to finance publication of his *Tropic of Cancer* (1934)—a book that brought Miller little in the way of immediate fame or fortune. Instead, its language, subjects, and candid sexuality brought censorship in the United States and Britain until the 1960s.

Miller did not think much of, or about, politics. Nor did he think much of so-called normality, which he considered a state of existence inimical to the truly interesting people in life. But he didn't think much of Salvador Dalí, either, despite the fact that Dalí made a career out of being outrageous. For four years, Dalí lived just down the street from Miller, at 101 bis Rue de la Tombe-Issoire, at the corner of Villa Seurat, and Miller seems to have ignored him. As far as Miller was concerned, Dalí was a complete fraud— although he put it more colorfully.

Parc Montsouris is little known except to those who live near it, and they prefer to keep it that way. This is one of those lovely green expanses introduced into Paris in the mid-nineteenth century by Baron Georges Haussmann, under the active encouragement of Emperor Napoleon III, who was crazy about English parks and squares. Napoleon III (who took this title out of respect for his deceased cousin, Bonaparte's young son, who had been known in certain quarters as Napoleon II) had fond memories of these parks and squares from his pre-imperial days, when (as a member of the extensive Bonaparte family) he was exiled from France following Waterloo.

Napoleon III (or Louis-Napoleon Bonaparte, as he was named at birth) introduced green spaces, small and large, throughout Paris—the small ones being called "squares," in the English fashion, which the French pronounce as "skwars." Until then, Paris had only four public parks: the Luxembourg

Gardens, the Jardin des Plantes, the Tuileries Gardens, and the gardens of the Palais Royal, all in the city's center. But Louis-Napoleon saw a need for parks on the city's growing outskirts, which had become vastly larger after the city's boundaries were moved from the newly demolished Farmers-General tax wall to the more recent Thiers fortifications (dating from the 1840s), located about a mile outside the former tax wall. In the process, Paris enlarged its population by one-third and more than doubled its surface area. It was then that the city was divided into twenty rather than twelve arrondissements, or municipal administrative districts, which bore no resemblance, whether in shape or numerical order, to the original twelve.

Parc Montsouris, a forty-acre landscape park, is specifically modeled after an English landscape garden, complete with expansive lawns, trees, rustic walks, cascades, and a lake. It is a beautiful place to come and relax. And if you keep your eyes open, you may spot a mysterious train track, romantically overgrown with vines, that cuts right through the park at a subterranean level. Oddly enough, it isn't headed for the center of Paris and, if anything, it parallels the nearby Périphérique, Paris's unloved and unlovely beltway.

This train track belonged to the **Petite Ceinture**, or Little Belt, the small railway that once encircled Paris. Back in the mid-1800s, during Napoleon III's Second Empire, railroads were beginning to converge on Paris, and the new Thiers fortification had risen on the city's outskirts. There was considerable need for a railroad to serve as a connecting link between the various railroad lines entering the city, in addition to connecting and provisioning Paris's defenders on the Thiers fortifications (sixteen substantial forts lay just outside the walls). The outcome was the Little Belt encircling Paris, just inside what then was the Thiers fortification, with spurs leading to major commercial ventures such as the massive slaughterhouses of La Villette in the northeast and Vaugirard in the southwest (the one that wafted unpleasant odors toward La Ruche).

At first the Petite Ceinture served solely as a freight carrier, but then it opened to passengers, and by the turn of the century it was carrying millions of riders every year. But then, during the early years of the twentieth century, the construction of the Métro system sounded the Petite Ceinture's death knell. Today, the RER (Regional Express Network) runs on a portion of its tracks, in the northwest of Paris, but the rest has been abandoned and locked up—although the homeless find refuge here, and there are secret entrances to be found to the quarries below (entries that are well-known to *cataphiles*, as the French call these urban underground explorers).

Fans of the Petite Ceinture were hoping that the new tram system around the south and east of Paris would run on at least a portion of the old tracks, but the city of Paris opted for a new ground-level system. So, for the time being, you will have to content yourself with views of the old tracks, such as this one at Parc Montsouris—although a couple of the Petite Ceinture's stations still exist, converted to other uses. La Gare is now an upscale restaurant in the sixteenth arrondissement, near La Muette Métro. Another converted Petite Ceinture station, La Flèche d'Or in the twentieth arrondissement, was a popular rock club, but it has been encountering rough times of late.

Looking down at the overgrown tracks, it is difficult to imagine this once-busy little railroad, which carted freight and people around the outskirts of Paris. A blessing for many, it also annoyed some of the well-to-do on the city's western outskirts, such as the acerbic writer and journalist Edmond de Goncourt. In 1868, Goncourt and his brother had just moved from the heart of the city to what they termed "the country" in Auteuil, in search of peace and quiet. Consequently, both brothers were deeply dismayed by the noise of the Petite Ceinture, whose trains ran nearby, "rumbling and whistling and disturbing our insomnia."[8]

Then again, the neighbors' children and a nearby horse also disturbed the Goncourts, spoiling what they had hoped would be perfection.

You can catch another glimpse of the Petite Ceinture in **Parc Georges-Brassens**, an attractive park virtually unknown to tourists, created on the site of the Vaugirard slaughterhouse, whose fumes once enveloped the impoverished residents of La Ruche. A recent addition to Paris's park system, Parc Georges-Brassens' only remnants from the slaughterhouse are the bronze bulls at the park's main entrance and the bell tower that originally tolled for auctions. There is also a brick structure, bedecked with a sculpted horse's head, that originally housed the horse market. This now serves on weekends as a market for used books.

The park is a pleasant oasis of trees, lawns, and a small lake, as well as rose gardens and a winding stream. But my favorite spot is the bridge that crosses over the train tracks of the Petite Ceinture. The tracks below are overgrown and lush, a true jungle. But best is a sign that warns people not to throw trash onto the railroad's right-of-way. The sign is old and rusted, and it gives as its authority a decree dated 22 March 1942—a date that goes back to the German Occupation of Paris. This is a startling memento of a dark and difficult time, and I hope no one removes it.

Not far from Parc Georges-Brassens, and tucked into the southwest corner of the city alongside the Seine, is another recent addition to Paris's parks—**Parc André-Citroën**. This newcomer created a good deal of excitement at its inception in the early 1990s, not only for its considerable size but also for its innovative features and design.

Parc André-Citroën was meant from the outset to be spectacular. Described as a futurist space where technological innovation and nature live in harmony, it is arranged around a large lawn bordered at one end by two sizable pavilions housing exotic plants. These in turn bookend a paved area dotted with dancing fountains—multiple waterspouts that shoot up from the surface. A canal encircles all four sides of the lawn, while to one side is a series of small gardens, each with a theme (usually a color). On weekends, a tethered giant hot-air balloon makes its ascent from the lawn's far end.

The whole thing is striking, although I feel that it is a place to admire, not to sit and relax. In fact, there are few places to sit here, except in the small gardens, and these, with their trees and benches, seem to draw the most visitors. Yet even these gardens have a hard-edged look due to the large concrete structures that divide them—structures that are meant to carry water down into pools but at present are not working.

André Citroën, who made his fortune at the turn of the last century by inventing the double-helical gearwheel (think V-shaped teeth set together at an angle), amplified his wealth by moving into the mass production of artillery shells during World War I. It was only after the war that he launched into automobile production, for which he is generally known today. Parc André-Citroën is built on the site of Citroën's huge automobile works—an enterprise that rivaled that of his major competitor, Louis Renault, whose own automobile works spread across the river at Billancourt.

Citroën was a businessman with a sense of adventure, not a mere mechanic, and he might well be intrigued by the park that now bears his name. The dramatic architectural features would interest him, and the tethered balloon that regularly ascends and descends here would probably catch his eye, inviting him to take a ride.

But I like to think that he would especially enjoy the dancing fountains.

As you have no doubt noticed, the last three parks we have visited all stretch across the southern rim of Paris's city limits, as defined in 1860. Parcs Georges-Brassens and André-Citroën have risen on previous industrial sites, while Parc Montsouris occupied land riddled by played-out quarries. But all have shared a common link to Paris's last and largest wall, the Thiers fortifications.

Paris had been surging into areas such as Passy, Montmartre, and Belleville well before 1860, when the Farmers-General tax wall at last came down. Reflecting this new ring of growth, the government had already enclosed Paris within yet a larger and more bristling wall, this one named after its then premier, Adolphe Thiers. The Thiers fortifications (1841–1845) eventually marked Napoleon III's administrative limits for Paris, complete with the arrondissements as they exist today. Yet unlike the Farmers-General Wall, which it replaced as a tax barrier, the Thiers wall's chief function was defensive, reflecting concern for Paris's security in in an increasingly dangerous world.

The enemy no longer was England but Prussia and a reunited Germany—reunited after almost a millennium, under the military leadership of Otto von Bismarck. Unfortunately for the French, the Thiers fortifications did little to stop the Germans during the 1870 Franco-Prussian War, and these fortifications never saw action during World War I. As a result, one of the first things the French did to inaugurate the peace in 1919 was begin to pull these ineffective ramparts down.

Not surprisingly, the site of this last wall offered a huge land grab once the fortifications came down—a process that was not completed until 1932, but when finished offered up an enormous chunk of unoccupied land. The fortifications themselves belonged to the military, but the land around them—a barren military sector called the Zone—belonged to a hodgepodge of private and public owners, including the villages and communes outside the wall. The Zone itself had been for decades a dismal no-man's-land, a dangerous dead end inhabited by tramps, thieves, ragpickers, and the outcasts of society. The idea that this last reserve of unoccupied land in the city could become something better had for decades aroused interest, and when France passed its first national planning law in 1919, there already were optimists with dreams of new housing as well as hospitals, schools, and parks for this insalubrious ring around Paris.

One plan was to create attractive open spaces by constructing a ring of landscaped parks. These in turn would be linked by an irregular boulevard that incorporated gardens and courtyards in the spaces between buildings and streets. But contrary to hopes and expectations, the land was developed piecemeal, with most built up helter-skelter by private developers. Hammered by real estate interests and hampered by the cost of expropriation proceedings and clearance operations, the government seemed paralyzed.

There were, however, exceptions, one of the most notable being the **Cité Internationale Universitaire de Paris**, which went up just to the south of Parc Montsouris on land that once had been part of the Zone. This experiment in international living—one of the most concrete examples of the post–World War I international peace movement—got its start when the wealthy French industrialist Emile Deutsch de la Meurthe decided that he wanted to create some sort of tangible legacy and contacted the rector of the University of Paris, who at that moment was despairing over the postwar dearth of student housing. Together with the minister of public instruction, they came up with the idea of a *cité universitaire*, or campus of residence halls—not a novel idea in itself, except that this particular group of residence halls would have a unique and heartfelt purpose: true to the spirit of the times immediately following World War I, which then was widely viewed as "the war to end all wars," the Cité Internationale Universitaire de Paris would be dedicated to promoting international peace.

The idea was that if enough students from the four corners of the world lived together in close quarters, they would form friendships and learn to understand and appreciate one another. Walls of bigotry and misunderstanding would crumble, and wars like the terrible one from which they had just emerged would never again engulf the world. In this spirit, the first buildings of the experiment were opened in 1925 on an eighty-five-acre strip of land deep in the fourteenth arrondissement that became available when the Thiers fortifications there were torn down.

Other buildings on this international residential campus quickly followed, thanks to generous support from numerous governments, corporations, and private individuals, including John D. Rockefeller Jr., who was a major donor. Oddly, given the original purpose of the place, most of the residences were set up as national houses, with students of a particular nation residing in that nation's building (Americans, for example, in the Fondation des Etats-Unis, and Japanese in the Maison du Japon). In response to this potential clannishness, the various houses now reserve at least a third of their rooms for students from other countries and consciously mix their residents. In addition, students mingle in the campus restaurants, library, theater, orchestra, chorus, team sports, and sports facilities.

Although the original concept of national houses may be outmoded, the resulting architecture is always interesting and sometimes striking. Nations responded to the call with architecture that either reflected their national identity or represented the latest and best of what their architects could do, creating a kind of world's fair of architecture. Brazil House is a frankly

Le Corbusier's Swiss House, Cité Internationale Universitaire de Paris. © J. McAuliffe

aggressive piece of architecture designed by Lucio Costa. Japan House, on the other hand, looks a bit like a Nipponese temple, while Greek House looks like the Parthenon, and the Deutsch de la Meurthe group is cozily reminiscent of Oxford or Cambridge.

But the prize of the entire campus is Le Corbusier's 1932 Swiss House, a clean-lined and airborne structure that is open on its ground level, resting its entire weight on a mere set of elongated pillars or piles. Unfortunately, it turned out that almost everyone, especially the Swiss, had expected something more like a Swiss chalet. According to Le Corbusier, the inauguration ceremony for Swiss House was more like a funeral.

But Le Corbusier's Swiss House has earned plaudits in the years since, even though, much like its neighbors, this designer structure requires considerable upkeep and care. As for the entire project, Cité Internationale Universitaire de Paris is still going strong, linked with other student International Houses around the globe and actively promoting its vision for a better and more peaceful world.

Certainly a success story for at least this small portion of an outmoded fortification.

Square des Peupliers. © M. McAuliffe

CHAPTER ELEVEN

~

Lost River

Once upon a time, not so very long ago, there were two rivers in Paris—the Seine and the Bièvre. The Seine bisected Paris from east to west, while the little Bièvre entered Paris from the south, winding its way through the Left Bank before depositing its waters in the Seine.

Once a bucolic stream where, according to legend, beaver thrived (possibly giving the watercourse its name), for centuries the Bièvre had meandered through a countryside dotted with watermills and rustic villages. Within Paris, its waters flowed past mills and gardens, its tree-lined banks providing shade and beauty.

But then, Jean Gobelin, a dyer—attracted to the Bièvre by its minerals—set up shop in what now is the thirteenth arrondissement. By the seventeenth century, his small venture had blossomed into the renowned Gobelins tapestry workshops, attracting a plethora of tanners and dyers to the area. By the eighteenth century, Paris's Bièvre had grown dark and polluted, and even its upstream waters suffered from considerable contamination after Christophe Philippe Oberkampf began to manufacture his famed toile print fabrics in the little riverside village of Jouy-en-Josas.

Industrialization completed what the early polluters began, and by the nineteenth century the Bièvre had become little more than a fetid sewer that coursed its way through the most poverty-stricken parts of Paris. No one objected when the city of Paris dealt with this horror by gradually relegating it underground, as a sewer. There it continues to run, in pipes.

Since that time, the industrial slums through which the Bièvre flowed have made way for a far more welcoming environment, and a series of pleasant parks and intriguing nooks now dot the stream's original course. This has led to considerable interest in bringing back the Bièvre, although little has been done so far to implement this revival. Yet despite the river's disappearance from view, you can still follow its winding course, wandering through some interesting and picturesque neighborhoods along the way.

Originating in Guyancourt, near Versailles, the Bièvre enters Paris through the site of the once-bristling Thiers fortifications. After these came down, more than a dozen acres along the Bièvre, in the thirteenth arrondissement, became **Parc Kellermann**—one of the loveliest parks in Paris that has, if anything, become even lovelier over the years.

From the formal French gardens at the park's entrance, descend through lush greenery to a romantic setting punctuated by weeping willows, streams, and pools. Most dramatic of all is the monumental waterfall that plummets down a high retaining wall before pouring into a succession of rocky basins. These in turn flow into a small lake that shelters heron and other birds among its ornamental grasses.

The Bièvre once flowed freely here, and it still runs beneath your feet. The wooden walkway informs you that this is a "symbolic course of the Bièvre," but in fact, the river does flow there, or at least nearby—through a large conduit, the Collecteur Pascal. Centuries ago, some enterprising Parisians divided the Bièvre right about here into two roughly parallel streams. By banking up an artificial riverbed higher than the original, they cleverly provided power for a number of watermills farther downstream. The Collecteur Pascal follows this upper course, skirting to the right of the playing fields and crossing beneath Boulevard Kellermann to Rue de l'Interne-Loeb.

Since you cannot cross Boulevard Kellermann here as easily as does the river, you may prefer to follow the course of the lower Bièvre along Rue de la Poterne-des-Peupliers to the Poterne des Peupliers (Poplar Gate), where it passed through the now-vanished Thiers fortifications and beneath the Petite Ceinture. The poplars that once lined the riverbank still border this narrow thoroughfare, while the viaduct under what now is Boulevard Kellermann contains some vestiges of the old walls.

Continuing along the lower Bièvre's winding course, follow Rue des Peupliers uphill—yes, uphill—to the pleasantly old-fashioned **Place de l'Abbé-Georges-Hénocque**, a quaint tree-shaded place where neighbors gather to chat at a small outdoor café. Continue uphill, noting occasional sidewalk medallions marking the River Bièvre's course, to where Rue des Peupliers intersects with Rue du Moulin-des-Prés. This is the approximate site of an old watermill that once operated on the upper Bièvre.

If you find this a strange location for a watermill—after all, how could a river flow up the considerable hill you've been climbing since Boulevard Kellermann?—be assured that the mill's actual site was about sixty feet beneath where you stand. Rivers do not run uphill, even in Paris. Instead, the landscape in this part of town has changed dramatically during the past century or so, thanks to some massive earthmoving. Just to give you an idea: Rue du Moulin-des-Prés once crossed far below Rue de Tolbiac, which formed an impressive viaduct high above the Bièvre.

If you follow present-day Rue du Moulin-des-Prés to Rue de Tolbiac, you will find the **Square des Peupliers**, a tiny jewel of a cul-de-sac at 72 Rue du Moulin-des-Prés. Shade-drenched and bordered with wisteria-covered houses, this cobbled lane lies at the point where both branches of the Bièvre bumped up against the rocky Butte-aux-Cailles (Quail Hill). From here they looped south, the lower course following Rue de la Fontaine-à-Mulard to Place de Rungis.

Long ago, when winter came and the river froze, young people came to skate in these pond-filled lowlands, known as La Glacière. Others came to chop up portions of the frozen water into blocks of ice, which they stored in icehouses (*glaciers*). Eventually the marshy lands of La Glacière were filled in to make room for new housing, but happily this included the charmingly eccentric **Cité Florale**. Located immediately to the west of Place de Rungis and just a few minutes' walk from Parc Montsouris, the Cité Florale is a village of tiny houses so picturesque that one is amazed that it has remained relatively unknown. Enter by Rue Brillat-Savarin and wander down the flower-named lanes. My favorite entrance is via Rue des Liserons, which leads to the minute Square des Mimosas and picture-perfect Rue des Iris.

This jumble of tiny streets, all named after wildflowers and vines, is lined with equally tiny cottages of every imaginable style. All, with the exception of unfortunate Rue des Orchidées, which has succumbed to a batch of apartment buildings, are an oasis miraculously preserved in the midst of uninspired high-rises. One of the main reasons the Cité Florale still survives is that the ground beneath it will not support anything much taller and heavier. Built on the low-lying marshy area where the Bièvre spread into ponds, this small village grew up in the 1920s, just inside the no-man's-land that bordered the Thiers fortifications. When these came down following World War I, development of the area soon followed. The Cité Florale was certainly the most inspired of this postwar building boom, and soon its winding streets and vine-covered cottages attracted a loyal group of residents, including writers and artists in search of low rents and charm.

Wander through this cluster of small streets and cul-de-sacs and soak up the beauty and the peace. No wonder flowers do well here, and one assumes that its residents—and their artistic endeavors—are also thriving.

If you are paying attention to your map, you'll note the Bièvre's imprint everywhere—on the placement and curvature of streets as well as on place-names summoning up images of trees, flowers, and country mills. From Place de Rungis, the lower streambed curves around what now is the Cité Florale via Rue Brillat-Savarin to Rue Wurtz. Along the way you will find other jewels, such as **Petite Alsace** (10 Rue Daviel), a picturesque enclave of half-timbered houses, and Rue Le Dantec, a lovely old street at the base of the quiet and village-like Butte-aux-Cailles.

Crossing under Petite Alsace, the upper Bièvre met up with its sister branch at Boulevard Auguste-Blanqui. Here the two passed through a double watergate in the old toll walls (the Farmers-General Wall, demolished in 1860) and once again divided. The higher stream flowed along what now is Rue Edmond-Gondinet, where it passed another watermill (the Moulin Croulebarbe, at the corner of Rue Corvisart), while the lower stream ran along what now is Rue Paul-Gervais. Together, the two arms enclosed a lush enclave that once provided kitchen plots for Gobelins workers and now is the **Square René-Le Gall**, a secret garden and small wood that encompass the course of the Bièvre. The river's waters emerge on the western side of the park, where they burble their way along a pathway beside a school, ending in a small pool within the park.

This place has a history: here, long ago, during a violent thunderstorm, a tormented young man stabbed to death a beautiful shepherdess who had spurned him. If this sounds like something from a Victor Hugo novel, you are not far wrong, for the beautiful Square René-Le Gall spreads over the former Champ de l'Alouette, or Field of the Lark, where the young shepherdess died. Attracted by the story's dark drama, Hugo used this spot as the site that so magnetically drew Marius, the yearning young lover of *Les Misérables*.

While in the vicinity, Victor Hugo frequented the rustic tavern that still stands at 41 Rue de Croulebarbe, along what once was a riverbank path. Nowadays, this tavern—which still sports the name "Cabaret de Madame Grégoire" on its façade—is a Basque restaurant, the **Auberge Etchegorry**, whose cassoulet is worth sampling. Nowadays, this rustic auberge overlooks

Square René-Le Gall's gently flowing water and densely forested interior—a haven of peace and greenery on the banks of the river's ancient course.

From Rue de Croulebarbe, follow the upper Bièvre's curve along Rue Berbier-du-Mets, behind the venerable Gobelins textile workshops. Nearby is the **Hôtel de la Reine Blanche** (at 17 and 19 Rue des Gobelins), twin Gothic mansions where a royal queen (we do not know which) dwelled during her widowhood, when white still was the prescribed color of mourning for widowed queens. Legend has it that the queen in question was Blanche of Castille, mother of Saint Louis, but there are other candidates. And although the original mansion, dating from around the year 1300, was razed after a tragedy took place there (a ball during which several died when their costumes caught fire), another mansion was eventually built on the site. This one, Gothic in style with twin buildings, dates from around 1500 and is still one of the oldest domestic buildings in Paris—a remnant of late medieval times.

Before following the Bièvre across Boulevard Arago, take a quick detour to look at another floral enclave, the **Cité Fleurie**, whose entrance opens along the boulevard at number 65. This beguiling bower grew up a century and a half ago in what then was a wasteland on the city's outskirts. Much like the nearby artist colony at La Ruche, it was built from remnants of a world's fair—in this case, the one of 1878. Hauling the materials here from the fair site, the builder constructed a series of rustic half-timbered artists' studios in long rows, divided by a long, woodsy garden.

The results, still enchanting today, soon drew a clientele of appreciative and impoverished artists, including many who would eventually become famous. Both Rodin and Maillol sculpted here, while Modigliani stayed at no. 9 and Gauguin (always impoverished) camped out with a friend.

Anti-fascism as well as artists thrived in these sheltered studios. As early as the mid-1930s, an anti-Nazi library flourished at no. 18, where one could read literature unobtainable in Germany. During the German Occupation, the Gestapo got wind of this subversive cache and shut it down, but only after it had been operating for several years.

After the war, the Cité Fleurie continued its bucolic existence, but its low two-story buildings seemed a waste of space to some insensitive souls, who almost succeeded in demolishing it. Fortunately, its occupants, led by artist Henri Cadiou, tenaciously fought to protect it. At last, in 1973, they succeeded in making Cité Fleurie a protected site—a boon for the entire quarter as well as for those visitors fortunate enough to see it. Appropriately, the small next-door park is named for the Cité's tireless protector, Henri Cadiou.

⁓

Much like the Collecteur Pascal, you will find it easier to cross Boulevard Arago at Rue Pascal, following both streams' approximate course to the busy intersection at the foot of Montagne Sainte-Geneviève, where Rue Mouffetard, complete with its famous street market, begins its climb. Here as well is the small peaceful park adjoining the church of **Saint-Médard**, where you can rest and picnic on your finds from the market.

Nearby, on tiny Rue de l'Arbalète, is the birthplace of **Auguste Rodin**. This quarter may look charming now, but in 1840, when he was born, it was a slum—originally part of a village surrounding the old church of Saint-Médard and the old Roman road to Orléans. It was and still is a bustling place, the sort of environment that would quicken the imagination of an intelligent child. But as a youngster, Rodin showed no particular aptitude for anything. The third child and only son of a lowly office worker at the Préfecture de Police, Rodin seemed distinctly unpromising. Perhaps, though, his inability to read, write, or do sums was simply a sign of his complete indifference to those subjects. For from an early age, the only thing that genuinely interested him was drawing.

Young Rodin wanted to draw, and he wanted more than anything to become an artist. Finally, at a loss for any other alternative, his despairing father at last agreed to send him to the Ecole Gratuite de Dessin (the free school of design), then located in the former School of Surgery at 5 Rue de l'Ecole-de-Médecine (6th). There, this ungainly lad with carrot-colored hair labored to make his mark. He quickly learned that the school's goal was to produce craftsmen—highly skilled young men prepared to join the ranks of the Parisian artisans who specialized in one of the decorative arts. Those in training to become ornamental carvers could take classes in sculpting, and it was in such a class that Rodin, after mastering the basic drawing classes, first encountered modeling clay. "I felt as if I were ascending into heaven," he later wrote, describing how he "grasped the whole thing in a flash."[1] It was more than a revelation—it was a calling. He would be a sculptor.

But there would be many years between this epiphany and Rodin's first real success. Along the way, the Ecole des Beaux-Arts—which found his emerging naturalism completely out of step with its traditionalism—rejected him three times. He spent twenty years barely supporting himself in the decorating end of the building trades. It was during these years that

Rodin began to fill in the sizable gaps in his education, learning to read with comprehension and gravitating toward the passionate poetry of Hugo and Lamartine. He spent several years in Brussels and made a pilgrimage to Florence, to study the work of Michelangelo. "I believe," he wrote his longtime mistress, Rose Beuret, "that the great magician is revealing a few of his secrets to me."[2]

Before his Italian trip, Rodin had begun work on a life-size sculpture of a man, using a Belgian soldier as his model. Upon his return, he finished the work and showed it, under the title *The Age of Bronze*, at the prestigious Salon in Paris, which accepted his creation. But as this vibrant sculpture from an unknown sculptor started to attract attention, rumors began to circulate that Rodin had cast it "from life"—that is, from plaster casts of the model. How could anyone, his critics whispered, create such a sculpture without casting it "from life"?

This scandal blazed throughout artistic circles, but fortunately, several prominent artists came to Rodin's defense, and the tempest subsided. Rodin won the battle, and having won, benefited from the ugly controversy that had at first threatened his career. He now found a public that was aware of him and his prodigious talents.

Although he did not yet know it, Rodin's most difficult days were behind him.

Here at the foot of Rue Mouffetard, where the old Roman road to Lyon crossed the Bièvre, two medieval mills—the Moulin Saint-Marcel and the Petit-Moulin—ground wheat into flour. And here, at last, the two arms of the Bièvre rejoined into one.

Skirting Montagne Sainte-Geneviève, the newly unified river plunged onward, toward the Seine. Originally it followed a course that took it along what now is Square Adanson and between Rue Buffon and Rue Poliveau, where it ran past another mill at Rue Geoffroy-Saint-Hilaire. From there it flowed through what now are the grounds of the Museum of Natural History and beneath the curve of Rue Nicolas-Houël to its final destination, just upriver from the present Pont d'Austerlitz.

There it might have stayed, had it not been for the monks of the Abbey of Saint-Victor, who in 1151 received permission to re-route it through their lands to irrigate their extensive gardens and power a mill. Virtually nothing remains of this once-powerful abbey, but you can follow the Bièvre's artificial course—through the Jardin des Plantes and along Rue Jussieu—to where it emptied, just downstream of the Pont de l'Archevêché. En route, you will find one of Paris's most exciting archaeological discoveries of recent years, the **Arche de la Bièvre**, marking the place where the re-routed stream passed through Paris's twelfth-century walls on its way to the Seine.

Built about a half-century after the Bièvre's alteration, these moated and towered fortifications completely encircled the city. Yet what to do about the recently redirected river? The monks certainly were not interested in putting it back, which left the king's engineers with the task of constructing a gate capable of letting the Bièvre in while keeping the enemy out.

They succeeded, creating a dramatic stone arch guarded by a portcullis, through which the water—but not the enemy—could enter. In time, this wall lost its usefulness, and the arch disappeared under the dirt and rubble of the centuries. Few even remembered that it existed until recently, when excavations for a post office on Rue du Cardinal-Lemoine (at the corner of Rue des Ecoles) uncovered this eight-hundred-year-old treasure. Now carefully restored, it can be seen (via an underground parking garage) on the first Wednesday afternoon of each month.[3]

Two centuries after Philip Augustus's engineers created this magnificent structure, Charles V incorporated the river's waters into a new set of defensive moats around the old medieval walls. Responding to this challenge, the monks got to work upstream and dug yet another canal, leaving the moats and first canal to fester. This unhealthy state of affairs lasted until the reign of Louis XIV, who ordered both canals to be filled. The river then returned to its original course—until the nineteenth century, when it was buried and ignominiously dumped into the Paris sewer system.

Still, for more than two hundred years, the Bièvre was content to follow the first canal that the monks of Saint-Victor made for it—through the city wall and on to its final destination, at the tip of Rue de Bièvre. This narrow lane, just off Place Maubert, is steeped in history and is a fitting place to end your journey. Admiring these wonderful old houses, it is difficult to imagine that once, like so much of the route through which the Bièvre passed, this ancient street was a slum. Completely rejuvenated, Rue de Bièvre now is a fashionable district where former President François Mitterrand made his home, at no. 22.

A happy ending—at least for the areas through which the Bièvre once flowed. But what about the river itself? Could it once again flow through the city of Paris? Upstream, thanks to the coordinated efforts of the towns through which it passes, the revived Bièvre now flows *à ciel ouvert* from its source in Guyancourt to the suburbs of Paris, with pleasant riverbank paths along the way. This would be difficult if not impossible in Paris's dense urban fabric, but some dream of reviving the river and bringing it back in places.

A dream, perhaps. In the meantime, take a few hours to explore the Bièvre's old course. You will be traveling through history, and you will undoubtedly enjoy where it takes you.

Jardin Berthe-Weill. © M. McAuliffe

CHAPTER TWELVE

~

Into the Marais

My favorite starting point for a walk into the Marais, on the Seine's right bank, begins in the middle of the Seine, on the small island called the **Ile Saint-Louis**. Long ago this small island consisted of two even smaller islets, unpopulated except for a few cows. But by the 1600s, as central Paris was becoming crowded, royal decree brought the two islets together into the splendid (and expensive) residential area it quickly became.

Always a high-rent district with little elbow room for even the most luxurious structures, the island's mansions are narrow but deep. Those amazing carriage doors hide courtyards, often quite lovely, which you can glimpse if any of the huge doors are open. Stroll here early in the morning, when the tourists haven't yet gathered and the mist is still rising off the Seine. One can choose from two levels of walkways, one hugging the stone embankment just above the river and the other alongside the narrow street that borders the island's northern edge.

At the island's eastern end is the beautiful **Hôtel Lambert**—where Voltaire resided with his aristocratic mistress during the 1740s. Owned in the twentieth century by the Rothschilds, it was recently sold to an Arab prince, who encountered considerable opposition over his plans to install air-conditioning, elevators, and an underground car park (what, no swimming pool?). Not surprisingly, this wrangle went on and on, complicated by a fire; but now, to the relief of many, the renovation has been completed, with the building's historical character intact.

The view from nearby Pont de Sully—especially from its span connecting this end of the island with the Right Bank—is gorgeous. But my favorite spot on the Ile Saint-Louis is at the island's western tip, high above the Seine. The lower-level walkway here is a popular site for fashion shoots and wedding parties, grouped around an especially picturesque tree. But I prefer the higher level, where one can look out over the Ile de la Cité (linked to the Ile Saint-Louis by the Pont Saint-Louis), as well as the Hôtel de Ville and the Right Bank, while watching the barges and boats go by.

Crossing Pont Louis-Philippe to the Right Bank, over the **Parc Rives de Seine** below (formerly the Pompidou Expressway, now a justly popular riverside parkway for anyone and anything but automobile traffic),[1] continue up an ancient pedestrian footpath called the **Rue des Barres**, which climbs up broad, shallow steps behind the beautiful Church of Saint-Gervais-Saint-Protais. This wide pathway may well follow the course of the first wall on Paris's right bank, a wall that probably was a wooden stockade dating from sometime between the ninth century's Viking invasions and the city's twelfth-century recovery.

This is the heart of an especially ancient part of town. Passing some evocative buildings (especially the half-timbered Hôtel de l'Abbaye de Maubuisson at no. 12, which dates from 1540 and has roots that go back even earlier), you will soon find yourself on **Rue François-Miron**. This, too, is an ancient byway, part of the old Roman road eastward and, until the creation of the Rue de Rivoli in the mid-nineteenth century, the only road directly connecting the eastern outskirts of Paris to the Hôtel de Ville and the city's center.

Long ago, this was a ceremonial route, one that Louis XIV entered after his marriage, and one that foreign dignitaries and royalty used to enter the city, passing through the massive city walls at the gate guarded by the formidable Bastille fortress. Over the years, this route went by many names, but for centuries it was called Rue Saint-Antoine (after the Abbey of Saint-Antoine-des-Champs that once lay outside the city walls, on the site of today's Hôpital Saint-Antoine). This is the way it was until Baron Haussmann, carrying out the wishes of his emperor, Napoleon III, drove the Rue de Rivoli in a straight line from the Place de la Concorde to the Place de la Bastille, with plans for this byway to continue its arrow-straight course through to the Place de la Nation and beyond (Haussmann would in fact use the Rue du Faubourg Saint-Antoine, beyond the Place de la Bastille, to divide this ancient workmen's quarter between two newly arranged arrondissements, the eleventh and the twelfth).

As Haussmann's plans became known, shopkeepers all along this ancient route begged to keep it as the main thoroughfare, rather than substitute the straight one that Haussmann proposed. After all, business was at stake, and the new route threatened to drain business from the old. But Haussmann was deaf to their pleas and pushed the Rue de Rivoli straight on from the Hôtel de Ville, as planned. He then renamed the original Rue Saint-Antoine as Rue François-Miron, while the new eastward extension of the Rue de Rivoli became Rue Saint-Antoine, all the way to the Place de la Bastille.

Although Haussmann did not intend to preserve this part of Old Paris—his mission was to eradicate the old and bring in the new—his action here resulted in preserving much of the old quarter along Rue François-Miron, an unintended gift to future generations. Two of the most remarkable of these remnants are the half-timbered houses at **11 and 13 Rue François-Miron**. These tall gabled structures date from the fourteenth century and give perhaps the best feeling of what medieval Paris looked like. Although various ordinances and age itself have greatly altered their appearance over the centuries, these houses have in recent years been restored to their former glory, with plaques proclaiming that no. 11 is the House at the Sign of the Mower (reaper), while no. 13 is the House at the Sign of the Sheep.

Farther along, at 68 Rue François-Miron, is the seventeenth-century **Hôtel de Beauvais**, the beautiful mansion where pint-sized Wolfgang Amadeus Mozart was an honored guest during his first visit to Paris (a plaque suitably commemorates this event). Actually, his first two visits here were both part of the same concert tour that his father, Leopold, had arranged to show off his musical children (Wolfgang and his sister Nannerl) at the courts of Europe. In November 1763, the family arrived in Paris, where they received such a warm welcome that they remained until the following April. Young Wolfgang was only seven at the time, and he took Paris by storm, providing what can only be called musical spectacles. He improvised on difficult themes, sight-read whatever was put before him, and (a real audience-pleaser) played on a cloth-covered keyboard.

Soon the very heavens seemed to open for this young prodigy, capped by an invitation to dine with the royal family at Versailles, followed by a performance. The queen made much of little Wolfgang, inviting him to talk with her (he never was shy) while she fed him sweetmeats and encouraged him to kiss her hands. Dazzled with such attention, and showered with expensive gifts, the Mozarts finally departed for London, where they met with similar acclaim. Two years later, they returned to Paris en route home. By this time

Wolfgang was ten years old and a seasoned performer as well as a fledgling composer (he had published his first sonatas on his earlier Paris visit and composed his first symphonies in London). Once again, he performed for the wealthy and the high-born.

But unfortunately for Mozart, the grandeur and the glamour did not last. By the time he returned to Paris in 1778, he was twenty-two, and public interest in him had evaporated. "People pay plenty of compliments," he wrote to his father, "but there it ends." The problem, as he clearly recognized, was that everyone still thought of him as seven years old, "because that was my age when they first saw me."[2] He was regarded as little more than a faded child star.

Not finding anyone willing to offer him a permanent position, Mozart kept knocking on doors. At last a prestigious musical group commissioned a symphony (Symphony No. 31 in D Major, K297/300a), which has become known as his Paris Symphony. This was well received, but Mozart's world soon darkened with the illness and death of his mother, who had accompanied him on this (his last) trip to Paris. Funeral services for her were held at the ancient church of Saint-Eustache, where a plaque on the church's southern wall commemorates Anna Maria Mozart.

Not many months later, and still jobless, Mozart left Paris for good. He would never return.

The word "marais" means "marsh" or "swamp" in French, accurately describing the marshy bogs that once characterized this side of the Seine. Long ago these extended far into the Right Bank's interior, the remains of a prehistoric Seine riverbed that once arched northward, bumping up against the hills of Montmartre and Belleville before moving (in a massive geological shoulder roll) to its present course. Over the centuries, much of this swampy land was reclaimed, but the marshy quarter most prone to flooding retained the name Le Marais.

The quarter became popular with the aristocracy after Charles V—escaping mobs of hostile Parisians, who objected to raising taxes—abruptly left his palace on the Ile de la Cité for new quarters, the Hôtel Saint-Pol, or Saint-Paul, located comfortably near his Right Bank fortress, the Bastille. Royalty subsequently occupied the nearby Hôtel des Tournelles, which met its end when Catherine de Medici had it razed following the death of her husband, Henri II, in a freak accident that took place there. Catherine may have moved out, but the aristocracy continued on in the Marais, most notably following Henri IV's decision to build the gorgeous Place des Vosges on the site of the Hôtel des Tournelles' garden.[3]

The aristocracy remained in the Marais until Louis XIV established Versailles as the more fashionable as well as politically astute place to be. After that, the neighborhood gradually changed, and with their owners long gone, these beautiful mansions, dating primarily from the seventeenth century, were left to go to seed. In time, many of these run-down *hôtels particuliers* became small factories and workshops, while others provided homes to waves of immigrants, especially Jewish immigrants, who were at long last granted civil rights during the French Revolution. These immigrants were returning to Paris, and the Marais, for the first time since they had been expelled centuries before. More Jewish immigrants followed during the years of persecution in Russia and eastern Europe, especially around the late nineteenth and early twentieth centuries, until the Marais became the major Jewish quarter in Paris.

Fittingly, the memorial dedicated to the nearly six million Jews who lost their lives during the Holocaust, or Shoah, is located in the Marais. The **Mémorial de la Shoah** (17 Rue Geoffroy-l'Asnier) rises above a crypt containing the ashes of victims from the different death camps and the Warsaw Ghetto. Walls leading into the building list the names of the approximately 76,000 French Jews whom the Nazis deported and murdered. Near the crypt is a room containing the files created by France's collaborationist Vichy government to identify Jewish citizens, which were used by the Nazis to locate Jews for deportation.

The memorial's permanent exhibit documents the history of French Jews during the Holocaust, while outside, alongside the memorial, is the Wall of the Righteous, listing more than three thousand non-Jewish French who helped save Jews during the war.

Before World War II, the Marais was home to one of the largest Jewish communities in Europe, but almost three-quarters of its population died in Nazi death camps. The heart of the Marais, especially around Rue Pavée and Rue des Rosiers, is now the vibrant center of a revived but much smaller Jewish quarter. But notice the plaques on buildings here and throughout the Marais that commemorate those who lived, worked, or went to school here and never returned.

⌒

Rue Vieille-du-Temple and Rue des Rosiers are now heavily touristed, with boutiques, bars, and restaurants lining Rue Vielle-du-Temple, while kosher bakeries, restaurants, and falafel joints crowd the Rue des Rosiers. Among the falafel purveyors, the crowds outside L'As du Fallafel are the longest, the noise inside the loudest, and the food (many argue) the best—although Mi Va Mi falafel, across the street, has its ardent defenders. Try both and see.

This is the heart of the revived Marais scene, and weekends—with everything open on Sundays, which can be pretty dull elsewhere in Paris—attract mobs of tourists, who treat the whole thing as a party. Farther down Rue des Rosiers, though, is an unexpected island of tranquility. Keep your eyes open for a doorway at 10 Rue des Rosiers, and you will follow a narrow entry into an unfolding series of peaceful gardens. This is the **Jardin des Rosiers-Joseph Migneret**, which actually is a composite of gardens from two surrounding *hotels particuliers*, the Hôtel de Coulanges and Hôtel d'Albret, both noble relics of the seventeenth century. Wander here among chestnut and fig trees as well as bamboo and roses, and don't overlook the fine remnant of an ancient tower, a piece of the twelfth-century fortified wall that Philip Augustus built to keep his arch enemy, Richard Coeur de Lion, out of Paris. Philip's wall passed through here, all those centuries ago, as it curved down to the Seine.

These lovely gardens, with memories of medieval times as well as the seventeenth century, also summon up recollection of the devastation that the twentieth century inflicted on the Marais. This quiet place is named in honor of Joseph Migneret, who was director of the neighboring elementary school of the Hospitalières-Saint-Gervais. During World War II, Migneret actively resisted the German occupiers and the collaborationist Vichy government, saving dozens of Jewish children from deportation and death.

Migneret was valiant, but he was unable to save all the children: near the garden's entrance is a plaque listing the many Jewish children from the neighborhood who were deported to the death camps, some of them only several months old. Between 1942 and 1944, more than 11,000 children were deported from France to their deaths in Auschwitz, and more than 500 of these lived here, in the fourth arrondissement. Among these, 101 were too tiny even to have begun school.

A quiet garden seems an appropriate place to read their names and ponder the evil that ended their brief lives.

Nearby is one of my favorite museums in Paris, the **Musée Carnavalet**, or the museum of the history of Paris. I call it Grandma's Attic, because of all the wonderful and unexpected things you will find here. Housed in a glorious sixteenth-century mansion where the illustrious Madame de Sévigné lived the last twenty years of her life, the Carnavalet has the most amazing conglomeration of stuff (Proust's bed, antique shop signs, relics from the Bastille, Gallo-Roman findings, Neolithic canoes, and so on). Much as if your grandma and her forebears had been collecting relics of Paris history for centuries.

After having expanded during the 1980s into the adjoining Hôtel Le Peletier de Saint-Fargeau, the Carnavalet has recently undergone a complete renovation. Its lovely garden has been much changed, to make way for tables to feed visitors coffee and cakes, and the entire indoor layout has been rearranged, to the confusion of longtime visitors. But as a whole, the renovation has been useful, much as if someone vigorously shook out the cobwebs. The overall design has been updated, contemporary architectural features have been added, and additional treasures from the attic have come to light, especially in the newly opened lower level, where the Carnavalet now has the space to fill its once-lengthy omission from the Gallo-Romans to the sixteenth century. Some lovely finds from medieval Paris are now on display, and the museum now even takes small steps in the other direction on the timeline, moving closer to the present.

I find myself heading for those galleries containing the paintings that inspired my first books on Paris, *Dawn of the Belle Epoque* and *Twilight of the Belle Epoque*, as well as Alphonse Mucha's fabulous art nouveau Boutique Fouquet, a jewel box of a shop designed, appropriately, for a jeweler. The Cour Henri IV, a small interior garden, is now lovelier than ever, while the newly opened medieval rooms yield treasures such as a poignant element from the tomb of Louis of France, heir to Louis IX (Saint Louis), showing a portion of the young man's funeral procession in bas-relief. On a similar note (and in a different part of the museum), I am always moved by the room containing the humble bed and table of Madame Elisabeth, sister of Louis XVI, which she used while imprisoned in the Tour du Temple.

Then again, for comic relief, you can always get a chuckle from the grotesquely over-the-top cradle that once held Napoleon III's heir, the little Prince Imperial. This "very decorative cradle," as the museum so discreetly understates, was a gift from the city of Paris, and one is gratified to learn that all the materials from which it was made were crafted by Parisian artisans.

There are a number of small parks, or pocket parks, nearby—as one might expect, given this quarter's prevailing architecture. The mansions in this quarter were typically built with a courtyard in front and a garden behind, all shielded from public view by high walls whose only openings were protected by huge carriage doors. In recent times, many of these walls have fallen or been removed, revealing the gardens they once hid. A number of these are now public spaces, often including children's playgrounds—such as the **Square Léopold-Achille**, just to the north of the Musée Carnavalet, which features a serpentine-shaped hill that children love to roll down, and where parents gather to rest and chat while keeping an eye on their offspring.

Some of these little parks, such as the **Jardin Mark Ashton** or Jardin de l'Hôtel-Lamoignon, are lovely at times and a bit worn late in the season, as befits this one's location on the major tourist route along the Rue des Francs-Bourgeois. Still, it offers a reasonably attractive and quiet place to sit, just across from the Musée Carnavalet. Once the garden of the Hôtel de Lamoi-gnon, which now houses the Bibliothèque Historique de la Ville de Paris, its carpet of grass, flowers, and benches welcome footsore and lunch-toting tourists as well as anyone who simply wants a quiet place to sit.

Around the corner is the imposing gate leading into the courtyard of the **Hôtel de Lamoignon**, one of the oldest mansions in the Marais. Now home to the splendid Bibliothèque Historique de la Ville de Paris, this striking building once was carved into apartments, whose residents included the novelist Alphonse Daudet. Regularly making their way to Daudet's door was an impressive literary bunch, including Emile Zola, Edmond de Goncourt, and Gustave Flaubert. Goncourt's journal records many a relaxed and gossipy evening spent there in Daudet's company.

Adjoining these walls, where Rue Malher meets Rue Pavée, is a section of wall that once belonged to the notorious **La Force prison**, originally a man-sion known as the Hôtel de la Force, which during the Revolution housed many aristocrats en route to the guillotine. One of these was Adrienne de Lafayette, wife of the dashing young general, the Marquis de Lafayette, who had made quite a name for himself in the New World, assisting American revolutionaries in their fight for liberty. These exploits have become the stuff of legends, but less well known is the impact that Lafayette's American adventures had on his and his wife's fate.

It started out sunnily. Upon returning to France, Lafayette took advantage of his illustrious reputation to press for a solution to his own country's ills—his dream being that France would become much like America, but with a constitutional monarchy. But even Lafayette was not capable of leading France into such brave new realms, for which centuries of royal absolutism had not prepared it. As the storms of France's own Revolution gathered, even this remarkable man—equipped with a broad military mandate and a stately white horse—was not able to control the mobs. Soon he became an anathema to royalists and Jacobins alike, and when the Jacobins proclaimed him a traitor and demanded his execution, Lafayette fled from France.

In revenge, the Jacobins destroyed his house on the Rue de Bourbon, confiscated his assets, and arrested Adrienne de Lafayette, taking her to the La Force prison. Only the end of the Terror and the intervention of James

Monroe, the new American ambassador to France, prevented Adrienne's execution and won her release.

But by this time Lafayette had fallen into the hands of the Austrian emperor, who—like other monarchs of Europe—held him responsible for instigating the Revolution that now threatened their thrones. As it happened, by remaining in prison, Lafayette was safe from the Jacobins, whose guillotines were slicing away at a grisly pace, claiming among their Parisian victims Adrienne's grandmother, mother, and sister. But Lafayette's Austrian prison was ghastly, which made it all the more admirable that Adrienne, upon her release from La Force, traveled to Austria, where she and her equally determined daughters joined Lafayette in his prison cell—enduring unimaginable hardship for almost two years in order to call worldwide attention to his incarceration.

In time, he was released, and the family—stripped of almost all its assets—returned to a crumbling family château outside of Paris. There Lafayette survived the Napoleonic years by remaining in obscurity, working his lands (much like George Washington) as a gentleman farmer. Adrienne gladly joined him in this rural life, but her health had been shattered by her imprisonment, and she died at the age of forty-eight. Heartbroken, Lafayette buried her in **Picpus Cemetery** (35 Rue de Picpus, in Paris's twelfth arrondissement), near the mass grave holding her guillotined relations.

Since you are no doubt interested in what became of the dashing young general, now a grieving middle-aged private citizen, you will be glad to know that after the Napoleonic years, Lafayette once again returned to Paris and to the political scene, serving in the Chamber of Deputies. Again he became the leader of the liberal opposition to increasingly restrictive regimes—those of Louis XVIII, followed by Charles X, both younger brothers of the guillotined Louis XVI—of whom it was said that they forgot nothing and forgave nothing. When Charles X's actions set off the July Revolution of 1830, Lafayette once more found himself at the head of a widespread revolt in the cause of those principles he held dear.

The outcome, the installation of the more moderate Louis-Philippe, duke of Orléans, did not turn out as Lafayette had hoped, and in 1832, another smaller and abortive revolt (immortalized by Victor Hugo in *Les Misérables*) yet again found Lafayette at the center of the fray. This time, though, he retired in dismay from the fighting, which reminded him all too bleakly of the Jacobin-inspired mobs he had encountered all those years before.

It was a discouraging end to a valiant life. Nevertheless, a life well lived—principled, and packed with glory. When death came, in 1834, Lafayette joined his wife in a simple grave at Picpus, where an American flag always flies. During the German Occupation of Paris, even the Nazis did not have the nerve to take this flag down.

～

Just up the road, alongside the Musée Carnavalet, is yet another small park, the **Square Georges-Cain**, named for the museum's former chief curator. Arranged in a circle around a Maillol sculpture (*L'Ile-de-France*) and rose bushes, with a modest stepped rise between the center and the park's rim, this garden was created almost a century ago on the site of the grand garden of the Hôtel Le Peletier de Saint-Fargeau—a mansion that since 1989 has served as an extension to the Musée Carnavalet (the Carnavalet's recent renovation has brought the two original mansions more closely together into one entity). Around the park's sides are vestiges of long-disappeared structures from around Paris, including columns from the pediment of the Palais des Tuileries and a ceiling rosette from the Hôtel de Ville—both buildings that succumbed to flames during the 1871 Commune uprising. Along one side of the park is the Hôtel Le Peletier de Saint-Fargeau's original seventeenth-century orangerie, one of the last remaining in Paris.

Around the corner is yet another small oasis of greenery, this one the formal French garden behind the Hôtel Donon, now the **Musée Cognacq-Jay**. Ernest Cognacq and his wife, Marie-Louise Jay, never lived here, but it now houses their extensive collection of eighteenth-century paintings, sculpture, porcelain, and furniture. It's a lovely old mansion, and you can wander through its permanent collections free of charge.

The story behind this mansion and its collections is one of a meteoric rise, through work, work. and more work. The hard-driving Ernest Cognacq began his life in Second Empire Paris as an impoverished fifteen-year-old, unsuccessful at numerous jobs before he at last set up shop in one of the arches of the Pont Neuf, across from the site of the great water pump known as the Samaritaine (its name came from the bas-relief of Jesus and the Samaritan woman that adorned the pump's façade). Although the city demolished the pump in 1813, memories of it still lingered when Cognacq began his sales pitch on the bridge, which was a popular place to saunter. As it happened, Cognacq was a gifted salesman, and by 1870, his small venture had turned enough profit that he took the next big step and rented a shop on the quay by the Pont Neuf. He named his store **La Samaritaine**.

La Samaritaine was not the first department store in Paris, and in fact, the young woman who became Cognacq's wife had worked at Le Bon Marché,[4] which began its illustrious career in 1852. The entire point of such an enterprise was to sell large quantities of merchandise to large numbers of buyers,

Garden of the Musée Cognacq-Jay, Hôtel Donon (Jardin Lazare-Rachline). © M. McAuliffe

at lower prices (and a lower profit margin) than ever before. Consumers flocked to Le Bon Marché and La Samaritaine, drawn by the lower (and fixed) prices as well as by the delightful ambiance that these stores offered. Rather than stuffy and uninteresting destinations, shoppers (usually women) found themselves in huge and utterly tantalizing emporiums where goods one didn't really need suddenly became irresistible.

Despite the new department stores' encouragement of their bourgeois customers to overspend on needless "necessities" and luxuries, Cognacq recognized that the bulk of his customers were not wealthy and knew the value of a sou. He strove to give them their money's worth, and soon he was famous for his motto, "the customer is always right!" As for his own personal life, Cognacq was remarkably frugal. He regularly worked fifteen-hour days and never took a vacation. His wife, Marie-Louise Jay, was equally prudent, agreeing to put off marriage for more than eight years until Cognacq's financial situation was more stable, all the while continuing to work at Le Bon Marché, where she became head of the clothing department.

After marriage, the two continued their grueling work routine, with Marie-Louise now running La Samaritaine's clothing department. Already, hard work was paying off handsomely, and La Samaritaine was expanding rapidly. La Samaritaine and the Cognacqs thrived, and Ernest Cognacq soon became a very rich man. In time he and his wife moved into a large mansion on the Avenue du Bois (now Avenue Foch), which was big enough to accommodate his growing art collection—a collection that would eventually be open to the public in the Musée Cognacq-Jay.

Cognacq died in 1928, but not before he saw sales at La Samaritaine pass the one-billion-franc mark and construction begin on his iconic Art Deco building on the Seine. Dearly beloved by bourgeois shoppers, this Samaritaine may have become old fashioned by the twenty-first century, but it was sadly missed when it closed in 2005, for safety reasons. Talk circulated that it would never reopen, that it would be razed to make way for luxury condominiums, and so on. Its actual fate has turned out to be something more complicated: the completely renovated La Samaritaine still is, at its core, a department store, with its fabled glass roof and dramatic central stairway restored and intact. But it has emerged as a luxury destination, including expensive restaurants, an over-the-top beauty department, and a luxury hotel with a spa that is supposed to have the biggest pool in Paris. This is no longer a destination for the average Parisian, even one with dreams. This Samaritaine unabashedly and unapologetically caters to a wealthy clientele.

This certainly is not the Samaritaine that Ernest and Marie-Louise Cognacq built up from scratch, whose clientele were of more modest means. Still, the new Samaritaine is amazing, and I am pleased that the original structure has been so carefully preserved and restored. We now shall see how many folks actually shop there. Perhaps it will only take a few, if they are sufficiently wealthy.

Just north of the Musée Cognacq-Jay and the Musée Carnavalet is the **Musée Picasso**, housed in the magnificent Hôtel Salé (meaning "salted"). Why the name? This seventeenth-century mansion's original owner was (among other lucrative pursuits) a tax farmer, who collected the substantial taxes on salt in the name of the king. Over the years the Hôtel Salé passed through several hands, and for much of the nineteenth century it housed the municipal Ecole Centrale des Arts et Manufactures, the school of civil engineering that young Gustave Eiffel attended (an indifferent student, he had been unable to get into the more prestigious Ecole Polytechnique). Since then it has been restored and now houses Picasso's extensive personal art collection—his heirs' gift to France in lieu of inheritance taxes.

Recently, the mansion has undergone a huge and lengthy remodeling, opening up the museum's public space, which now spreads through numerous white-walled galleries that could be part of any modern building. These do, however, include a delightful raftered area under the eaves, where one of my favorite Picasso owls hangs out. In addition, this recent overhaul most fortunately retained the *hôtel particulier*'s magnificent bifurcated central staircase and surrounding gallery.

Next door to the museum is a small terraced garden that most museum visitors overlook, the **Jardin Berthe Weill**. Weill was an art dealer who became legendary in the modern art world and gave Picasso his first break at the turn of the last century. She also backed Matisse when he was still an unknown and gave Modigliani his first one-man show. Key to enjoying this garden—in addition to appreciating the woman for who it is named—are the bookcases, with books available for reading on any of the nearby benches. Such an enchanting idea, even if you choose to bring your own book!

Long ago, this part of Paris—much like its counterpart across the Seine—was dotted with convents and monasteries. The largest, the abbeys of Saint Lazarre and Saint-Martin-des-Champs,[5] were major powers, placing their stamp on history, but a multitude of smaller religious houses existed as well, ones that have left little but their names. These include the Boulevard des Filles du Calvaire (Daughters of Calvary) and the Rue des Blancs-Manteau (Order of the White Cloaks)—although the Church of Notre-Dame-des-Blancs-Manteaux, built on the site of its much earlier predecessor, still survives. Then there is the Marché des Enfants Rouges, the oldest covered market in Paris, named after the red-clad children from the nearby charity orphanage. This orphanage no longer exists, but the market still thrives and is beloved by those living nearby.

Not far away, on Rue des Archives, is a more solid remnant of the past, the **Cloître des Billettes** (Cloister of the Billettes), the last remaining medieval cloister in Paris. It dates from 1427 and, remarkably, three of its original four galleries are still standing. The church itself, which is more recent, is now Lutheran and currently under massive renovation. But when this has concluded, watch for art exhibits in the cloister, which open this piece of the past to the public.

Nearby, on Rue du Temple, is the **Musée d'Art et d'Histoire de Judaïsm** (MAHJ), housed in the beautiful old Hôtel de Saint-Aignan, one of the gems of the Marais. Like so many of its seventeenth-century neighbors, this lovely mansion underwent years of decline after its residents left the Marais, first being carved into apartments and then being turned into an unfortunate warren of commercial enterprises. When, in the mid-twentieth century, the city of Paris stepped in to save it, as it did for so many of the quarter's beautiful but decayed *hôtels particuliers*, the Hôtel de Saint-Aignan was in such bad shape that it took more than twenty-five years to recover the original.

The result is magnificent, and after crossing the expansive courtyard—featuring a replica of Louis Mitelberg's (TIM) dramatic tribute to Captain Dreyfus—you will find the totally reconstructed grand staircase, which leads into a vast chamber that features those thirteenth-century Jewish tombstones that so intrigued me when I first spotted them in the Musée du Moyen Age. They are on permanent loan here, amplifying MAHJ's aim of presenting two millennia of Jewish community presence in Paris, and placing this within the general history of Judaism. Frequent exhibits expand on this theme, and the central presence in the courtyard of the memorial to Captain Dreyfus sets an appropriate tone.

Behind, and accessible through tiny Impasse Berthaud, is the **Jardin Anne-Frank**, which spreads over the former gardens of the Hôtel de Saint-Aignan. Fittingly, a chestnut tree has been planted here, an offshoot of the very one that Anne looked out on from her Amsterdam window while in hiding from the Nazis. Here, in this place of peace and quiet, one can find respite within one of the busiest quarters in Paris.

Bois de Vincennes. © J. McAuliffe

CHAPTER THIRTEEN

~

Points East

For color and excitement along the streets of Paris, there's nothing quite like the unexpected appearance of the cavalry regiment of the **Republican Guard**. The first time I encountered it, on the Rue de Lyon, the horsemen (they were all men at the time) were in full military dress, helmets shining and plumes flying, their horses beautifully matched and precisely prancing. As I later learned, they were headed back from some ceremony, probably at the Palais de l'Elysée, to their headquarters in the nearby Caserne des Célestins.

The last remaining unit of the French army with horses, this mounted regiment has ceremonial as well as security duties and is based on the Right Bank's Boulevard Henri IV, a short but major connector between the eastern end of the Ile Saint-Louis and the Place de la Bastille. Eager to get a closer look, I signed on for a tour with several others (all tours at present are in French). Entering the well-guarded gates of the Caserne des Célestins, I found myself in a huge nineteenth-century facility centered around a large riding ring. Here, in ringside stables, some 140 horses of the First Squadron are maintained in considerable comfort, even horsey elegance. Their riders (who now include several women) are part of the French Gendarmerie and train daily. You may even spot some, as I did one morning, trotting along the pedestrianized Pompidou Expressway (now the Parc Rives de Seine), where they calmly join other walkers, bikers, and runners.

After such a perky beginning to the day, one is well fortified to encounter the challenges of the Place de la Bastille, once the site of a formidable fortress that famously met its end at the hands of a Paris Revolutionary mob. Little of the Bastille remains, although small medallions in the Place de la Bastille now mark the vanished fortress's outlines, and a dogged search will reward you with the remnant of the Tower of Liberty—one of eight Bastille towers, which was uncovered in 1899 during construction of the Métro. This unremarkable-looking circle of stones was painstakingly removed and rebuilt, stone by stone, in the **Square Henri-Galli**, a pleasant little park at the point where Boulevard Henri IV meets up with the Seine and the Pont de Sully. As the sign there reminds us, before being a prison, the Bastille anchored the Saint-Antoine gate through the Charles V wall that once encircled the Right Bank.

Vestiges of the Bastille's counterscarp have also been found and duly flagged for passersby in the Bastille station of the No. 5 Métro line. But the fortress's destruction has not lessened the challenges that the Place de la Bastille presents the pedestrian, even after extensive and excruciating works that have snarled traffic for what seems like an eternity. We were promised, in government-speak, "a new metamorphosed place, more accessible and more welcoming, . . . which will allow a more balanced and peaceful use for the benefit of all." Right. Just take my suggestion and get around or across and through it as best you can, and as quickly as possible.

If you take the western route around, from Boulevard Henri IV, you will cross Boulevard Richard-Lenoir, which covers a surprising body of water, the **Canal Saint-Martin**, a hardworking stretch that does a major job of connecting several waterways to the Seine. Completed in the 1820s, it was designed to extend two other canals, the Ourcq and the Saint-Denis (which meet just above the Bassin de la Villette at the northern edge of Paris), into a waterway cutting across one of the Seine's many wide-ranging loops, linking it with the river Ourcq. Napoleon Bonaparte originally conceived of this canal network as a means of bringing the Ourcq's waters to Paris, which badly needed clean water (the Seine's waters simply weren't sufficient or sufficiently clean). Unfortunately, these waters remained pristine only briefly. Soon the Industrial Revolution flooded in, blighting everything it touched. Where there once had been grassy banks, there now stood warehouses and foundries. Abject poverty soon followed, accompanied by radical politics and readiness for mob uprisings.

Eventually Baron Haussmann ordered the southern third of the Canal Saint-Martin covered over, between Place de la République and Place de la Bastille. But while government troops could now march unhindered into this center of unrest, little else changed. Poverty and blight continued a century longer, until land shortage and soaring property values in western Paris encouraged a new look at this area to the east. By the late 1970s, cleanup had begun.

Nowadays, the tree-lined Canal Saint-Martin is an attractive daytime destination, drawing throngs of couples and families along its three-mile stretch. But more than a popular place to stroll, the canal is still a hardworking transportation system, with barges slowly moving underground and through its locks, economically cutting across a huge loop of the Seine. These locks manage the large drop from one end of the canal to the other, while the canal's significant bend circumvents the Hôpital Saint-Louis, still a working hospital that retains its beautiful seventeenth-century quadrangle and chapel.[1]

The waterside walk south from the Bassin de la Villette ends at Rue du Faubourg-du-Temple, where the canal continues under a cover of gardens and playgrounds that extend from block to block down the avenue that becomes Boulevard Richard-Lenoir. Here neighbors congregate to chat, enjoy the flowers, and watch the children play, oblivious of the canal that flows directly below their feet. If it weren't for the occasional mysterious-looking ventilation domes rising out of the earth, it would be easy to forget that a canal exists here at all.

Gardens make way for an extensive outdoor market, which continues all the way to the Place de la Bastille. There the canal reappears, this time in the form of a marina—the sparking boat basin of the Paris Arsenal. You can walk the canal's length or, if you prefer, barge cruises are available between the Paris marina and the Parc de la Villette. Yes, you will spend some of the trip underground—spooky and claustrophobic or thrilling and adventurous, depending on your point of view.

Just a few steps from Boulevard Richard-Lenoir is a surprising little street, the **Cour Damoye**, an artistic enclave that has somehow survived the furor around it. Locked gates at night certainly help, preserving the peace if not the quiet, but if you arrive in daytime, wander through and enjoy. At its far end pick up the Rue de la Roquette, a major if narrow thoroughfare that leads directly across the eleventh arrondissement to Père-Lachaise Cemetery. This is a lively and vibrant neighborhood, filled with a variety of small restaurants, cafés, and noise. This was once part of the extensive network of workshops that characterized the entire Saint-Antoine quarter, with side alleys off the main roads leading into courtyards where cabinetmakers, carpenters, and metalworkers handcrafted elaborate furnishings for the French aristocracy and courts of Europe.

As gentrification has moved in, so have up-market artisanal firms, such as **La Manufacture du Chocolat Alain Ducasse**, located in a converted car garage at 40 Rue de la Roquette. Here, in a trendy industrial-chic setting, Ducasse makes his chocolate on the spot, in huge vats and grinders that one can watch at work from behind glass windows. Ducasse of course has a dizzying number of restaurants around the world, and his name sparks controversy—prompted at least in part, I suspect, by his success as well as by his audacity. Many, in this city of more than three hundred gourmet chocolate shops, seem to have hoped that his chocolate enterprise would fall flat on its face. After all, what business did a latecomer like Ducasse have to barge into this tight-knit community of chocolatiers! But whatever his rivals may think, Ducasse's chocolate-making has been a success, in quality as well as in sales. He has opened other chocolate shops around Paris and now has opened a shop next to the original that sells ice cream and sorbet, including several flavors based on chocolate.

Turn into the little courtyard (dodging carts of cocoa beans as you cross) and enter this small enterprise, where everything to do with chocolate-making takes place, from roasting to tempering and molding. The atmosphere is aromatic and hushed, with salespersons dressed in lab coats offering assistance in debating the merits of one source of chocolate over another (all of Ducasse's chocolates are sourced). It feels much like debating one fine wine versus another, and just as satisfying. Ducasse's focus is on purity and source rather than variety, and soon you will find yourself considering whether, among many other possibilities, a dark chocolate from Colombia (73 percent) or one from São Tomé and Príncipe (75 percent) will best satisfy your particular taste.

Whatever you get, or choose not to get, you will have just visited a typical artisans' courtyard of the Saint-Antoine quarter, albeit much gussied up.

~

Not far away, along Avenue Daumesnil, stretches another group of artisanal shops, the **Viaduc des Arts**, a relatively new venture installed under the arches of the railway that once chugged back and forth between the Place de la Bastille and the city's eastern edge. These ateliers have emerged as a showcase for a wide variety of crafts, whose workers invite you to watch them as they ply their trades—either over their shoulders or through huge windows fronting the street. Appropriately located in this historic quarter of Parisian crafts, each of the Viaduc's many arches houses specialists, from glassblowers, leatherworkers, tapestry-weavers, and silversmiths to repairers of antique fabrics, musical instruments, and dolls. Check out the stonecutter or the porcelain painters, or any of a variety of makers of furniture and cabinets along the way. If retouching photographs is not your interest, then perhaps the hatmaker will appeal. There is a world of creativity here, to purchase or simply to enjoy.

Above these shops is one of the best walks in Paris, the **Promenade Plantée**. Starting just beyond the Bastille Opéra, this walk raises you up along the abandoned railway's right-of-way through the heart of the twelfth arrondissement. More than twenty years ago, the city of Paris made a wonderful decision to turn this right-of-way into an extended garden, and I have watched it grow—in beauty and popularity—from the outset. To join the many who love this walk (and jog), take any of several stairways along the Viaduc des Arts up to this narrow urban oasis that stretches imaginatively through eastern Paris, providing flowers, trees, pools, and architecturally interesting walk-throughs between buildings. Here along the rooftops you will find arbors and trellises, comfortable benches and trees. Well-designed and maintained, the Promenade Plantée rewards strollers with unfolding variety, including an abundance of roses in season, changing colors in the autumn, and two decorative pools that draw appreciative wedding parties.

After crossing the Jardin de Reuilly via a long pedestrian arch—on the site of the railway's vanished switching yards (the railway's handsome old Reuilly station still exists nearby) and the location of the long-ago summer residence of Merovingian kings—the Promenade turns into a street-level boulevard. It then dives below street level into a kind of lush jungle world, where waterfalls drip down the sides of tunnels into pools surrounded by hanging vines. There are any number of small delights along the way, such as a maze, where you can cheat a bit by climbing a small stairway to an observation deck.

You can branch to the right at Square Charles-Péguy, an attractive and well-shaded bower commemorating a young poet from the neighborhood who died in the early days of World War I. Or you can continue on a bit to the Périphérique, where a spiral staircase takes you to a small frontage road and another bike path. From either there or Square Charles-Péguy, you are within a breath of the Bois de Vincennes, with its lake, islands, romantic little pavilion, and even a grotto.

〜

Originally, the **Bois de Vincennes** was intended to be the workers' equivalent of the upper-class Bois de Boulogne on Paris's western side. After all, when the workers were behaving themselves, Emperor Napoleon III (Bonaparte's nephew) was inclined to be generous. As he put it, "The faubourg Saint-Antoine should also have its Hyde Park."[2]

The Bois de Vincennes had been a pleasure ground for royalty since the twelfth century, when Louis VII built a hunting lodge there. The forest's importance grew over the years, especially in the fourteenth century, when Jean II and Charles V erected the huge and heavily fortified Château de Vincennes there, with its village of support buildings, a moated eight-foot-thick curtain wall, and a bullying keep, or donjon, that was the highest in France. By 1860, soon after Paris tore down its Farmers-General Wall and absorbed its surrounding suburbs, the emperor prompted the legislature to cede the Bois de Vincennes to Paris on the condition that the city convert it into a public area for walks—while keeping the castle and its surrounding military installations, including the camp and grounds used for army maneuvers.

Years later, writing his memoirs, Baron Haussmann complained about the cost of creating the Bois de Vincennes. "Exceeding all forecasts," he wrote, it "made a large breach in the city's finances."[3] He had never been enthusiastic about this park, which he sourly pointed out was to be for the working classes of Paris's newly created eleventh and twelfth arrondissements, especially the workers of the fractious Faubourg Saint-Antoine. Emperor Napoleon III, however, was a keen backer of the project, viewing this enormous green space on the eastern edge of Paris as part of his efforts to better the lives of Parisian workers, who largely inhabited the eastern portions of the city. He also had an interest in cajoling them, given their increasing discontent with imperial rule. After all, the rich were getting richer under Napoleon III, but the poor certainly were not benefiting from all the new wealth. The emperor thought that a lovely park, where the workers and their families could stroll (during their admittedly limited leisure hours), would be of benefit both to them and to him.

Well, Haussmann was right—the Bois de Vincennes certainly blew a hole in the imperial budget (although it certainly did not stop Haussmann from spending still more on other major projects around town). Creating the elaborate system of artificial lakes as well as the extensive lawns and specimen trees that the landscaped areas required, in addition to grottoes, cascades, cafés, restaurants, and a racecourse, all cost money, lots of it. In addition, the area suffered, most surprisingly, from sandy soil, which made everything undertaken there far more difficult and expensive. Despite all this, and contrary to the emperor's hopes, this new pleasure ground did not mollify the workers nor avert their volcanic eruption in 1871's Commune uprising.

Nowadays, this extensive park, or series of parks, does clearly operate as a kind of lungs for this part of the city, where families gather on weekends to boat, ride ponies, visit the zoo, or picnic. Crowded on weekends, it is a lovely place to visit during the week, to rest, relax, and enjoy the beauty. You might prefer to explore this vast space in at least two excursions, focusing first on Lac Daumesnil and second on the château and nearby Parc Floral. The Promenade Plantée leads most easily to the Lac Daumesnil sector, entering from Porte Dorée and taking visitors past the large sculpture and fountain dating from the huge 1931 Paris Colonial Exposition. This exposition's purpose was to glorify France's imperial mission by highlighting the cultures and resources of her still-extensive colonial empire, and almost eight million people came to gawk at native huts and Buddhist temples, some of which still remain. The pagoda representing Togo and Cameroon has been preserved and is now an active Buddhist temple. Nearby is a small Tibetan Buddhist temple, while another small temple on the same grounds is being renovated. If you are lucky, you will arrive on the autumn weekend when the Buddhist temple holds its festival, complete with singing, dancing, crafts, and lots of food.

Back in 1931, Josephine Baker, the fabulous stage and film star, was elected queen of this exposition, but she never managed to be crowned. Protesters complained that she wasn't even French (American born, Baker did not become a French citizen until 1937). Perhaps her then-current show at the Casino de Paris had confused those who voted for her, because in it she portrayed several glamorous versions of France's colonized women. In any case, Baker was consolable, as her career surged on. Later, during World War II, her work for the French Resistance and the Free French forces earned her a Croix de Guerre and made her a member of France's Legion of Honor. More recently, she became the first Black woman and first person of American origin to be interred in France's Panthéon.

Lac Daumesnil, at the heart of this part of the Bois de Vincennes, is a lovely manmade lake with two sizable islands, the Ile de Reuilly and the Ile de Bercy, reached by a rustic bridge that leads to the Ile de Reuilly's enchanting gazebo and grotto. Another bridge connects the two islands, and for those who reach the tip of the Ile de Bercy and do not relish the walk back, there is a kind of ferry service: for a small fee, a boatman will respond to your call and row you back to mainland. More athletic folks can rent boats and row along the islands' shorelines, enjoying the waterfowl that nest here in the spring.

From here one can return to the heart of town via Métro Line 8, Porte Dorée stop, to return to complete the Bois de Vincennes another day. Or, one can take the little tramline to Porte de Vincennes, where Métro Line 1 will take you to the eastern end of the line at the **Château de Vincennes** and Parc Floral (reachable by a short walk or bus ride). The château, a spectacular castle with a massive keep, or donjon, was the product of the Hundred Years' War with England, and for three centuries royalty enjoyed the pleasures as well as protection that the luxuriously appointed castle of Vincennes afforded. Louis XIII lived there during the dangerous years of his minority, and Louis XIV (who built extensive new quarters for royalty there) arranged on his deathbed for his successor, the five-year-old Louis XV, to stay at Vincennes for safekeeping. But by this time, the court had removed to Versailles, and except for the occasional hunting party, Vincennes no longer saw much of royalty.

In fact, despite the occasional royal drop-in, the Château de Vincennes increasingly served as a prison, whose "guests" included such notables as Henri de Navarre (the future Henri IV), Denis Diderot, and the Marquis de Sade. Under German Occupation, the château imprisoned members of the Resistance, many of whom were shot by firing squads against its walls as the Allies were entering Paris. Look for the cross in the fortress's dry moat that marks the spot.

The walkway over the moat into the keep is dramatic, matched only by the drama of the keep itself, an intimidating affair. From here, as an antidote to the castle's militant history, you can head down the road to the **Parc Floral**, an extensive park and horticultural garden where, between spring and autumn, a carefully planned series of flowers is always in bloom. First tulips, then a spectacular display of azaleas and rhododendrons, followed closely by iris, peonies, and a wealth of other blossoms, this is a favorite destination for Parisians, who love its many quiet nooks and heavenly views. On most days I find at least several readers on benches tucked away among the trees and flowers or overlooking the cascade and small lake. Like its sister park at Lac Daumesnil, this park can be busy on weekends, and for a bit of quiet I would recommend weekday mornings, followed by a picnic lunch. This being Paris, there are also several small cafés and restaurants available, should you be so inclined.

But I would truly recommend a picnic on a quiet bench, nestled in among the towering azaleas and rhododendrons. The book is optional.

Tomb of Abelard and Heloise, Père-Lachaise Cemetery. © J. McAuliffe

CHAPTER FOURTEEN

~

Onward and Upward

Not far to the northwest of the Bois de Vincennes is **Père-Lachaise Cemetery**, the final resting place for so many famous people, including Sarah Bernhardt, Frédéric Chopin, Isadora Duncan (in the Columbarium, by the ashes of her adored children), and Oscar Wilde.

Bernhardt arrived in style. Thousands lined the streets, ten deep, to watch her funeral procession. This followed a three-day period of mourning, in which mourners filed past her body, now permanently ensconced in the white satin-lined coffin in which, as an aspiring star, she had famously had herself photographed, and in which she had claimed to sleep.

Chopin had just as splashy a send-off. Nearly three thousand people attended his funeral at the Church of the Madeleine—an event that was delayed for several days in order to organize a performance of Mozart's Requiem, as Chopin himself had wished.

The tragedy of Isadora Duncan's death—a dramatic leave-taking, in which the long fringes of her shawl caught in the spokes of her car's rear wheel— was only rivaled by the tragedy of her two children's deaths, drowned several years earlier when their automobile rolled over an embankment into the Seine. Her dearest friends gave her a huge funeral, with heaps of the flowers she so loved. Thousands awaited her body in Père-Lachaise, where as many as could fit crammed into the crematory chapel.

By contrast, Oscar Wilde was penniless at the end, and it was only at the instigation of a friend that his body was at last disinterred from a less prestigious cemetery and brought to Père-Lachaise. There, his massive tombstone now draws scores of visitors, many of whom left lipstick marks on the stone before it was cleaned and placed behind a protective barrier.

In addition to tombs of the famous (pick your own to visit), this enormous cemetery holds monuments in memory of victims of the Holocaust, as well as memorial monuments to victims of warfare. In a dramatic understatement, a simple plaque on the southeastern wall (the Mur des Fédérés) marks the spot where the last fighters of the Paris Commune were shot in May 1871.[1] Here, multitudes of left-wing sympathizers and political gatherings have gravitated over the years.

But the favorite Père-Lachaise destination for many people, especially for lovers, is the neo-Gothic tomb of **Abelard and Heloise**. After his final meeting with Heloise at Le Paraclet, in Champagne, Abelard continued to teach in Paris, but peace eluded him. In the end it was not his affair with Heloise but his insistence on applying reason to theology that did him in. Abelard dared to raise dangerous questions, and eventually he was condemned for heresy. Misunderstood and shattered, this powerful and original thinker went into severe decline following his condemnation and soon died.

Heloise, by now an abbess, grieved bitterly for him and brought his body back to Le Paraclet. There, following her own death, she was buried by his side. Following the Revolution and the destruction of much of Le Paraclet, these tragic and endlessly fascinating lovers at last returned to Paris, the city where their love began.

They now lie side by side in Père-Lachaise Cemetery, beneath a bower of trees. You will find their tomb to the right of the cemetery's western entrance, where their final resting place continues to draw flowers from a steady stream of lovers and strangers who—despite the passage of nine centuries—know their story and wish them well.

Just below Père-Lachaise, to the southeast, is a remarkable little garden, the **Jardin Naturel—Pierre-Emmanuel**, where the city of Paris has successfully set out to return this once-bucolic landscape to its natural state. This is not a large garden, but its location, by a school and in an urban setting, make it all the more welcome. At its center is a small pond, where a special enclosed walkway below water level allows visitors to view the aquatic activity beneath the pond's surface—a brilliant idea and surely a wonderful experience for children as well as adults.

Continuing along Rue de Bagnolet, this unremarkable city street leads over the now-abandoned railroad tracks of the Petite Ceinture and past its Charonne station (a revived but still grungy Flèche d'Or café) into the heart of the old **Village of Charonne**. Turn onto Rue Saint-Blaise, a charming cobblestoned street, and peer into courtyards—especially that of number 5. Neighboring Rue Riblette reveals still more gorgeous courtyards and leads, via Rue des Balkans, to the Jardin de l'Hospice Debrousse and the **Pavillon de l'Ermitage**, once part of the long-gone estate of the Château de Bagnolet.

I have long been a fan of Rémi Rivière, ever since I first met him at the opening of the restored Tour Jean-sans-Peur in 1999.[2] At the time, having just completed one demanding project, he was already contemplating his next, the Pavillon de l'Ermitage—a lovely but then-derelict eighteenth-century "folly," or ornamental structure, at the eastern edge of Paris.

After years of determination and hard work, the Pavillon opened to the public. Originally it was part of the domain of Bagnolet, the estate of the duchess of Orléans—the legitimized daughter of Louis XIV and Madame de Montespan and wife of Philippe d'Orléans (Regent of France during the minority of Louis XV). The duchess spared no expense on Bagnolet, remodeling the chateau and landscaping its extensive grounds. Sometime between 1723 and 1727, she built the Ermitage at the park's far edge, near the village of Charonne. Much like other "follies" of the period, the Ermitage lacked heat and was only used in fine weather. But despite its small size and limited function, it was designed elegantly, in what has become known as Regency style.

The highlights of the décor, then and now, are the original mural paintings (attributed to Jean Valade) of hermit saints—a subject that gave the Ermitage its name. Three of the tall slender murals miraculously remain in the vestibule and former gallery, painted in the soft dove colors called "grisaille." At their inception, Valade's murals represented the height of fashion. But the duchess's son, Louis the Pious, found portions of these murals offensive and had them whitewashed. Following this, the duchess's grandson updated the Ermitage in the new neoclassical style, giving it a mural of the goddess Flore over the northern salon, surrounded by wall-to-wall trompe-l'oeil, including a painted garden, Roman columns, false marbling, and Cupids. A rapid series of subsequent owners turned the little structure into a habitable house, complete with fireplaces. The hermit paintings survived all these renovations and updates, while the northern salon, with its remarkable collection of trompe-l'oeil, survived intact.

History came knocking when the vastly altered Ermitage passed into the hands of the Baron de Batz, best known for his plots to save Louis XVI and Marie Antoinette from the guillotine. The baron carried out his political intrigues in the Ermitage, which was conveniently outside of, yet not far from, Paris. Still, this kind of caution proved insufficient, and one night in

September 1793, some two hundred guardsmen surrounded the little structure. They managed to arrest several of the plotters but did not catch the baron, who fled through the park's shrubbery and escaped.

After the baron and Revolution, the Ermitage passed through more hands, until 1887, when it was sold to the Assistance Publique (the French authority that manages social services and state-owned hospitals). The Assistance Publique built a home for the aged (l'Hospice Debrousse) on the Ermitage's grounds and turned the Ermitage over to the hospice director, who used the ground floor as offices and the upstairs as an apartment.

Eventually, as the hospice expanded, the Ermitage was abandoned, although by this time it fortunately had been classified as a *monument historique*, preventing its destruction. But despite this, the structure had deteriorated badly by the time Rémi Rivière and the Association des Amis de l'Ermitage (Association of the Friends of the Hermitage) undertook to save it and open it to the public. This took time, money, and considerable effort, but, as Rivière puts it, all the hard work was worth it. The Pavillon de l'Ermitage, he has explained, is unique and "très français." Above all, he adds, it is "très, très charmant."

Indeed, the Pavillon de l'Ermitage is extraordinarily charming. Visitors are now privileged to enter this long-padlocked vestige of the eighteenth century, learn from the accompanying texts, and admire its beauty. Above all, they can gaze out the tall, arched windows into the small adjoining park and imagine what it must have been like to be a member of the French court in the early 1700s, attending the duchess at a party here on a fine summer day.

Climbing upward through Ménilmontant to the slopes of Belleville (or taking the zigzag route of the Métro uphill, via Line 3 bis, Line 11, and the crazily circular little Line 7 bis), you will find, near the Place des Fêtes, a small garden containing a mysterious round building with a distinctive cupola. The garden is the Jardin du Regard-de-la-Lanterne, and the little building is the **Regard de la Lanterne**. Windowless, and with its one solitary door bolted shut, it looks like a secret meeting place for some forgotten sect. But the Regard de la Lanterne had quite a different—and unexpected—function: it once presided over an ancient source of water, the medieval aqueduct of Belleville.

Oddly enough, for a city built along a major river, Paris and Parisians have spent the better part of two thousand years battling a chronic lack of water.

Regard de la Lanterne © J. McAuliffe

The Gallo-Romans tackled the problem first, building the ancient aqueduct that led the way, more than a millennium later, for Marie de Medici to carry out another aqueduct along approximately the same route—from the south, to her vast Luxembourg Gardens.

In the meantime, a vast number of Parisians were digging wells—although this turned out to be far easier on the Right Bank than on the Left, where the water table lay much deeper beneath the surface. The Right Bank's well water seemed clean enough, but unfortunately the very fact that it lay close to the surface meant that it received runoff from Paris's notoriously muddy streets, as well as seepage from its open sewers.

But no one until well into the nineteenth century drew a connection between the quality of the water they drank and the epidemics that regularly swept the city. Indeed, the main qualification for water was availability, and the hunt for water began as early as the twelfth century, as Paris began to revive from its earlier encounters with the Vikings. Competition became especially fierce on the Right Bank, whose population was booming. Increasingly, those who lived a fair piece from the Seine found they couldn't rely on well water alone, and before long two wealthy Right Bank abbeys began to scout out the possibility of bringing in spring water by aqueduct from the north.

In those days, lots of little springs trickled down the bucolic hills of Belleville and Ménilmontant (street names like Rue des Cascades and Rue de la Mare still summon up their memory). These *sources du Nord*, or springs of the North, looked especially promising, since they burbled out of the ground at a height that made it possible to bring their waters down by simple gravity.

The monks of Saint-Lazare were probably the first to tap these waters. Their priory was located well outside the medieval city of Paris, along the route then known as the Chaussée de Saint-Lazare (now Rue du Faubourg-Saint-Denis), at present-day Boulevard de Magenta. Toward the end of the twelfth century, these monks began to harness the spring waters that spurted up near the village of Le Pré-Saint-Gervais, just over the present-day northeastern boundary of Paris, bringing these waters by conduit to their priory.

At about the same time, or perhaps a little after, the monks of Saint-Martin-des-Champs harnessed the waters of Belleville, bringing them by conduit to their abbey, located along the old Roman road into Paris (now Rue Saint-Martin) at present-day Rue Réaumur. The shell of their extraordinary abbey church now houses a portion of the Musée des Arts et Métiers.

The waters of Belleville at first flowed through several different aqueducts, or below-ground channels, including a joint effort between Saint-Martin-des-Champs and the Knights Templar, whose land it crossed. Eventually, another small system brought water to Henri IV's seventeenth-century Hôpital Saint-Louis. In time, as the city of Paris took over this water supply, these systems were linked, combining their flow.

But at first, these aqueducts were separate and surprisingly simple affairs, with the spring water collected in covered stone-lined trenches known as *pierrées*. These *pierrées*, which ran just above a bed of impermeable clay, ended at small basins or settling pools placed inside buildings called "regards."

This is where the Regard de la Lanterne came in. Much like Marie de Medici's later regards, its job, as the head regard in its system, was to collect the water from its *pierrées* and send it, via aqueduct, along its way. It also served to protect the precious water it collected from pollution and thieves.

Once a year, during Paris's September Journées du Patrimoine, this and other regards in the system are open to the public. All are interesting, but it is the Regard de la Lanterne that is the most thrilling. Descend the hidden steps that sweep downward in a double staircase just inside the regard's door. There, at the bottom, you will see three pipes leading in from the regard's *pierrées*, whose water flows into a small pool. From there, the water flows out via an ancient aqueduct, built during the fifteenth and sixteenth centuries, replacing the far simpler version that preceded it.

There, in the flickering light, you can make out a name carved in 1586, shortly after this regard was built. You can also stand at the entrance to the aqueduct, which is an elaborate stone tunnel more than six feet high and three feet wide. Here the water flows from the basin along a shallow channel in the aqueduct's floor.

From the Regard de la Lanterne, the water of Belleville once traveled along this ancient aqueduct, encountering other regards along the way. Originally there were about forty of these in the Belleville and Le Pré-Saint-Gervais systems, which either collected water from several sources or divided water to send it to its users. Still other regards simply served as settling pools. Their functions varied, and few regards still remain—although all the survivors are now protected as *monuments historiques*.

Oddly enough, there never was much water in either the Belleville or Le Pré-Saint-Gervais systems. To make matters worse, the water itself, although reasonably pure, was heavily flavored by the limestone and gypsum through which it passed, making it unpleasant to drink. Still, monarchs and the city of Paris all tried over the years to make as much of this water as possible available to the people of Paris. As early as the twelfth century, King Philip Augustus arranged with the monks of Saint-Lazare to take some of their water, via pipes (probably lead), down present-day Rue Faubourg-Saint-Denis to the Fontaine des Innocents (grandly rebuilt in the 1500s and later moved to what now is Place Joachim-du-Bellay). This water also supplied a fountain in the covered markets, or Halles. Other fountains followed, and during the Middle Ages, water from Le Pré-Saint-Gervais ran in all the public fountains located on or to the west of Rue Saint-Denis, while fountains located to the east received their water from Belleville.

During the fourteenth and fifteenth centuries, the city of Paris—aided by the upheavals of the Hundred Years' War—gradually took over the water and aqueducts of Belleville and Le Pré-Saint-Gervais. But these waters never supplied more than a fraction of what was needed, and in any case seemed better for washing than for drinking. By the mid-eighteenth century, the water of Belleville primarily cleaned the sewers, while the somewhat better-tasting water of Le Pré-Saint-Gervais supplied Paris until the 1860s, when it was routed into the sewers—where some still runs today.

Just as several of the historic regards still remain, so do portions of the aqueducts that once served them. A section of the narrow aqueduct leading to the Hôpital Saint-Louis has somehow survived the inroads of urbanization, while several pieces of the Belleville aqueduct still run beneath the houses and streets of Belleville. Its course is marked by ancient stone markers, to facilitate repairs as well as to protect it from damage—although much damage has already been done. Still, what remains is protected as a *monument historique* and, with the active oversight of a group of committed preservationists (Association Sources du Nord—Etudes et Préservation), its survival seems more secure.

It was Baron Haussmann who, with his determined engineer, Eugène Belgrand, established the far-flung water system that, with modifications and updating, still supplies Paris today. Well before the role of water in spreading epidemics became widely known, Haussmann set to work to create a vast system of covered aqueducts and reservoirs to convey and store enormous quantities of pure spring water from afar. It was a daring move, but in a sense no more so than that of the Gallo-Romans who engineered their aqueduct of Arcueil, or the medieval Parisians who built the little Regard de la Lanterne.

～

Not far from the Place des Fêtes spreads one of the most beautiful places in Paris, the **Parc des Buttes Chaumont**. Little known to tourists, this gem is savored by Parisians, especially those who live nearby.

It owes its existence to Baron Haussmann, who was good at creating parks in places where parks had never been before, especially on the city's outskirts. During the middle years of the Second Empire (mid-nineteenth century), Haussmann cast his eyes northward to the heights of Belleville, where a shantytown stretched through a huge garbage dump that had risen around former gypsum quarries. Impatient with obstacles, Haussmann cracked the whip and, despite enormous obstacles, the sixty-two-acre park of Buttes-Chaumont emerged within five years, turning a major eyesore into one of the city's most dramatic beauty spots.

Here Haussmann oversaw the creation of a lake, a towering island topped by a small temple, several waterfalls, two dramatic bridges, and panoramic views. Filled with roads and paths, lawns and hillsides, precipices and grottoes, it's a place for walking and running or simply resting and rejuvenating. Some of Paris's most famous landscapers and gardeners helped to create it, and even Gustave Eiffel got into the act, designing the suspension bridge that takes you across the lake to the belvedere.

Much as with the Bois de Vincennes, the idea was to provide Parisians of this part of town, primarily workers, with a pleasant destination of their own, and Napoleon III was wholeheartedly in support of the project. Yet as it turned out, neither this nor the Bois de Vincennes made much of an impact on those they were meant to gratify. Grinding poverty eclipsed pretty walks, and within a few years, the Paris Commune would erupt, with the workers of Belleville providing much of the impetus.

But this is history, and a century and a half later, the Parc des Buttes Chaumont is a peaceful spot, from whose belvedere you can look across to its sister mound, Montmartre, and over all of Paris below.

Avenue Frochot. © M. McAuliffe

~

CHAPTER FIFTEEN

From the Heights

Having explored two of the highest points in Paris—Belleville and Montmartre—it is time to make our way back down to the center of town, starting at the foot of Montmartre.

Pigalle, a busy and heavily touristed neighborhood at Montmartre's base, has for years been the center of naughty sex shops and strip joints—although gentrification here as elsewhere in Paris is on the rise. But it looked quite different back in the early years of the nineteenth century, when this was the northern part of a vibrant quarter of successful artists, musicians, and writers known as the Nouvelle Athens. Those who lived here included Chopin, George Sand, Hector Berlioz, the Goncourt brothers, and Victor Hugo.

One lovely remnant of these olden times is the tiny, winding **Avenue Frochot**, near (but not to be confused with) Rue Frochot. This unexpected delight is a private street and is both gated and guarded. But peer through the gates into the enticing trees and greenery and, if you can, persuade one of the residents to let you inside to glimpse the charming rose-covered houses. One of the loveliest of these, at no. 7, was long occupied by Jean Renoir, son of Pierre-Auguste Renoir and a famous film director in his own right. Long before him, Alexandre Dumas *père* occupied this address, and Victor Hugo is supposed to have once lived nearby.

More accessible is the nearby **Musée de la Vie Romantique**, once the home of the prominent painter Ary Scheffer, who lived here and entertained a stellar collection of artists, musicians, and poets during the 1830s and 1840s. These included Delacroix and Ingres (never together, one presumes,

given Ingres' cool classicism and contempt for Delacroix's dramatic romanticism), and especially Chopin and George Sand. The museum is the recipient
of a large amount of the novelist's memorabilia, including a plaster cast of
Chopin's left hand.

This is an especially lovely spot when the roses are in bloom, and one
can take tea, with appropriate goodies, in the adjoining greenhouse or
courtyard, billed (correctly) as a haven of peace in the heart of the ninth
arrondissement.

Chopin had arrived in Paris from his native Poland in 1831, at the age of
twenty-one (his father was French, hence the French surname), and moved
into a fifth-floor walk-up in the bustling quarter of Boulevard Montmartre
and Boulevard des Italiens. There, he immediately fell in love with Paris.
"You wouldn't believe what a charming place I have," he wrote a friend, with
all the enthusiasm of a college student. "A little room, handsomely furnished
in mahogany, with a little balcony on the boulevard from where I can see
from Montmartre to the Panthéon and all along the finest districts." Still,
Paris overwhelmed him: "You find here the greatest splendor, the greatest
filthiness, the greatest virtue and the greatest vice," he wrote, and added,
"You can enjoy yourself, get bored, laugh, cry, do anything you like, and no
one takes any notice because thousands here are doing exactly the same.
Everyone goes his own way."[1]

Quickly establishing himself as a chamber pianist for the elite and piano
teacher for their children, Chopin soon moved to a series of better quarters,
furnishing them to his exacting taste. In time he met and began his famous
relationship with the novelist Amandine-Aurore-Lucile Dupin, who went by
the pen name of George Sand. Already renowned for her refusal to conduct
herself as was expected of women of her times (she frequently strode the
streets of Paris in male attire and engaged in lesbian as well as numerous
heterosexual affairs), Sand was a famous author by the time she and Chopin
began to live together, on Rue Pigalle.

But this was a noisy spot, and so both moved to more comfortable quarters in nearby **Square d'Orléans**, an elegant enclave surrounding a series of
linked courtyards. Beautifully preserved, this site is well worth a visit even
without its claim to fame. Here, Chopin lived at no. 9, while Sand lived at
no. 5. He had already learned that he could not compose with Sand's two
young children underfoot.

Several blocks to the east is a remarkable remnant of Emperor Napoleon III's efforts to improve the lives of Paris's workers. After coming to power (by a bloody coup, let us not forget), he took an interest in workers' housing, which was becoming an ever-greater problem during his years in power, with tenements in central Paris being widely eradicated. This destruction, a major characteristic of 1850s and 1860s Paris, aimed at making way for new roads and better housing; but better housing on cleaner streets was unfortunately well out of financial reach for these neighborhoods' former residents.

The first fruits of Louis-Napoleon Bonaparte's efforts to provide decent workers' housing in Paris opened in 1851. It was a large complex called the **Cité Napoléon**, and it still is located at 58 Rue de Rochechouart, at the foot of Montmartre. Comprised of several buildings grouped around a garden courtyard, it originally contained more than two hundred small subsidized apartments that were priced within the range of what workers could pay.

Although the buildings' exteriors were unattractive (likened to a barracks), their interiors were unusually light and airy, featuring open double staircases leading to floors arranged along wide corridors and lighted by an overhead glass roof—astonishingly modern in concept and appearance. Each unit contained a kitchen and was heated and ventilated. Each floor had water pumps and toilets (this was well before the era of private bathrooms), and the buildings contained communal laundries and children's nurseries.

It certainly sounds attractive. Yet unfortunately, the idea behind this well-meaning but ultimately unsuccessful endeavor was that, through careful management of the tenants' lives and surroundings, they could be improved out of poverty. There were many restrictions, most especially a ten o'clock curfew, as well as police surveillance. The emperor wanted to place at least one of these housing blocks in each of Paris's arrondissements, and shortly after this one appeared, he subsidized the construction of a similar housing block on Boulevard Diderot, near the Gare de Lyon. A decade later he made yet another attempt, on Avenue Daumesnil.

But the poor of Paris did not want to be regimented, and in any case, the supply of workers' housing was woefully inadequate. The Cité Napoléon and its offshoots never succeeded as workers' housing, and today, ironically, this and its sibling on Avenue Daumesnil (now called Villa Daumesnil) are gated apartment complexes, serving the well-to-do.

Despite its locked gates, the Cité Napoléon is relatively easy to access and explore. As you do, you will probably encounter groups of architectural students trooping through, for this is an amazingly contemporary structure, and the idea of glass roofs and open double staircases filled with plants—looking for all the world like a very large hothouse—is one that certainly found its way into the architectural vocabulary of the twentieth century.

⌣

And what happened to the displaced workers of central Paris, as Baron Haussmann's juggernaut rolled on? They simply moved to cheaper quarters on the city's outskirts, where tenements and slums would rise up that were as derelict as the ones being destroyed.

It was this continued poverty and escalating despair that fueled the Commune uprising of 1871—a revolt that left its mark throughout Paris, not only with the famous destruction of the Tuileries Palace, the Palais de Justice, and the Hôtel de Ville, but also lesser-known examples, such as the **Hôtel Thiers** on Place Saint-Georges. This magnificent dwelling belonged to Adolphe Thiers, the first president of the new Third Republic and leader of the troops that so furiously put down the uprising.

This bloodbath originally broke out on the Butte of Montmartre, in a now-obscure spot located just behind Sacré-Coeur, at 6 Rue des Rosiers (now 36 Rue du Chevalier-de-La-Barre). Here, in March 1871, all hell broke loose after the government sent troops to recover multiple cannons that the citizens of Montmartre had dragged all the way from the Place de Wagram to the top of the Butte. Having subsidized these cannons through public subscription during the Franco-Prussian War, the men, women, and children who participated in this dramatic transfer believed them to be theirs and were determined to keep them safely out of Prussian hands. The government strongly disagreed on the question of the cannons' ownership and certainly did not want to see such weapons in the hands of Paris's volatile poor. A confrontation ensued, during which two generals were captured and dragged to 6 Rue des Rosiers and shot.

Following these opening shots, Paris's workers quickly established their own government, the highly contentious but socially conscious Commune, which took over the Hôtel de Ville. Members of the official French government, under Thiers, raced for the safety of Versailles, well beyond Paris's massive walls. Ironically, these walls (and the sixteen muscular forts just outside them) had been built during the 1840s at the instigation of none other than Theirs himself, then prime minister under King Louis-Philippe. Thiers well knew these fortifications' strengths and weaknesses and proceeded deliberately. Finally, on the night of May 21—after the capture of several of these forts and a lengthy cannon bombardment of western Paris—government troops poured into Paris.

Georges Haussmann's broad boulevards—newly created under Napoleon III's Second Empire—had not only cleaned up some of the most insalubrious slums of central Paris but also provided wide and straight thoroughfares on which troops could march. Unquestionably, the Communards found it difficult to build and defend their barricades in the new Paris. But one unforeseen consequence of Haussmann's slum clearance was the removal of Paris's poor from the center of town to the outskirts—to Montmartre, Belleville, and all those impoverished communities in the eleventh, eighteenth, nineteenth, and twentieth arrondissements. Here, in their home territory, the Communards put up a fierce fight.

Withdrawing from the Hôtel de Ville to the *mairie* (town hall) of the eleventh and then of the twentieth arrondissement, the Commune's headquarters was pushed into a corner, even while its supporters continued to fight tenaciously in Belleville and Ménilmontant. During this terrible May week, since known as "Bloody Week," reprisals triggered reprisals as fury and despair escalated. Seething at the brutality of Thiers' troops, Communards destroyed Thiers' stunning mansion on Place Saint-Georges and then set to work on other monuments linked with the Ancien Régime and both Napoleonic empires, destroying Bonaparte's massive Victory Column and statue in the Place Vendôme and setting the torch to the Palais des Tuileries, the Palais Royal, the Palais de Justice, and the Hôtel de Ville.

By the week's end, only a few pockets of resistance remained—the largest being the famed cemetery of Père-Lachaise. Here, a macabre nighttime gun battle took place among the tombstones, until by morning the remaining Communards had been driven into the cemetery's far southeastern corner. Lined up against the wall, all 147 were summarily shot and buried in a communal grave. The site, now a place of pilgrimage, is marked only by a plaque dedicated "Aux Morts de la Commune, 21–28 Mai 1871."

At least twenty thousand Communards and their supporters died—a figure that dwarfs not only the Communards' own well-publicized executions, but even the grisly body count of the Reign of Terror. This, and a Paris filled with smoking ruins, was the legacy of these terrible weeks and months.

Paris did rebuild, but not in entirety. Bonaparte's Victory Column in the Place Vendôme went up again, with a copy of Bonaparte's statue (clad, Caesar-like, in a toga) reinstalled on top. The Palais de Justice and other buildings were repaired, and the Hôtel de Ville was rebuilt almost from scratch. The Palais des Tuileries was another matter. As with the Hôtel de Ville, a stone shell of the palace remained, making restoration possible, albeit exorbitant. Still, the palace—the royal and imperial residence ever since Napoleon Bonaparte—was such a vivid symbol of monarchy and empire that the Thiers government hesitated. Torn between whether to demolish the ruins or restore them, it procrastinated. In the end, the blackened shell remained an eyesore for a decade, with a sufficient number of monarchists in the Chamber of Deputies to hold open the possibility of rebuilding. Finally, a surge of republicans voted into government, along with the onset of economic hard times, made rebuilding unthinkable, and in 1883 the Chamber of Deputies at long last voted to demolish the palace's blackened ruins.

The Hôtel Thiers was another matter. Although razed to the ground, Thiers' famous library and art collection survived, thanks to the intervention of painter Gustave Courbet—an enthusiastic supporter of the Commune but, as it turned out, an even more committed supporter of the arts. The mansion was soon rebuilt (Thiers had a wealthy wife) and, after the deaths of Thiers and his wife, it was donated, along with its extensive library (the Bibliothèque Thiers, specializing in nineteenth-century French history) to the Institut de France.

The mansion itself remains a luxurious vestige of the late nineteenth century. It is accessible to scholars of French history and, during September's Journées du Patrimoine, to the general public.

Several blocks downhill, after Rue Notre-Dame de Lorette passes the church of this name and becomes Rue du Faubourg-Montmartre, there is an enchanting little corner confiserie, **A la Mère de Famille**, which has been delighting chocolate and bonbon lovers since 1761. That is more than two centuries, during which it has survived world wars and any number of uprisings and revolutions.

A la Mère de Famille now has a number of boutiques carrying its confections, but its original shop, at 35 Rue du Faubourg-Montmartre, is a step back into another age. Occupying a corner spot in this old quarter, it is a charmer, loaded with a rainbow array of house-made treats and presided over by an antique cashier's booth, where one lines up to pay for purchases. There is quite an array of possible choices, but you might want to consider their famous wafer-thin dark chocolate palets, which come with an assortment of praline or ganache fillings. These are for the adults; children gravitate to the more colorful nougats and marzipans.

The sweets, of course, are delectable, but the shop itself is a treat, a visit to a land of sugarplums.

A la Mère de Famille. © J. McAuliffe

You are now almost at the Grands Boulevards—a major contribution of Louis XIV, the Sun King, to all those generations of flâneurs and boulevardiers who have enjoyed this lively semicircular stretch that grew up along the course of the Right Bank wall that Louis triumphantly pulled down. The Grands Boulevards have been famous ever since for their theaters, their restaurants and cafés, and their nightlife. Almost at the corner of Boulevard Montmartre is an especially hardworking remnant of the past, the landmark **Bouillon Chartier**, now a *monument historique*, which since 1896 has been serving up basic French fare at low prices in a cavernous Belle Epoque setting. There are no reservations, and one can avoid long lines only by coming off-hours. This is not the place for gourmet fare. But stick to the basics, and you will join the throngs of Parisians as well as tourists who happily crowd in for a brief and noisy meal, entertained by gruff waiters who are as much a part of the experience as the beautiful tiling, mirrors, and globe lighting.

Cut through the nearby Passage des Panoramas to yet another historic chocolate shop, **Debauve & Gallais** (33 Rue Vivienne), self-described as chocolatier of the kings of France ever since Sulpice Debauve, the royal family chemist, successfully disguised Marie Antoinette's medications in flat chocolate discs, or pistoles, that enchanted her and generations of chocolate lovers to come. No, these no longer include the queen's medications, but the chocolate is still some of the best. I dote on their dark chocolate ganaches, but others (including Napoleon Bonaparte) prefer their croquamandes, or caramelized almonds in dark chocolate, as well as other delights The shop itself is a little jewel box, reminiscent of Marie Antoinette, and all the offerings, although not cheap, are seriously good.

Since you are now near the Boulevard des Italiens, don't hesitate to take a peek inside the majestic building that for generations housed the French bank **Crédit Lyonnais**. It's a beauty, in the Second Empire style known as Haussmann style, and dates from the 1870s. The workshops of Gustave Eiffel provided the stone building's metal frame, and inside you will find vast halls, impressive open spaces, plus an astonishing double revolution (or double helix) staircase that made it possible for the upper echelons and their underling staff to climb up and down without actually encountering one another.

After a damaging fire in 1996, the building was divided into two parts, with the back portion sold off. Only the part facing the Boulevard des Italiens remains open to the public, but you are welcome to enter. Don't hesitate.

～

A couple of blocks down the boulevards to the west rises a magnificent building, the Paris Opéra, or the **Opéra Garnier**, as it is known, in honor of its distinguished architect, Charles Garnier.

Like Auguste Rodin, Garnier also came from humble origins in the Left Bank's rough Mouffetard quarter. The son of a blacksmith and wheelwright, Garnier—like Rodin—embarked on his artistic career at Paris's Ecole Gratuite de Dessin. But unlike Rodin, Garnier succeeded in getting into the Ecole des Beaux-Arts, where he carried off the Grand Prix de Rome. It was a brilliant start to a career that began to sag in the middle until, during the years of the Second Empire, Garnier unexpectedly won the competition to design Paris's newest opera house.

Defeat in the Franco-Prussian War and the end of the Second Empire, followed by siege, uprising, and a new republic, almost prevented the completion of Garnier's magnificent structure, but the Third Republic finally agreed to complete his Opéra—a lavish gilt-encrusted edifice that would soon be known as the Palais Garnier.

Garnier had beaten out 170 other architects by his frank recognition of this opera house's basic purpose. Rather than directing attention to the stage and what went on there, Garnier's Opéra showcased the audience, providing a glittering backdrop for the social encounters that constituted the true heart of a night at the Paris opera. Vast and richly decorated foyers allowed audience members to stroll and mingle, but it was the Grand Staircase that was and remains the Opéra Garnier's special glory. Henry James may have thought this opulent branching stairway "a trifle vulgar," but he allowed that, "if the world were ever reduced to the dominion of a single potentate, the foyer would do for his throne room."[2]

Garnier adored this staircase, and he could often be found on opening nights near its foot, gazing contentedly upward at the surging throng. It was, as he often said, his favorite view, a stage in itself. By now a dapper member of Paris's elite, Charles Garnier gave no indication of his humble roots.

As the golden bust commemorating him outside the Opéra indicates, Charles Garnier had successfully crossed a great divide—and he had no intention of looking back.

High above the gilt-encrusted auditorium of the Opéra Garnier hangs a magnificent eight-ton chandelier with a past. For this is the chandelier that fell one fateful evening in 1896, killing a member of the audience and inspiring a story that still captivates theatregoers today.

The story, of course, is **The Phantom of the Opera**, which has appeared in numerous movie versions as well as the lushly romantic Andrew Lloyd Webber musical that has already spent decades on Broadway. But none of these renditions come close to capturing the original, a novel written in 1911 by a colorful French journalist named Gaston Leroux.

Leroux's singular combination of romantic dash and investigative know-how was perhaps surprising, given his solidly respectable and unimaginative middle-class upbringing. Born in Paris in 1868 (on Rue du Faubourg-Saint-Martin) to a public works contractor and the daughter of a shipbuilder, he was raised in Normandy, near his grandparents' shipping company. A promising student, he nevertheless had no intention of joining the family business. Instead, he dreamed of becoming a writer, in the footsteps of Victor Hugo and Alexandre Dumas. This made no sense at all to his father, who insisted that he study law. Eventually Leroux capitulated and went to Paris, where he majored in revels rather than in studies. Still, he did manage to receive that all-important law degree, although his father did not live long enough to enjoy the triumph. Dying prematurely, the senior Leroux bequeathed a large fortune to his heir, who now added to his already-considerable reputation as a man-about-town by going through the entire legacy in a matter of months.

Now Leroux had to earn a living, but the law still did not interest him. Fortunately journalism did, and eventually he landed a position as drama critic for a Paris newspaper. This led to a stint as a courtroom reporter, followed by more than a decade as a foreign correspondent. Showing up in a variety of exotic trouble spots around the globe, Leroux covered the 1905 Russian Revolution as well as simmering situations in Egypt, Morocco, and Korea. At the same time, he began to try his hand at writing fiction.

Four novels later, he decided that what he really wanted was to outdo Conan Doyle and Edgar Allan Poe at their own game. His *Mystery of the Yellow Room*, probably his best, may have done exactly that. This classic "locked-room" mystery wowed readers at the time and has remained popular to this day, being a diabolically clever puzzle with all the shivers of a Gothic horror tale. But Leroux's final touch of genius was his ability, based on long experience as a journalist, to present his tale as if it were breaking news in a sensational case. Interlacing his narrative with invented but completely plausible interviews, news stories, and snippets of memoirs, Leroux manipulated readers' sense of reality while propelling them forward with all the driving force of a tabloid headliner.

It was exactly this combination of ingredients that Leroux brought three years later to *The Phantom of the Opera*. He began with a real setting, the magnificent Opéra Garnier, which in fact was built on an actual water table, and whose labyrinthine corridors and underground cellars were rumored to harbor a ghost. Leroux understood his readers' fascination with dark corridors and endless underground cellars, and when he learned of the discovery of a skeleton in the Opéra's deep recesses, he seized upon this as the key to his "Phantom" story.

He tells the reader that for several years he had searched the archives of the National Academy of Music for evidence of the Opéra Ghost and had conducted numerous interviews of those who had witnessed the ghost or its ghostly activities. But this skeleton, he claims, offered the final proof. And then he begins his tale.

It is the tale of Erik, a horribly disfigured musical genius, who lives in the underworld of the Opéra basements (yes, that lake) and loves a beautiful young opera singer, Christine. Christine in turn loves Raoul, the handsome young Vicomte de Chagny, who returns her devotion, but the madly jealous Erik is determined to put an end to their love affair. As some have pointed out, this Gothic romance bears some resemblance to various "Beauty and the Beast" stories, except that in this case, Christine does not return Erik's love. Although she pities and is grateful to him (for his amazingly effective private voice lessons), she cannot overcome her horror of Erik's hideous appearance, nor does she wish to abandon Raoul. In the end, after a series of terrifying events, the Phantom finally allows her to join her lover, and the Phantom—with nothing left to live for—dies.

Leroux's Phantom is unquestionably mad, but he is also an architectural as well as musical genius, responsible for constructing the Opéra Garnier itself, with all those hidden passageways and trap doors that subsequently enable him to rule his Opéra kingdom. As we follow Christine and Raoul in their attempt to escape Erik's all-seeing eyes, we climb through the Opéra's dizzying heights, feeling that we are accompanying them every step of the way. This is not surprising, for Leroux studied Charles Garnier's architectural plans and knew Garnier's opera house well. Much, including Leroux's description of the famous backstage Foyer de la Danse and the lofty Opéra roof, is pinpoint accurate. When he chose to embroider on fact, whether the plummeting chandelier or the Phantom's underground lake, Leroux merely was elaborating on what already was there—a terrible accident within the opera house or a water table (contained by a massive structure) that still lies beneath.

Unlike Leroux's mysteries, his *Phantom of the Opera* did not meet with instant success. But over the years it gained in popularity, especially after the silent film version with Lon Chaney appeared in 1925. Today, it is one of the best known stories anywhere, and there are few people who, on encountering Paris's Opéra Garnier for the first time, do not wonder about that chandelier, the Phantom, and the underground lake.

Tour Saint-Jacques. © J. McAuliffe

CHAPTER SIXTEEN

~

Grande Croisée

Traveling into Paris from the north, or making your way out again in the same direction, has always involved taking the road between two heights, Montmartre and Belleville. This roadway, sloping downward toward the Seine, was originally paved by the Romans and still exists as Rue Saint-Martin. Beyond medieval city limits, it proceeds north as Rue du Faubourg-Saint-Martin—the dividing point between what lay within and without Paris proper grandly marked, by the Sun King himself, as the Arc de Triomphe de la Porte Saint-Martin (Louis was never shy about celebrating himself or his military victories).

Another newer route paralleling this one grew up during medieval times, connecting Paris with the important Abbey of Saint-Denis, and is now known as Rue Saint-Denis, with its extension northward as Rue du Faubourg-Saint-Denis. Its dividing point is also marked by a Louis XIV arc of triumph, this one the Arc de Triomphe de la Porte Saint-Denis.

Both Saint Denis and Saint Martin were important saints in Paris from Christianity's earliest times, and the roadways bearing their names were for centuries essential entries into and exits from the city. In addition, they linked up with bridges crossing the Ile de la Cité to the Left Bank and points south. Then, in the middle years of the nineteenth century, a major change occurred: Baron Georges Haussmann flatly decided against using either of these for the north-south portion of his famous *Grande Croisée*, his major new arteries slicing through Paris.

Haussmann had his reasons and, as it turned out, his emperor, Napoleon III, totally agreed.

⌒

Louis-Napoleon Bonaparte, born in 1808—the son of Hortense de Beauharnais (daughter of Napoleon Bonaparte's wife Josephine, by Josephine's first marriage) and Louis Bonaparte, younger brother of Napoleon Bonaparte—was the product of a scheme to provide Napoleon and the now-infertile Josephine with an heir. This scheme was successful, in that Hortense and Louis produced two sons, but the marriage itself was a dismal failure. Still, being unaware of his parents' personal antipathy, little Louis-Napoleon enjoyed a childhood ensconced in imperial splendor at the Tuileries, Saint-Cloud, and Fontainebleau, thoroughly spoiled by his mother and by his maternal grandmother, Josephine.

Like his mother and grandmother, young Louis-Napoleon was a charmer, and he maintained his ability to captivate throughout his life. Certainly he was not a warrior leader in the image of his uncle: Louis-Napoleon's military exploits were embarrassingly slight and came to unfortunate ends, although everyone who knew him insisted that he looked good on a horse. Instead, exiled (along with the rest of the Bonapartes) from France after Waterloo, he focused on seducing women, spending money, and enjoying himself. At the same time, this playboy-prince took considerable pride in his name and never ceased to dream that someday he would rule France.

This dream, as well as a longing for a dashing military role, led Louis-Napoleon into two abortive coup attempts, the second of which landed him in a French military prison, where he studied, wrote, and consorted with a mistress with whom he had two children before he eventually escaped to London. But his prison stay had not been without benefit, for during those years he widely published his political ideas—including a growing concern for the poor—in numerous articles and pamphlets, drawing a significant number of reformers and workers to his cause.

His cause became clearer with the deaths, first, of his older brother, then that of Napoleon Bonaparte's only son, the young duke of Reichstadt, and last, that of Louis-Napoleon's father, all of which left Louis-Napoleon as the foremost Bonaparte claimant to France's imperial throne. By the 1840s this position had become markedly more significant because, two decades after his death, Emperor Napoleon Bonaparte had surged back into popularity in France, signaled by the 1840 return of his ashes to Paris, where he was interred with great ceremony in the Invalides. The Bonaparte name was now one that Louis-Napoleon could flaunt with pride in his native land.

This opportunity presented itself in 1848, as revolution toppled yet another French monarch, the Orléanist Louis-Philippe (who in turn had benefited from the revolution of 1830). Using charm and wile, Louis-Napoleon insinuated himself into the good graces of those French political figures who mattered, and then into the hearts of the French people, who (males only in those days) voted him into the office of president of the Second Republic. Of course, despite his fervent promises, Louis-Napoleon never had any intention of upholding the republic. Within a short time, he was able to overthrow it in a bloody coup and install himself as Emperor Napoleon III of the Second Empire, heir to Bonaparte's First Empire. (Louis-Napoleon graciously reserved the title of Napoleon II for Bonaparte's deceased young son.)

Of course, power was the main point, but for years Louis-Napoleon had also entertained dreams of grandly improving the city of Paris, and now he had the opportunity to carry these out. When he first arrived in Paris in 1848, at the Paris embarkation point of the great Northern railway (now the Gare du Nord), the emperor-to-be had carried with him a color-coded map of Paris that set out his plan for renewing the great city, along with his dreams for improving the lot of workers and the entire nation. (The narrow and easily overlooked plaza in front of the Gare du Nord is now called the **Place Napoléon III**, the only memorial to him in all of Paris.)

Looking at Paris today it is difficult to imagine what the city looked like as Louis-Napoleon set about to transform it. Much of it, especially in its center and eastern districts, consisted of a tangle of dark and narrow streets lined with aged and sinister tenements. Bridges linking both banks of the Seine with the Ile de la Cité were guarded by tollgates, and any effort to get goods or people across town was blocked by an impossible obstacle course of circuitous and filthy lanes. Paris had changed little since medieval times, and in fact had kept the worst and elaborated on it. The rich, as always, kept to themselves—largely in the western part of town. But the poor eked out their existence in the rest of the city, on the margins of society.

Louis-Napoleon wanted to tear down the old and rotten and create a city that was far more welcoming to commerce as well as a pleasanter place in which to live. This meant, to his way of thinking, the necessity of creating unimpeded east-west arteries on both the Right and the Left Banks as well as a central route leading directly from the northern to the southern gates of the city. It also meant connecting the warehouses and passenger stations of the new railroads—not only with each other, but with the city's vital center. For in that era of booming new industrialization, the magic word was "railroads."

Already Paris had a scattering of embarkation points and stations around its outskirts, marking the end points of several different railway lines.

Unfortunately, these were not connected, nor were they linked in any meaningful way with the center of Paris. Predecessors of the Gare du Nord, Gare de l'Est, Gare de Lyon, Gare d'Austerlitz (originally the Gare d'Orléans), Gare Montparnasse, and the Gare Saint-Lazare existed but remained awkwardly unconnected and difficult to reach, whether for freight or passengers.

Louis-Napoleon, now Napoleon III, wanted to move fast, and he soon found precisely the man to carry out his wishes: Georges-Eugène Haussmann, a Frenchman with a German name who was about to become the second most powerful man in the empire.

⌒

Born in Paris not far from l'Etoile (now Place Charles-de-Gaulle) to a prosperous and well-connected Protestant family, Georges Haussmann studied hard, worked hard, and did all the right things as he climbed his way up the ladder as a public administrator, honing his organizational and management skills along the way. He had earned a reputation for tirelessly exploring the geographical areas for which he was responsible and for introducing significant improvements, whether for draining swamps or building roads, canals, and suspension bridges. He had also earned a reputation for being curt, inconsiderate, and arrogant, and he was not shy about pulling strings or letting his ambition show.

Haussmann married wealthily, fathered two daughters, and was living comfortably in the Bordeaux area, where he was prefect, when he gave Louis-Napoleon an especially regal welcome as the prince-president prepared for his final power grab. Where votes were required to place an imprimatur of legitimacy on Louis-Napoleon's coup and proclamation of empire, Haussmann delivered. His reward came shortly thereafter, when the newly minted emperor appointed him prefect of the Seine—a position that put Haussmann in charge of Paris (the office of mayor, created during the height of the Revolution, had been largely abolished—the volatile Parisian populace being regarded with distrust by whoever was in charge at the time).[1]

Napoleon III had already begun work on remodeling the city even before Haussmann arrived in Paris, focusing on creating north-south and east-west transportation arteries as well as green spaces throughout the city. And yes, he wanted to open up areas that had been bastions of insurrection to facilitate troop movement—on wider streets that could not be easily blockaded by a few mattresses and a pile of junk. Order and prosperity marched together to his way of thinking, and he was convinced that his *grands travaux* would not only create prosperity but would improve the morals of the people who lived there.

The new emperor jump-started the efforts, begun under Bonaparte, to create a major Right Bank east-west thoroughfare, the Rue de Rivoli, starting at the Place de la Concorde—work that had stalled in its eastward course alongside the Louvre's uncompleted northern wing. He also had his sights on a major Left Bank thoroughfare parallel to the Rue de Rivoli, which (until Haussmann talked him out of it) involved piercing through the Rue des Ecoles. (Haussmann did not hesitate to point out to his boss that, most unfortunately, the Rue des Ecoles was located along the slopes of Mont-Sainte-Geneviève, where it could not be broadened sufficiently to safely carry the large volumes of traffic that the emperor had in mind. Instead, Haussmann recommended another route, on level ground closer to the Seine. This would become the Boulevard Saint-Germain.)

Linking these east-west arteries on both banks, in the emperor's design, would be a major thoroughfare from north to south. This was to begin at the current Gare de l'Est and extend as far as the Grands Boulevards, with the prospect of continuing all the way to the Seine. By the time Haussmann came into office, the northernmost portion of this great north-south axis, christened the Boulevard de Strasbourg, was already underway. From there, the emperor decided that this broad north-south route should meet up with the Rue de Rivoli at the Tour Saint-Jacques and continue on to the Place du Châtelet, crossing the Seine to the Ile de la Cité. It would then proceed south to the Observatoire, which was located just beyond the southern tip of the Luxembourg Gardens, and would then continue on to what then was the Barrière d'Enfer in the city walls (now Place Denfert-Rochereau).

Originally called the Boulevard du Centre as it moved south beyond the *grands boulevards*, this section of the major north-south axis soon acquired a new name, thanks to France's victory in the battle of Sebastopol during the Crimean War. But in the meantime, this route was strongly opposed by those who thought it should proceed along a widened Rue Saint-Denis or Rue Saint-Martin, both of which had carried traffic into and out of Paris for centuries. Haussmann retorted that if he took either of these routes, it would require years to cut through the urban fabric that had grown up around them. This new route, he argued, unfolding between the two ancient ones, could proceed relatively unimpeded through gardens, courtyards, and low-rise buildings, spreading to what then was an impressive width of ninety-eight feet.

Of course, Haussmann later conceded, this new Boulevard de Sébastapol, "ripped open Old Paris, with its riots and barricades, . . . piercing this almost impenetrable maze with a large central roadway."[2] Moreover, the resulting roadway would not only be wide, but it would be straight, unlike the narrow and somewhat meandering Rues Saint-Martin and Saint-Denis that flanked it. Haussmann could also do some chest-thumping by asserting that this route allowed him to spare buildings of historical merit, such as the priory church of Saint-Martin-des-Champs.

⁓

The Priory of **Saint-Martin-des-Champs** has roots going back to the sixth century and, much as with Saint Germain-des-Prés on the Left Bank, suffered terror and devastation in the ninth century when the dread sails of Viking dragon ships appeared on the Seine.

Parisians retreated to the walled Ile de la Cité, from where they fought the besiegers, until at length the Vikings moved on, leaving desolation in their wake. What remained, beyond the flattened Cité, were scatterings of dependent villages huddled around several abbeys, including two that exist today—or at least their churches do. The one is the Left Bank's Saint-Germain-des-Prés, and the other is the Right Bank's Saint-Martin-des-Champs.

Saint-Germain-des-Prés rose again, fostering security and prosperity in its environs. As for Saint-Martin-des-Champs, it too rebuilt, this time taking no chances and developing into a strongly fortified bastion with a moat, positioned in the midst of extensive fields that the monks cultivated ("champs" means "fields"). A Benedictine monastery subsidiary to the Abbey of Cluny, this was one of the major Cluniac houses, whose large landholdings made it second in importance only to the nearby Royal Abbey of Saint-Denis.

The Priory of Saint-Martin-des-Champs was dissolved during the Revolution, but its medieval church and refectory remain. The church now serves as the dramatic setting for a portion of the remarkable **Musée des Arts et Métiers**, dedicated to science and technology in all its possibilities—a storehouse of innovation and invention.

I am especially fond of this church's vaulted interior and its astonishing display of early automobiles and airplanes, suspended throughout the structure's soaring heights. These culminate at one end with Foucault's Pendulum and at the other with an original scale plaster model of the Statue of Liberty, standing on a dramatic rise. But one of my favorite exhibits, easily overlooked, is located in a nearby stairwell. It is Clément Ader's *Avion III*, a steam-propelled airplane built between 1892 and 1897, constructed of linen and wood along the lines of an enormous bat. Gabriel Voisin, who first encountered it at the 1900 Paris Exposition, was so overwhelmed by what he saw that it led him into a career of pioneering aviation work and aircraft manufacturing.

For his part, Voisin always insisted that Ader, in his first aircraft, the *Eole*, had in 1890 been the first to leave the ground "under his aircraft's own power, from a level surface, without the aid of up-currents" and had flown "about 260 feet (80 meters) in a straight line at a height of from three to six feet."[3] The Wright brothers, of course, begged to differ on who came first.

Charles V's medieval wall followed a course quite near the remarkable priory church of Saint-Martin-des-Champs, and in fact the spot where the Sun King later constructed the triumphal arch of Porte Saint-Denis marked the northernmost point of that wall. It then cut back toward the Seine, leaving a curiously angled parallel of streets in its wake, starting with Rue de Cléry and Rue d'Aboukir. This neighborhood, along what once was the old medieval wall, is where Victor Hugo placed his impoverished beggars and thieves of *Notre-Dame de Paris* (*The Hunchback of Notre-Dame*), after their day's work around Notre-Dame was done and they returned home. As they approached their destination, these experts at flimflam were "miraculously" cured of their lameness, missing limbs, and other piteous infirmities. Thus the sardonic name, the "**Court of Miracles**."

Moving south along the Boulevard de Sébastopol, one can almost envision Haussmann battling it out with Old Paris. Just to the east of Boulevard de Sébastopol, for example, at 51 Rue de Montmorency, remains the **Maison de Nicolas Flamel**, the oldest stone house in Paris, dating from 1407. You may recall the name, as Flamel shows up rather prominently in the first Harry Potter story, and Victor Hugo refers ominously to him in *Notre-Dame de Paris*. Flamel has gone down in history, or in the shadows of history, as a dedicated alchemist who discovered the philosopher's stone and its secret of eternal life. Since the philosopher's stone was also capable of turning base metals into gold, subsequent seekers have not been surprised to learn that Flamel was a wealthy man.

In addition to any time he may have put in at his laboratory, Flamel was a successful manuscript copyist and dealer (much like a publisher and book-seller today) as well as a major community benefactor. In 1407 he built the sturdy stone structure at what now is 51 Rue de Montmorency, setting aside the top stories as a kind of homeless shelter while turning the ground floor into a moneymaking tavern that supported the enterprise. If you look carefully, you can make out some of the original carvings on the façade, including angels, Flamel's initials, and a Latin inscription invoking the inhabitants' prayers.

Many years ago, when I first glimpsed this ancient structure, it was in terrible shape—dark, dismal, and certainly showing its age. More recently it has received a face-lift and now houses a popular restaurant, the Auberge Nicolas Flamel. Some of the inscriptions, including the words "Taverne Nicolas Flamel" over the door, have disappeared, and other carvings have grown even fainter, probably the result of its scrub down. But the Maison de Nicolas Flamel is still a remarkable little building—one that has managed to survive more than six hundred years.

Haussmann's Boulevard de Sébastopol proceeded to rip its way through some of the oldest and most dismal quarters of Paris, retaining only a few remnants of the past, such as the ancient church of **Saint-Merri**, which boasts the oldest bell in Paris (from the 1300s). It was here, in this quarter's narrow streets and teeming tenements, that the uprising of 1832 broke out, attracting the attention of Victor Hugo, who used its dramatic elements for *Les Misérables*. Legend has it that a small boy, gallantly waving a tricolor in the face of a volley of shots, became the model for little Gavroche.

Hugo's story spread, as did this small-scale uprising, to nearby streets and to the Corinth, the tavern where the student revolutionaries threw up their ill-fated barricade. Hugo gives precise directions, but these are based on what used to be—before Haussmann and a vastly remodeled Les Halles. Yet you can still find traces of the narrow alleyways that once wound through this quarter, from the spaghetti-like route of Rue Mondétour to the tiny Rues de la Petite-Truanderie and Grande-Truanderie, which meet in an equally diminutive square. The Corinth probably stood at the corner of Rue Rambuteau and Rue Mondétour, in the now-gentrified area just to the east of Saint-Eustache and north of **Les Halles**.

Since the twelfth century, when Philip Augustus built two market halls on this site, this has served as a major source of food for Parisians. Unfortunately, by the time Louis-Napoleon seized the imperial crown, it had become cramped and derelict, much like its slum-ridden surroundings. Others before Louis-Napoleon had studied and debated the problem, but it was the emperor who lit the proverbial fires beneath a host of slow-moving bureaucrats to get a move on. Haussmann, who needed no prodding, entered office just after the first demolitions in the quarter began and pressed successfully for even further demolition and roadwork. But the main problem was architectural: the emperor hated what his architect, Victor Baltard, had come up with as a replacement for the old market halls. Baltard, a prestigious architect and Prix de Rome winner, had designed eight pavilions, the first of which was completed just before Haussmann took office. Heavy, grandiose, and made of stone, it looked every inch the "Halles fortress" that derisive Parisians called it. The emperor agreed: what he had in mind was the sort of glass-covered metal frame that had caught public attention when the British presented the Crystal Palace to the world in 1851, at their world's fair. "What I must have are huge umbrellas," the emperor told Haussmann, and he sketched out what he envisioned.

Haussmann was careful to preserve the sketch. He then elaborated, adding a broad road with the eight pavilions distributed around it. He then handed the whole thing over to Baltard, who was a friend. "Quickly get me a draft following these basic ideas," he told him. Just remember, he added, "more iron, nothing but iron!"[4]

The use of iron rather than stone was of course heresy to a classically trained architect such as Baltard (an attitude that Gustave Eiffel would encounter almost thirty years later when he proposed his all-iron tower for the 1889 World's Fair). Baltard protested, but at last he came up with the design that Haussmann—and the emperor—asked for. It would remain a graceful presence for more than a century.

The recent renovation of Les Halles has brought new vitality to areas stretching northward, especially up Rue Montorgueil, which now is a busy and prosperous pedestrian byway. But a previous renovation, in the 1970s, infamously moved this ancient food market out of the center of Paris to neighboring Rungis, replacing it with a lackluster garden and underground mall, and leaving only the ancient Church of Saint-Eustache as a point of interest. Scandalously, this renovation resulted in the destruction of the famous iron and glass structures that Victor Baltard designed for Napoleon III in the 1850s. The Musée Carnavalet has recently displayed a picture of the destruction of these pavilions, titled, *L'Assassinat de Baltard*. Indeed.

However, one did survive and—if you are persistent—you can find it where it has been relocated to the eastern outskirts of Paris, in Nogent-sur-Marne. There, a **Pavillon Baltard** (currently closed to the public) has remained a graceful presence and reminder that Baron Haussmann and his emperor sometimes had some very good ideas indeed.

～

Haussmann's Boulevard de Sébastopol continued toward the Seine, leaving a juxtaposition of old and new in its wake. The new (definitely post-Haussmann) is most vividly on display in the nearby **Centre Pompidou** (the Centre national d'art et de culture Georges-Pompidou), Paris's extraordinary repository of contemporary art and culture.[5] Even if you are not a fan of modern art, you should take the breathtaking escalator up the building's front to the top, where you can rest with a drink and look out over the Paris scene below. If you are a modern art aficionado, then this is a must destination, not only for the Pompidou's permanent collections but for its many major exhibitions.

This is a building that is still avant-garde after almost half a century, its "inside-out" systems fully and colorfully exposed on the building's exterior. Nearby is another tribute to the new, the **Stravinsky Fountain**, whose jolly figures are the creation of Niki de Saint Phalle, who first gained fame for her "blasted" sculptures—collections of objects heaped with bags and cans of paint that Saint Phalle repeatedly shot with a pistol or rifle, sending out sprays of color and vaulting her into the avant-garde. This violent portion of her artistic life soon passed, and the colorful figures of the Stravinsky Fountain are happy examples of some of Saint Phalle's later output. (The fountain's black mechanical pieces are the works of Saint Phalle's sculptor husband, Jean Tinguely.)

Old and new continue to live side by side in this part of central Paris, with the nearby **Fontaine des Innocents**, the only Renaissance fountain in Paris, located at the southeast corner of Les Halles. Dating from the 1500s, it previously stood at what once was the Church of the Holy Innocents—adjoining the infamous Cimetière des Innocents, then the oldest and largest cemetery in Paris. Overcrowding and mass graves in this cemetery created such a hazard to public health that, by the late eighteenth century, the remaining corpses were exhumed and brought to the abandoned quarries in Montparnasse that we now know as the Catacombs. The cemetery itself was closed down, and the church was destroyed soon after, leaving this glorious fountain at the center of Place Joachim-du-Bellay, a lively gathering spot in this corner of Les Halles.

According to the emperor's wishes, the Boulevard de Sébastopol eventually met up with his east-west artery, the Rue de Rivoli, at the **Tour Saint-Jacques**. But for a long and uncomfortable moment, it looked like this was a disaster in the making.

A starting point for pilgrims en route to the Cathedral of Santiago de Compostela, the Tour Saint-Jacques dates from the early 1500s and originally was part of the Church of Saint-Jacques-de-la-Boucherie (the Church of the Butchers), patronized by prosperous butchers from the nearby Les Halles markets. Unfortunately, the church itself was destroyed during the

French Revolution, and its grand tower, which reaches for the Paris sky, almost met the same fate during Napoleon III's Second Empire.

The trouble began when emperor's engineers, who did not have good elevation maps to go by, misjudged the meetup point between the east-west Rue de Rivoli and the north-south Boulevard de Sébastopol—a point that was to mark the Right Bank crossing of the emperor's *Grande Croisée*. You might well ask why they did not have sufficient elevation maps, and Haussmann certainly was appalled when he made this discovery, shortly after becoming prefect of the Seine. The answer was that roadbuilding in Paris had always proceeded informally, and this way of doing things was now creating a huge mess with the Rue de Rivoli extension as it slowly made its way toward the Hôtel de Ville. Most unfortunately, when this much-ballyhooed east-west artery reached the Tour Saint-Jacques, workers were surprised to discover that the variations in land height between the road and its surrounding area was far greater than anyone had anticipated, being off by several feet. This was an astonishing difference, and something that immediately raised the question of how to join the new Rue de Rivoli with the streets attempting to cross it, as well as with its access to the Pont Notre-Dame, whose entrance was already sufficiently steep to cause comment. Even the stability of the Tour Saint-Jacques was threatened, and there was talk about having to pull it down.

Fortunately, Haussmann soon found the kind of expertise he needed, resulting in a complete land survey, including spot heights, for the entire area of Paris within the Farmers-General Wall. Haussmann then proceeded to solve the problem of the difference in ground levels around the Tour Saint-Jacques by razing most of the neighborhood surrounding the tower. He then retained the tower's original elevation by placing it on an enormous pedestal surrounded by a small park, the first of many small parks or squares that Napoleon III would introduce to Paris. The difference in elevation between the tower and its surrounding area can be seen by the stair steps leading from nearby Rue Saint-Bon up to the original street level, now on Rue de la Verrerie, a startling difference of almost five feet.

In passing, don't overlook the statue of Blaise Pascal at the tower's base, which Haussmann placed there as a commemorative of Pascal's gravity experiments—noteworthy events that probably took place from the tower's top. You might also be interested to know that one of the church's foremost patrons was Nicholas Flamel, whose ancient stone house on Rue de Montmorency stands nearby. Flamel's importance as a benefactor to the Church of Saint-Jacques-de-la-Boucherie can be seen from the street named after him (Rue Nicholas-Flamel), which runs directly north from the small park surrounding the Tour Saint-Jacques. A small cross street, Rue Pernelle, is named after Flamel's wife.

Just beyond the Tour Saint-Jacques lies the **Place du Châtelet**, since ancient times one of the most important—and fiercely defended—spots in Paris. For centuries, a massive fortification stood here, first of wood, then of stone, protecting the bridge (originally the Grand Pont, now the Pont au Change) leading to the Ile de la Cité. This fortification, called the Grand Châtelet (there was a Petit Châtelet guarding the island's southern entrance, at the Petit Pont), harbored fiercesome dungeons in its depths, and after Philip Augustus's twelfth-century wall diminished the Grand Châtelet's importance as a fortress, it became a notorious prison, not abolished until the early 1800s.

It was Baron Haussmann who abolished the worst of the slums in this neighborhood, as elsewhere in Paris, expanding the square, creating two identical theaters facing each other (the Théâtre du Châtelet and the Théâtre de la Ville), and moving the huge Fontaine du Palmier to the center of it all. The Théâtre de la Ville would for many years be known as the Théâtre Sarah Bernhardt, who produced and starred in productions there for almost two decades. It lost this name during the German Occupation of Paris, on account of Bernhardt's Jewish ancestry.

The fountain, known as the Fontaine du Palmier because of the sculpted palm leaves at its top, is modeled (like so much of Bonaparte's monuments) after a Roman triumphal column and grandly commemorates Napoleon's Egyptian Campaign as well as his other major victories. Probably of most importance to the people of Paris at the time, though, was the fact that this was one of a series of fountains that Bonaparte commissioned to bring fresh drinking water to the quarter. Another massive one, the Fontaine de Mars, still exists in the seventh arrondissement.

Perhaps now is a good time, as we approach the center of Paris, to note that Napoleon III was not the only Bonaparte to inscribe his imprint on the City of Light. His uncle, **Napoleon Bonaparte**, is not, and never was, about to be overlooked. To this end, this imperial dynamo left permanent legacies of his event-filled reign in Paris. "I intend to make Paris the most beautiful capital in the world," he once said, and set about this with dizzying focus and energy. He thought in terms of monuments—such as his statue (dressed in a toga, like Caesar) at the top of the famed column in Place Vendôme, celebrating his victory at Austerlitz. Also, the iconic Arc de Triomphe as well as the Arc de Triomphe du Carrousel and the grand Fontaine du Palmier (also known as the Fontaine de la Victoire) in the Place du Châtelet.

Bonaparte redesigned whole sections of central Paris, from the National Assembly (the Palais Bourbon) to the Church of the Madeleine, and he began that new and imposing east-west artery, the Rue de Rivoli, starting from the Place de la Concorde—a major undertaking that his nephew, Napoleon III, would complete. And because Paris, despite the presence of the Seine, lacked water for its growing population, he dotted the city with imposing drinking fountains, including the Fontane du Palmier and the Fontaine de Mars.

There is so much else that Bonaparte bequeathed to Paris, including the Palais Brongniart, to house La Bourse (the Paris stock exchange), and the commencement of the northern wing of the Louvre (he filled the Louvre with his war loot, much of which had to be returned after Waterloo). He was responsible for the stone embankments around the Ile de la Cité and along portions of the Right and Left Banks. He also added the popular footbridge linking the Ile de la Cité and the Ile Saint-Louis, the stone Pont d'Austerlitz and Pont d'Iéna (both named in honor of his victories), and the iron footbridge, the Pont des Arts, linking the Louvre and the Institut de France.

For Bonaparte's beginnings in Paris, don't overlook the Ecole Militaire, with its traditional marching grounds on the Champ de Mars. And then, for a grand finale, visit the Little Giant's remains in Les Invalides. These were not returned to France until two decades after his death, due to fears that his very presence would prompt an uprising in his name. Remarkably, Queen Victoria requested a visit to Bonaparte's tomb during her visit to the Paris World Exposition of 1855. There, she paid her respects to England's great enemy while the organ played "God Save the Queen."

One of those heart-stopping moments in history.

Jardin de la Vallée Suisse (Jardin de la Nouvelle France). © M. McAuliffe

CHAPTER SEVENTEEN

~

Welcoming the World

The Paris World Exposition of 1855, which Queen Victoria so memorably visited, was the first in a long line of Paris expositions—many of which left significant vestiges long after the festivities disappeared.

The first of these Paris expositions, in 1855, was the outcome of Napoleon III's fascination with the very first world's fair, held in London in 1851. He was especially impressed with the Crystal Palace, a huge cast-iron structure whose walls and ceiling were filled with the greatest area of plate glass ever before seen. Light flooded through its ceiling and walls, amazing visitors and inspiring France's emperor to build such a structure of his own—one that would be even better.

Unfortunately, this attempt did not work quite as he had anticipated. The exposition's centerpiece, the Palais de l'Industrie—constructed between the Seine and the Champs-Elysées—was immense and sufficiently well-lit from the acres of glass in its barrel-vaulted roof. But to its detriment, it was sheathed in stone—as tradition and traditionalists required—and looked far heavier and certainly less exciting than the Crystal Palace. Despite this disappointment, the exposition did have its highlights, especially in the fine arts, which were housed in a temporary Palais des Beaux-Arts. This attracted a good deal of interest—especially those paintings that allowed spectators to view the dramatic contrast between Jean-Marie-Joseph Ingres (bastion of neoclassicism) and Eugène Delacroix (leader of the French Romantic school). But it was the arrival of Queen Victoria and Prince Albert (whom the emperor personally drove around Paris) that significantly raised the excitement level, drawing some 800,000 people to greet the royal couple's arrival. These crowds lined the entire length of the royals' crosstown arrival route, from the Gare de l'Est to the Château de Saint-Cloud.

In 1867, Napoleon III tried again. This time, more than ten million people pushed through the exposition's entrance gates at the Champ de Mars to view the latest industrial wonders, to partake of foods from other lands, and to revel in scenes of supposed lifestyles from far-off places (Arabs in a tent, Chinese women in a pagoda). Crowned heads decided that this was the place to be, and Baron Haussmann's reception at the Hôtel de Ville honoring King Wilhelm of Prussia and Czar Alexander of Russia was especially dazzling, with eight thousand guests illuminated by a sea of twinkling lights. "Before the queen that is Paris," the czar graciously observed, "we are no longer more than bourgeois."[1]

The year 1878 rose as a challenge to Paris, so recently defeated in the Franco-Prussian War and reduced to ashes during the Commune uprising that followed. The spacing of little more than a decade between the two previous French expositions meant that this was the year to do something, if anything, and national pride demanded a fitting celebration of France's recovery. The exhibition opened to the accompaniment of a national holiday, whose festivities Claude Monet captured on Rue Montorgueil, festooned with flags. As national pride required, it was the largest exposition held anywhere to date, stretching from the Champ de Mars to a Moorish-style palace constructed on the Place du Trocadéro, across the Seine. It was here, in the palace garden, that Bartholdi displayed *Liberty*'s colossal head, after being transported through the streets of Paris in a celebrational parade of its own.

Like its predecessor expositions, this one starred the newest inventions of the industrial age, including Alexander Graham Bell's telephone and Thomas Edison's phonograph. It also featured a dazzling display of electric lighting that illuminated the exhibition's two main concourses. All told, it was a grand success. But as it turned out, it would pale by comparison with the exposition that followed, the one of 1889 celebrating the centennial of the French Revolution.

The uncontested star of the 1889 Paris universal exposition was the **Eiffel Tower**, the outcome of a desire to feature something truly spectacular—an enormous tower that at three hundred meters (one thousand feet) would be higher than anything ever before built. Gustave Eiffel's subordinates first came up with the idea of an iron tower made of lattice-like girders splayed apart at the base and united at the top, with trusses joining the girders at regular intervals. The addition of enormous arches at the base of the four uprights completed the design, which looked a lot like bridge piers—something that

Eiffel's bridge-building team knew well. Aesthetics played little role in this tower's design: every feature was the product of careful computation based upon in-depth knowledge of stresses, weight, gravity, and wind forces. Even the tower's splayed legs were designed for wind resistance.

But there were other contenders for the thousand-foot behemoth, the most serious being the prominent architect Jules Bourdais, who was a staunch proponent of stone. Bourdais's proposed tower was to be built entirely of granite, constructed like a huge wedding cake in five successively smaller tiers. Each layer was to be swathed with decorative sculptures and columns, with an enormous electric-powered beacon at the top that could sweep nighttime Paris with its powerful beam.

Eiffel, by this time the well-established "wizard of iron," understood that metal better than anyone else on the planet and firmly believed that the age of stone was over. According to him, the medieval cathedral builders had pushed their medium about as far as it could go. To build higher and larger, it would be necessary to rely on iron and steel. A tower of one thousand feet could not be made of stone, he stated decisively, and certainly could not be built within the required time. After all, the Washington Monument, at half the size, had taken several decades to build. In addition, as Eiffel pointed out, Bourdais had not properly calculated wind resistance, nor had he planned any foundations for his stone monolith, whose base would rest directly on the ground.

Fortunately, Eiffel's proposed tower won the competition, and work began in 1887, first by going downward—an essential step that Bourdais, with all his refined asceticism, had overlooked. Since two of the tower's four feet stood on unstable land near the Seine, Eiffel probed fifty feet downward until he reached solid clay. He then sent huge sealed and electrically lit caissons seventy feet downward, well below water level, with workers breathing compressed air as they excavated (a system that Eiffel had successfully tested while building bridges). When all the enormous foundation blocks were in place and the equally huge anchoring bolts were inserted, Eiffel was ready to go up.

It was at this point that a wave of opposition emerged. A number of Paris's leading citizens were appalled by the idea of this "monstrosity" blighting their view. A Committee of Three Hundred quickly formed (one member for each meter of the tower's height), whose roster included some of the most celebrated artists, musicians, and writers in Paris. Led by Charles Garnier, of Opéra fame, the committee shot off a "Protestation des Artistes," to the exhibition's commissioner. As "enthusiastic lovers of beauty," they warned him in strongest possible terms against erecting this "useless and monstrous

Eiffel Tower." Such an eyesore, they predicted, would dishonor and devastate Paris, dominating it like a "gigantic black factory chimney."[2]

Eiffel dismissed these criticisms, retorting that beauty was not limited to richly decorated stone structures, and then set about to prove it. As with his previous structures, he first had drawings made of each of the tower's component parts, with the impact of gravity and wind on these parts precisely calculated. Then he had each one of these parts individually produced under his workshop's controlled conditions, including carefully drilled rivet holes, drilled to a tenth of a millimeter. These in turn were preassembled in manageable sections. At Eiffel's insistence, no drilling or adaptation was allowed on-site; if a part was defective, it was sent back to his workshop in Levallois-Perret, on the northwest outskirts of Paris. In all, some eighteen thousand prefabricated sections were eventually delivered to the tower site, forming a sort of gigantic Erector set—the classic children's toy that in fact was eventually created based on Eiffel's famed methods.

As the tower went up, the criticism continued—from fearmongers who predicted that the structure would collapse as well as from those who detested the tower's aesthetics. Yet after completing his mammoth undertaking in time for the exposition's opening in May 1889, Eiffel had the pleasure of seeing visitors surge up the steep staircases even before the elevators were working. Around two million people visited the tower during the exposition, and even some of the protesting artists were won over. The Eiffel Tower was the undisputed star of the exposition, the newest wonder of the world.

Auguste Rodin took time out from his sculpting to ride the tower's elevators to the first platform, where he joined Camille Claudel and others for lunch. Edmond de Goncourt, a staunch traditionalist who detested the tower, at last reluctantly agreed to join friends, including Zola, for dinner there. Taking the elevator up, Goncourt felt seasick, but once on the platform, he was struck by the view. It was a clear July evening, and he could fully take in the enormity of Paris, with "the steep, jagged silhouette of Montmartre" on the horizon, "looking in the dusky sky like an illuminated ruin." Rather than return by elevator, he gamely chose to go by foot. It turned out to be a somewhat terrifying experience. "One feels," he carefully reported afterward, "like an ant coming down the rigging of a man-of-war, rigging which has turned to iron."[3]

Eiffel never viewed his tower so poetically, but one senses that he might have been pleased by Goncourt's response.

The year 1900, signaling the start of a new century, prompted Parisians to put the ugliness of the Dreyfus Affair behind them and once more welcome the world to their door. To do this, the city undertook an enormous task, not only constructing major edifices for the exposition itself—including the Grand Palais and the Petit Palais, along with the spectacular Pont Alexandre III that linked them with the rest of the exposition across the Seine—but it also undertook a major new transportation network for the expected crowds. This meant building the present Gare de Lyon, including its famous clock tower and its equally famous restaurant, Le Train Bleu, and erecting the Gare d'Orsay (now the Musée d'Orsay) on the Left Bank site of the Palais d'Orsay, which had burned during the Commune. It meant adding a new spur to the Petite Ceinture, the passenger and freight railroad circling the city. And, in the most ambitious and forward-looking project of all, it meant digging an underground subway, the first stretch of the new Métro (now Line 1).

Not surprisingly, much of this huge undertaking remained unfinished on the exposition's opening day. Still, when everything was at last finished, the results were suitably impressive, and the crowds indeed came. The Petite Ceinture boosted its ridership that year to some forty million passengers, while the Métro carried some seventeen million passengers, many of them to points near the fairgrounds. Fifty million visitors swarmed into the exposition, almost half of them from France. Of these, nearly a million visited the star of the previous French exposition, the Eiffel Tower, which had survived various ill-conceived plans for its modification, including one that envisioned turning it into a Palace of Electricity and Engineering, with an enormous iron-and-glass structure added to its base.

Of course the Eiffel Tower has remained, despite efforts to dismantle it once its twenty-year permit expired. Gustave Eiffel always believed that his tower offered great possibilities for scientific research, and by 1908 it was proving valuable for radio telegraphy. The French army was able to use it to establish contact with its bases throughout France as well as with foreign destinations of interest, most notably Berlin. One of the Eiffel Tower's most famous exploits was the early 1917 interception of a message between Berlin and Spain that led to the identification and conviction of Mata Hari as a spy. She was executed by firing squad later that year.

⌒

Other vestiges of that 1900 Paris exposition remain on both sides of the Seine, notably the Petit Palais and Grand Palais, as well as the Gare d'Orsay, now the famed Musée d'Orsay.

The **Musée d'Orsay**, once a train station and, since 1986, a fabulously successful conversion to an art museum, houses works of art dating from where the Louvre leaves off, in the mid-1800s, and takes its collections through the early twentieth century, where the Centre Pompidou then takes over. Mobs regularly head for the museum's famed fifth floor, or upper level, where a treasure-house of Impressionist works are displayed, including all the Monet landscapes and Degas ballerinas that you could possibly wish.

This treasure trove includes Edouard Manet's scandal-causing *Le Déjeuner sur l'herbe* (*Luncheon on the Grass*), which has gone down in history for the pandemonium it created at the 1863 Salon (the official annual art exhibition of Paris's Académie des Beaux-Arts). The Salon famously rejected it, leading to an exhibition of this and other rejected works known as the Salon des Refusés. There, Manet's *Le Déjeuner sur l'herbe* quickly became a *succès de scandale*. After all, central to the painting is a completely unclothed young woman, with another in the background who is emerging from a dip in the pond, while two completely clothed young men surround the one woman and the luncheon in question. Not only are the young men clothed, but they are clothed in modern dress rather than in Grecian togas—which would have been far more acceptable to the largely bourgeois and prudish audience that found Manet's subject matter indecent and shocking, a sure sign of the decline of civilization. Not so, say today's viewers, and this remarkable painting has found its audience in the twentieth and twenty-first centuries. One of the painting's most obsessive viewers was Pablo Picasso, who created one hundred and forty drawings and twenty-seven paintings based on *Le Déjeuner sur l'herbe*, repeatedly returning to Manet and his vision.

But do not overlook the building's glorious interior, including its enormous clocks, especially the two exterior-facing ones, which you can view up close from the upper level. And in particular, do not overlook the treasures stashed downstairs, from the early years of the museum's collections. These include James McNeill Whistler's *Arrangement in Grey and Black No. 1*, more familiarly known as *Whistler's Mother*, and Edouard Manet's *Olympia*.

Manet's goal was to capture reality with a paintbrush, and two years after *Le Déjeuner sur l'herbe* he once again created an uproar with *Olympia*, a decidedly unromantic depiction of a cool and collected courtesan of Manet's own times. There is nothing respectable about Manet's courtesan: she is not partially concealed with carefully arranged drapery, nor is her direct gaze shielded from the viewer. She does not reference antiquity, nor is she surrounded by clouds and cherubs or depicted stepping delicately into pristine waters among flowers and butterflies. Instead, she calmly—and with an "I've seen everything" expression—awaits her client. In viewing Manet's worldly courtesan, startled female members of the ever-so-proper bourgeoisie would have realized, to their discomfort, that they had just seen the real thing.

Several years after Manet's death, his good friend Claude Monet set about raising the money to give *Olympia* to France, to hang in the Louvre. This is a painting, Monet wrote to the minister of public instruction, "in which [Manet] is seen at the height of his glorious struggle, master of his vision and of his craft." It was "unacceptable that such a work should not have its place in our national collections."[4] The Louvre turned it down, but the Musée du Luxembourg accepted it until the Louvre at length opened its doors—on the order of Georges Clemenceau, who by then was prime minister of France. Thanks to Monet and his good friend Clemenceau, *Olympia* did not leave France for America and its deep-pocketed collectors, as Monet feared, but now hangs in the Musée d'Orsay.

Claude Monet's cycle of *Water Lilies* (Nymphéas), perhaps his most famous paintings, are located just across the Seine in the **Musée de l'Orangerie**, a building that Napoleon III originally built to store the Tuileries Gardens' citrus trees during the winter. It now houses Impressionist and post-Impressionist art as well as the Jean Walter and Paul Guillaume collection of modern art, starring works by Chaïm Soutine and Amedeo Modigliani. But the museum's biggest draw remains the two oval rooms that contain Monet's *Water Lilies*, which the painter gave to France following World War I.

World War I (known in France as the Great War) had proved a ghastly bloodbath for all concerned, especially for France. Almost one and one half million French died in the war, with three million more wounded, many so severely that they would not be able to work or function normally again. This, out of a pre-war population of forty million. The numbers were shattering; the reality was even worse. Much of the northern third of France had been laid waste, and the nation's treasury had reached rock bottom, with staggering war debts as well. After Armistice, which Paris deliriously celebrated for three days straight, Claude Monet wrote his friend Clemenceau to offer two of what he called his *Grandes Décorations* (later known as his *Water Lilies*) to France. "It's little enough," he said, "but it's the only way I have of taking part in the victory."[5] It was, as their mutual friend and art critic Gustave Geffroy commented, as if Monet had offered a "bouquet of flowers to honour victory in war and the conquest of peace."[6]

By this time Clemenceau, as prime minister of France, had won the war for his nation and was now launched in the equally fraught process of winning the peace. But six days after receiving Monet's offer, Clemenceau dropped everything and went with Geffroy to Giverny to make his choice. At this visit, Clemenceau seems to have worked successfully to increase the number of canvases, but Monet now was reluctant to let any of them go. Thus began a long affair in which Clemenceau heroically worked to obtain Monet's water lily panels for the nation and, at the same time, valiantly sought to convince his longtime friend to undergo a much-needed operation to save his eyesight before it was too late.

Monet was by this time elderly, crotchety, and difficult to deal with, but Clemenceau (a doctor by training) at last convinced him to have the needed operation as well as give his water lilies to the nation, to be housed in the Orangerie. The Orangerie provided a perfect fit, especially as it could accommodate Monet's demand for an oval room. By the end, Monet even upped the number of donated panels from twelve to eighteen, so long as they could be hung in two oval rooms rather than one. This was in the building's basement, and Monet was never satisfied with the results, but in recent years, the Orangerie has completely redesigned the rooms, to much better effect. The crowds who pour in here certainly seem to agree.

Two other vestiges of the 1900 Paris exposition are the gorgeous Grand Palais and its smaller but still magnificent sibling, the Petit Palais. These were built on the site of Napoleon III's huge Palais de l'Industrie, from 1855, which served a variety of functions until it was demolished before the 1900 exposition, making way for its successors. The Grand Palais continues to serve as a venue for blockbuster exhibitions, while the **Petit Palais**, built in the Beaux-Arts style like its sibling, has become a museum—most fittingly the city's **Musée des Beaux-Arts**.

This wedding cake of a building, gorgeous inside and out (with its especially admirable wrought-iron circular staircases), houses an eclectic collection of art and artifacts, donations to the city of Paris from evidently well-to-do residents. These include a stunning collection of Art Nouveau ceramics (some of them life-size) and some fine examples of Art Nouveau jewelry and furnishings, where you will find contributions by Hector Guimard, of Métro fame. In addition, there is a wide range of other collections, many focusing on ancient Greece or Rome.

Keeping to the nineteenth century, I always enjoy Georges Clairin's painting of Sarah Bernhardt (one of the museum's prize possessions), which shows her leaning provocatively back into her divan, Russian wolfhound at her feet, and eyeing the viewer with what looks like a dare. Remember that Bernhardt's taste in men as well as in furnishings ran to the luxurious.

Among her escorts and lovers (over many years of escorts and lovers) was Charles Haas, a sophisticated and renowned man about town who would in time serve as a model for Proust's Charles Swann (much as Bernhardt would serve as an inspiration for Proust's actor Berma). Proust was not yet born when their affair took place, but it must have rattled the rafters at the time, given the numerous raunchy summonses that Bernhardt issued to entice Haas, including a sketch of a four-poster bed beneath which she dashed off the words, "Come! Come!! Come!!!"[7]

Hass came for a time, but Bernhardt may have amounted to little more than a pleasant diversion for this man who had scores of beautiful women vying for him. Their affair soon ended, with neither party brokenhearted. Still, although neither seems to have regarded it as an affair to remember, they remained friends until Haas's death.

While at the Petit Palais, I always look for Monet's *Soleil couchant sur la Seine à Lavacourt* (*Sun setting on the Seine at Lavacourt*), a twin to his earlier and more famous *Impression, soleil levant* (*Impression, sunrise*), which resides just a few miles to the west, in the Musée Marmottan. I also have a soft spot for the Petit Palais' *Trois Baigneuses*, a small oil painting by Paul Cézanne that served as an inspiration for Henri Matisse, who bought it back in the days when he was completely impoverished, with no hope in sight. His wife, Amélie, understanding the painting's importance to him, let him pawn a treasured ring to buy it. Many years later, when he gave *Trois Baigneuses* to the city of Paris, he said that it had "supported him morally at critical moments in my venture as an artist; I have drawn from it my faith and my perseverance."[8]

The exposition of 1900 came at an especially low point for Matisse. Its jury had turned down his one submission for its contemporary painting section, and he was reduced to taking a job gilding a kilometer-long swag of laurel leaves for the Grand Palais. Even this job did not last very long, for after three weeks his resentment boiled over and he was fired for insubordinate behavior.

Swags of similar gilded leaves can still be seen in the beautiful courtyard of the Petit Palais, a charming garden around a pool, designed to provide rest and refreshment to weary sightseers from the time of the 1900 exposition to the present. One of my favorite features here is a three-dimensional take on the coat of arms of the city of Paris, featuring its boat. Paris has long had its own coat of arms, going back to the thirteenth century.[9] Its central figure is a boat riding the waves, with a motto—in Latin—that lets the world know that Paris (and the boat symbolizing her) may encounter rough sailing, but will not sink. You can see versions of this boat everywhere in Paris, from

Métro stops to trash receptacles. There are some fine ones at Sacré-Coeur and the Hôtel de Ville, but this is probably the most dramatic and ornate.

⁓

Connecting the Grand Palais and the Petit Palais with the Esplanade des Invalides is the **Pont Alexandre III**—a magnificently ornate Beaux-Arts bridge that served as part of the grand design for the huge 1900 Paris exposition. By that time it had also performed its primary function, highlighting a major piece of diplomacy between France and Russia. Named after the Russian czar Alexander III, the bridge provided a symbolic affirmation of the Franco-Russian Alliance that the French had recently pulled off—signaling that France no longer was on its own in the increasingly dangerous arena of international power politics.

The czar's ceremonial arrival in Paris in late 1896 was a huge event, witnessed by nearly a million onlookers, including teen-aged Julie Manet, who had been orphaned the previous year by the unexpected death of her mother, the Impressionist painter Berthe Morisot—preceded, only three years before, by the death of Julie's father, Eugène Manet, brother of painter Edouard Manet. Coming from such a distinguished artistic family, it was no wonder that Julie's guardians were the Morisot-Manet family's close friends, Pierre-Auguste Renoir and Edgar Degas, as well as the poet Stéphane Mallarmé. (Neither Renoir nor Degas enjoyed each other's company, but they were united in their dedication to Berthe Morisot and to protecting young Julie.)

Julie, who kept a diary, noted the czar's arrival in Paris proceeded by a suitably grand procession, including hussars "all in blue and mounted on lovely white horses," and turbaned Algerian troopers dressed "in the most delicious tones of almond green, red, yellow, with greatcoats which flapped in the wind, riding ravishing Arab steeds." When the imperial carriage at last appeared, with the czarina dressed in white, Julie initially had little to say about the czar, although she would later report that he was blond and "looked very young," while the czarina "looked rather stiff and had a big nose." Julie snickered considerably, though, at the sight of the president of the Republic, Félix Faure, who by her account was sitting uncomfortably on the carriage's folding seat, where he seemed "very embarrassed to be where a child is usually seated," with his knees reaching his chin.[10]

The following day came the ceremonial laying of the cornerstone of the bridge dedicated to the current czar's father, Alexander III, the reactionary ruler under whom the Franco-Russian Alliance had been so lengthily negotiated. Immediately afterward, a barge appeared, from which sixteen young girls dressed in white descended to present the czarina with a silver vase overflowing with orchids. France was doing this event up properly, and rightly so, for with the Franco-Russian Alliance, France could boast (in the words of poet François Coppée) that it now held "the center of Europe between the two jaws of a vise. At the first insult, we will tighten that vise."[11]

The Pont Alexandre III was the visible symbol of that deeply nationalist spirit, which would soon be tested in the new century's first world war.

Just around the corner from the Petit Palais and Grand Palais, on Cours-la-Reine at Avenue Franklin D. Roosevelt, is an unexpected delight, the **Vallée Suisse** (now unimaginatively called the Jardin de la Nouvelle France). First you may notice a strange sculpture, which turns out to be a tribute to the nineteenth-century poet Alfred de Musset. Then you will see some steps that disappear down into rocks and greenery. These in turn lead into a delightful little world of grottoes, water, and enveloping wilderness. Who could have imagined such an unexpected treasure in such imposing surroundings! There is a pond, a waterfall, and a little footbridge, all wrapped in an atmosphere of enchantment. This romantic aura may continue even after you emerge, for you may well encounter a small wedding party, one of many that stage their photo shoots here.

The nearby Champs-Elysées itself, for the stretch from the Place de la Concord to the Rond-Point, is a kind of extended garden, fronting the French president's abode, the Palais de l'Elysée. Along the way you will pass that longtime presence, the elegant restaurant Laurent, where many celebrities have dined over the years—including George Gershwin, who was taking what he called a working vacation in Paris while composing his "orchestral ballet" that he would eventually title *An American in Paris*.

A nice guy, as his many friends agreed. Also an intense guy, who managed to cram more into a twenty-four-hour day than most people would ever care to consider. In Paris, where he and his brother and collaborator, Ira, arrived at the Gare Saint-Lazare with their sister, Frances, the social whirl began immediately. A crush of visitors constantly surrounded George, vying for his attention and feting him all over town. One of the biggest bashes was the one that Elsa Maxwell (the indomitable "hostess with the mostest") gave for him at the restaurant Laurent, following the European premier of his Concerto in F. There, he hobnobbed with a raft of celebrities, including Cole Porter, with whom he played piano until late in the night while Frances (known as Frankie) sang.

The date was 1928, and with the Roaring Twenties (or *Les Années folles*, as the French called them) in full swing, anything still seemed possible.

The **Champs-Elysées** was not always an elegant thoroughfare. Back in the early years of the Second Empire, around the middle of the nineteenth century, the Champs-Elysées was only a dusty road between the Place de la Concord and the Rond-Point, although it had been planted with lawns and trees. Beyond, the Arc de Triomphe simply marked l'Etoile, one of the entrances through the Farmers-General toll wall, while beyond this wall stretched a ring of rural communes, themselves encircled, or in some cases even bisected, by the Thiers fortifications.

It was Baron Haussmann who decided to smarten up the forty-six-acre strip from the Place de la Concorde to Rond-Point, renovating it with theaters, cafés, and restaurants, and creating enticing bowers of "choice trees and shrubs, and circular beds of plants and flowers," complete with fountains "to freshen the air with their gushing water."[12]

Now, footsore tourists tramp along this stretch, barely noticing their surroundings: the glittering lineup of stores beyond Rond-Point beckons. But do not overlook the well-tended landscape garden that here surrounds the broad Champs-Elysées, providing a much-needed respite between the Place de la Concorde and the commercial district that lies ahead.

Returning to the Seine, don't overlook the huge **Zouave statue** on the **Pont de l'Alma**, near the copy of the Statue of Liberty's torch in the Place de l'Alma, the latter having become an informal memorial to Princess Diana, who met her death nearby.

Originally there were four statues lining the bridge, twenty-foot sculptures of soldiers erected on stone foundations attached to the bridge, one of which—the most beloved—was of a Zouave, a colonial soldier in full dress and cape, who staunchly remains, even though the bridge has been rebuilt above him. Over the years he has served as an informal water level gauge, showing how high the Seine is rising in the months of late winter and early spring. (Look carefully and you may glimpse another water level marker farther upstream, on the Pont Neuf.)

Despite efforts to tame the Seine over the years, including raising the walls surrounding it and channeling and damming the river's tributaries, flooding has been more severe of late, prompting flood alerts and concerns about the impact of climate change. Still, thankfully, no flooding in the past century has been as bad as that granddaddy of Seine floods in 1910, when

The Zouave, Pont de l'Alma. © J. McAuliffe

the river crested at almost twenty-eight feet above its normal level and the water reached the Zouave's neck.

～

Just beyond the Pont de l'Alma, other remnants of Paris world expositions remain, from the Palais de Tokyo to the enormous Palais de Chaillot, which dramatically faces the Eiffel Tower from its hill across the river. The Palais de Tokyo, originally part of the 1937 world's fair (or International Exhibition of Arts and Technology, as it was called), is now the home (in its west wing) of a museum dedicated to temporary exhibitions of contemporary art and, in its east wing, the Museum of Modern Art of the City of Paris. Between the two wings is a terrace with a view of the Seine that is a lovely secret for those who know of it. Stop here for a snack or lunch break, or brown-bag it and eat on the steps. This is where Parisians love to meet, and you should consider doing likewise.

I have always enjoyed the **Museum of Modern Art of Paris**, in part because it is off the beaten track for most tourists, but also because of its riches. Chief among these is Raoul Dufy's *La Fée Electricité*, a massive and beautiful mural commissioned as part of the 1937 world's fair that surrounds the viewer in a room of its own. I also head for the two wonderful Matisse versions of *La Danse* (the third and final one now hangs in the Barnes Foundation in Philadelphia). There is a terrific Modigliani (*Femme aux yeux bleus*), and several works by Chagall, including a haunting *Le Rêve*. And among the museum's many Picassos, I am especially drawn to *Evocation*, or *L'enterrement de Casagemas*, a very early work that young Picasso painted after the suicide of his friend Carlos Casagemas, shortly after the two young men arrived in Paris in 1900.

The two, along with a third friend, had originally roomed in a scabby Montmartre studio already inhabited by three young women, one of whom, Germaine Gargallo, had earlier acquired and casually disposed of a husband. Casagemas, who was young and impressionable, fell passionately in love with Germaine, but she merely shrugged. After Picasso and Casagemas returned to Barcelona that Christmas, Casagemas went back to Paris, in the hope of changing Germaine's mind. Despite his pleas and repeated proposals of marriage, Germaine remained indifferent, and so finally, Casagemas announced that he was going to return home. To celebrate this decision, he invited Germaine and the rest of the gang to a dinner at a nearby hangout, to which everyone—looking forward to a free meal—enthusiastically agreed.

As it turned out, the entertainment turned out to be quite different from what anyone had expected. Casagemas seemed unusually nervous that evening, giving an edge to the proceedings. Still, all was well until, after rising to give a brief speech, Casagemas suddenly took out a pistol from his pocket and aimed it directly at Germaine. She promptly dived under the table and hid while Casagemas fired, crying "This is for you!" She fainted and slid motionless to the floor. Thinking that he had killed her, Casagemas then cried, "And this is for me!" and shot himself in the head.

It was ghastly. Germaine survived unharmed, but Casagemas died later that night at a nearby hospital. Later, his grieving friends buried him in Montmartre Cemetery—a scene that Picasso evoked in this painting. He had not been present for the shocking event, but its impact on him was enormous. He was stunned. And for the next several years the tragic specter of Casagemas would haunt him.

Just across the Avenue du Président-Wilson from the Palais de Tokyo is the **Palais Galliera**, a nineteenth-century neo-Renaissance palace built for a duchess to display her art collection (in a nod to the new technology, the stone superstructure is undergirded by an iron frame constructed by Eiffel's firm). The mansion is now, after a complicated history, the Musée de la Mode de la Ville de Paris, a museum dedicated to the history of fashion—an appropriate subject for the Ville de Paris. Keep an eye out for its exhibitions, some of which are huge draws.

For those who love the world of fashion, a visit here is a must. Even those with little interest in French couture may find the mansion itself, and especially its large courtyard garden, an off-the-beaten-path discovery. The garden, the attractive **Square du Palais Galliera** (or Square Brignole-Galliera), is easily accessible from Avenue du Président-Wilson and is open to the public—which is generally small in numbers, but appreciative.

Just around the corner from the Palais Galliera is yet another museum, one that was built for the purpose: the **Musée Guimet**, or the Musée National des Arts Asiatiques-Guimet. This is the outcome of the well-focused collecting of Emile Etienne Guimet, a nineteenth-century industrialist who traveled extensively in the Far East. The museum, which he built to house his extensive collections, first opened in 1889, complementing the 1889 Paris world exposition, and now contains not only Guimet's own collection but that of the Louvre's Asian art department, vastly expanding the Guimet's holdings.

Recently redesigned in a striking modern presentation, the Musée Guimet's stunning main floor beckons with lofty ceilings and open spaces anchored by an enormous twelfth-century sculpture from Preah Khan, Angkor, called *Chaussée des Géants* (*Road of the Giants*). After exploring this floor, return to the entry where, on each side, dramatic double staircases lead upward to more riches, culminating with a panoramic view of nearby Paris from the museum's rotunda. This is a museum devoted to the best of the best in Asian art, and the works it has chosen to exhibit are not only unusual (such as costumes from the Peking Opera) but also exquisite. The lighting is excellent, and exhibits are given plenty of space to breathe, allowing the visitor room to walk around, study, and admire in a peaceful atmosphere.

From the Musée Guimet, it is but a short walk around the corner to the Japanese garden and tea pavilion of the neighboring **Hôtel d'Heidelbach**, which is annexed to the Musée Guimet and included in the Musée Guimet's admission ticket. The Hôtel d'Heidelbach, which holds the collection of the wealthy collector who once lived here, has a small but choice exhibit of Japanese furnishings and tea services as well as Chinese artifacts, presented as they would appear in a Buddhist temple. But the star of the Heidelbach has always been the Japanese garden and tea pavilion at the rear, now reopened after a lengthy renovation.

Still a lovely, peaceful spot in the midst of the city, this Japanese garden may nonetheless disappoint visitors who have seen it before its renovation. The water, which provided special enchantment, has disappeared, leaving a Japanese *jardin sec*, or dry garden—entirely valid, but somehow more part of the urban fabric that surrounds it than an oasis from it. One senses, from the museum's new description, that the motivating factor behind this change was to make the garden and its teahouse more accessible to larger groups of people (such as conferences), who now need not worry about getting their toes wet as they navigate the garden's stony surface.

One sighs a bit for the past, but the present garden still is quite lovely. Despite the changes, it remains a peaceful and tranquil retreat from the everyday world.

Americans seem to have been world travelers from the outset, and among them were several of the new nation's Founding Fathers, who received a warm welcome in Paris. Benjamin Franklin arrived first and worked for years to obtain French recognition and assistance to the American colonies in their war against England. John Adams joined him and signed the final peace treaty here with him. Thomas Jefferson arrived last, as United States Minister to France. All fell in love with Paris, where you can find a number of statues and plaques commemorating America's Founding Fathers, especially Washington, Jefferson, and Franklin. You may also notice major avenues as well as Métro stops named for American presidents (Avenue Franklin-D.-Roosevelt, Avenue du Président-Wilson, and Avenue du Président-Kennedy).

Given France's role in helping the American colonies during their revolution, it is not surprising that there are a number of memorials to the Founding Fathers here. Jefferson receives a modern rendition at the Passerelle Léopold-Sédard-Senghor (formerly the Passerelle Solférino), while Franklin has a friendly-looking statue in the appropriately named Square de Yorktown, just off the Place du Trocadéro. Washington is rendered nobly mounted on horseback in the middle of Place d'Iéna, and if you look carefully, you will also find two plaques commemorating highlights in the French-American alliance that won America's independence: the Hôtel d'York (56 Rue Jacob), where the peace treaty with Britain was signed, and the magnificent Hôtel de Crillon in the Place de la Concorde, where Benjamin Franklin and two other Americans (Silas Deane and Arthur Lee) signed that all-important treaty of friendship, commerce, and alliance with France.

But my favorite is a statue of Washington and Lafayette, a work by the Statue of Liberty's sculptor, Frédéric-Auguste Bartholdi. This wonderful sculpture, which beautifully captures the two men's friendship, is located just north of the Musée Guimet in the **Place des Etats-Unis**. A memorial in the same little park pays tribute to the Lafayette Escadrille, largely made up of American volunteer fighter pilots during World War I.

Fittingly, an American flag always flies over Lafayette's grave in Paris's Picpus Cemetery (35 Rue de Picpus, 12th).[13]

Back to world's fairs, via Avenue du Président-Wilson, which brings us to the Palais de Chaillot—an overblown structure dating (like the nearby Palais de Tokyo) from the 1937 world's fair. Hitler famously posed here in 1940, after the Nazis occupied Paris—something that is enough to repel many folks from this site. Yet inside this gargantuan building is a relatively new and certainly worthy destination—unknown or at least overlooked by tourists: the **Cité de l'Architecture et du Patrimoine**. This enormous and fascinating museum is divided into two parts: a Museum of French Monuments, the heir of Alexandre Lenoir's original vision back in 1795, and a Gallery of Modern and Contemporary Architecture. Take your pick—anything from the twelfth century to the present day, whether original elements or scale replicas of stained-glass and medieval building elements, or the presentation of a number of seminal buildings from 1850 to the present, including work by Gustave Eiffel and Le Corbusier.

Outside, there remains that irresistible view of the Eiffel Tower, which is where you will probably be drawn next.

Eiffel Tower from Square d'Ajaccio. © J. McAuliffe

CHAPTER EIGHTEEN

~

Eiffel Tower and Beyond

Some people stand at the center of the Eiffel Tower's four legs and look up—a dizzying prospect. Just as dizzying is a ride by elevator to the top. Or you could choose, as Guy de Maupassant so famously did, to eat lunch at the tower's restaurant on a daily basis, because that was one of the few places in Paris where he could sit and not actually see the tower he so adamantly detested.[1]

If there are any who today dislike the tower, they wisely remain silent. It has become an icon of Paris, and even those returning to Paris after multiple stays find a thrill in seeing their first glimpse of the tower from their taxi or bus window. Still, I confess that I prefer to see it from a distance, well apart from the madding (and maddening) crowds. One of the best of these locations is the wonderful Seine-side walk, the **Parc Rives de Seine**, formerly the Pompidou Expressway, which hugs the river along its right bank. This provides walkers and bikers with an auto-free route all the way from the Pont de Sully in the east to the Pont Neuf and beyond, with unobstructed views of the Ile Saint-Louis and the Ile de la Cité en route. After the former expressway takes a dive under the city streets near the Pont Neuf, there still is a walkway to follow, along which the Eiffel Tower poses ever more enticingly.

The Pont Alexandre III also offers wonderful views of the Eiffel Tower, framed by the bridge's ornate lamps, while one of my favorite spots to view the tower is the lovely and generally overlooked garden adjacent to Les Invalides, the **Square d'Ajaccio** (formerly the Square des Invalides). Located at the northeast of Les Invalides, it was created as a pendant to another pocket park on Les Invalides' northwest corner, the Square Santiago-du-Chili. Originally designed by Haussmann's renowned director of parks and public works, Adolphe Alphand, the Square d'Ajaccio has recently undergone a much-needed renovation, bringing it closer to the way it looked when it was created, during the Second Empire.

The years have rewarded it with massive specimen trees, including chestnuts, plane trees, and a large magnolia, which shelter the flower beds below. A lovely place to rest and recharge.

From here it is but a short walk along the Esplanade des Invalides to the **Musée Rodin** and its renowned sculpture gardens, located in the buildings and grounds of the former Hôtel Biron.

This mansion has a noble past, having been designed, at least in part, by Ange-Jacques Gabriel, the architect of the Petit Trianon and the palatial residences flanking the northern entrance to the Place de la Concorde. It acquired its name from an early owner, the Duc de Biron, who was responsible for its extensive gardens. Unfortunately, the sisters of the Sacred Heart, into whose hands it eventually passed, ran a tough-minded boarding school for girls here and banished all signs of luxury, including hot water and heat. They also sold off the mansion's paneling, its huge wall mirrors, and its painted decorations, and they let the gardens go to ruin. Following the separation of church and state in France in 1905, neither the school nor the convent survived, and the mansion and its extensive grounds came under the charge of the government, which offered portions of it for rent at attractively low prices.

Henri Matisse now moved his studio and family here but stayed for little more than a year. The clamor of unwanted visitors pushed him from Paris—first, to the suburb of Issy-les-Moulineaux, then to Nice. Young Jean Cocteau on the other hand, being not troubled with unwanted visitors, wandered in at about the same time as Matisse and fell in love with the place. It was a "realm from a Perrault fairy tale," he wrote, bordered by romantically tangled gardens that were perfect for fêtes and poetry readings. Brambles and bushes overran "a little virgin forest, an impenetrable vegetable chaos." Even the tall windows to Cocteau's room were impeded by a thick carpet of forget-me-nots; once opened, they revealed "a veritable tunnel of greenery, leading to the unknown"[2]—much like the magic wood that would appear in Cocteau's classic 1946 film *La Belle et la Bête*.

Isadora Duncan also found her way to the Hôtel Biron, renting a long gallery there that she used for dance rehearsals. But it was Auguste Rodin who was to have the biggest impact on the derelict mansion. Early on, Rodin's friend, the poet Rainer Maria Rilke, discovered the property, took up residence, and told Rodin about it. After one look at the romantically run-down mansion, Rodin immediately rented the large ground-floor rooms facing the garden. He never lived there, but it was his favorite studio, where he loved to work and receive visitors.

Then, in 1909—much to Rodin's dismay—the government put his idyllic Hôtel Biron up for sale. The mansion's overgrown but glorious grounds were to be divided into forty-five lots, with a total price tag of more than five million francs. Rodin was devastated. After contemplating his alternatives, he contacted a deputy in the National Assembly to propose that he give all of his sculptures and drawings, as well as his by now extensive and valuable collection of antiquities, to the state. In return for this bequest, the state would keep the Hôtel as a Rodin museum and allow him to remain there for the rest of his life.

Astonishingly, no one jumped to accept Rodin's offer, and the government ordered all of the building's occupants to leave. Rodin's stay in this paradise looked like it was coming to a close. Fortunately, though, government bureaucracy moves slowly, especially when distracted by a major war, and by 1916, with Rodin's health declining, the state now found time amid the chaos of World War I to ensure the transfer of his massive donation to France—including the provision that the Hôtel Biron would henceforth be called the Musée Rodin. Unfortunately, there were some who opposed the idea, on the grounds that France had no need for another museum, and certainly not one that desecrated the memory of the Convent of the Sacré-Coeur, which had occupied the Hôtel Biron prior to the convent's expulsion. Most opposition, though, focused on the nature of Rodin's art, which his critics described as decadent, vulgar, and "tending toward the pornographic."[3]

Fortunately, when the final vote was taken, the bequest was overwhelmingly approved, and the former Hôtel Biron now houses the Musée Rodin and it extensive sculpture garden. The mansion itself, with its gorgeous staircase and famous sculptures, including *The Walking Man*, *The Kiss*, and a collection of works by Camille Claudel, as well as Rodin's private art collection (including works by Van Gogh, Monet, and Renoir), is a lovely place to browse on a quiet day. But it is the garden that I love the most, whether it is for such famous sculptures as *The Thinker*, *The Gates of Hell* (from which *The Thinker* is taken), *The Burghers of Calais*, and Rodin's magisterial sculpture of *Balzac*, or for its romantic beauty. This is at its peak in spring through autumn, but even in winter the garden here is a wonderful place.

The grounds include a small outdoor garden restaurant, although many simply bring their own edibles to consume in quiet nooks on the grounds. Here the tangled garden of Cocteau's time has been tamed but not snuffed out. Order has its demands, as can be seen from the manicured green lawns and perfectly clipped hedges, but paths wander among trees and flowering bushes that soften the landscape. From the garden's far end is a perfect spot from where to look back across a round pool and lawn to the mansion.

Rodin loved it here, and one can easily see why.

Since we are in the realm of sculptors and sculptures, it seems fitting to stop at the nearby **Musée Maillol**, a delightful small museum dedicated to the work of Aristide Maillol. You can find a large collection of his sculptures across the Seine, in the Jardin du Carrousel, but this is the museum that his model and muse, Dina Vierny, established to exhibit the full range of Maillol's work.

Maillol had not always been a sculptor. Born in the south of France in 1861, he moved to Paris at age twenty to become a painter, eventually trying his hand at ceramics and tapestry design as well. Only after the turn of the century did he return full-time to sculpture; but breaking with Rodin as well as traditional Beaux-Arts sculptors, he created a series of serene, almost abstract female nudes—expressionless or even headless creatures whose smooth sensual roundness and classical restraint revolutionized twentieth-century sculpture. Dina Vierny, who also modeled for Pierre Bonnard, Raoul Dufy, and Henri Matisse, was Maillol's flesh-and-blood realization of the perfect female figure, and their collaboration during the last decade of his life prompted a resurgence of his career.

Vierny risked her life during the German Occupation of France by helping other Jews escape the country, leading them over a long and difficult escape route across the Pyrenees. After the war and Maillol's death, Vierny showed this same courageous spirit in establishing her own Paris art gallery, promoting Maillol and other contemporary artists she deemed worthy of public attention.

Early on, as Vierny was building both her gallery and private collection, she made the gift of Maillol sculptures to the Tuileries Gardens that is now displayed in the adjacent Jardin du Carrousel, where they comprise a kind of "Musée Maillol en plein air." This was just a start, for she had already decided to establish a museum that would exhibit Maillol's work, in addition to displaying her own collection.

Musée Rodin (Hôtel Biron). © M. McAuliffe

Vierny began by acquiring the building on Rue de Grenelle formerly inhabited by the Convent des Récollettes, which in turn is fronted (on a thin strip of land that the nuns reluctantly ceded to the city) by the monumental eighteenth-century Fountain of the Four Seasons—a striking structure that looks like the façade of a palace but instead is a well-disguised public utility, originally built to bring water to the neighborhood. Little by little, Vierny was able to purchase the far-more-modest edifice housing the former convent, which in 1995 became the Musée Maillol.

Architecturally, the museum is a lovely conglomeration of the old and the new, which serves as a backdrop to Maillol's own work as well as to special exhibitions that are regularly held there. Enter alongside the glorious Fountain of the Four Seasons and enjoy.

Practically around the corner, on Rue Saint-Guillaume, is an extraordinary building that few seem to know even exists. It is the **Maison de Verre**, or House of Glass, located inside a block of residences on Rue Saint-Guillaume and accessed via a narrow passage between two courtyards. It was commissioned by a successful Parisian doctor, Dr. Jean Dalsace, and his wife, Annie Dalsace, who in the 1920s bought the site of an old apartment building, intending to remodel it in its entirety. Unfortunately, the elderly woman on the top floor refused to sell, forcing the Dalsaces to build underneath her— demolishing the first three floors without disturbing the fourth.

The Dalsaces enjoyed the newest of the new, and this house (designed by avant-garde architects and designers Pierre Chareau and Bernard Bijvoet) was at the forefront of architectural ideas of the time, and it still looks pretty modern today—especially in contrast with its older and more traditional surroundings. Its exterior, which is made of glass blocks supported by a steel frame structure, cannot be seen from the street. But from the courtyard, it looks like a translucent box embedded in the structures around and above it.

Inside, spaces are separated by movable, sliding, folding, or rotating screens of glass or perforated sheet metal, while other mechanical devices include an overhead trolley from kitchen to dining room, a retracting stairway from the private sitting room to Madame Dalsace's bedroom, and a bevy of complex cupboards and fittings throughout. The building's steel structure is clearly and intentionally visible, while a weight-and-pulley system opens the window panels, allowing for natural ventilation without interfering with the visual impact of the structure's glass façade.

I especially enjoyed the dramatic stairway that leads straight up to the Maison de Verre's double-height *salle de séjour*, where the Dalsaces entertained a coterie of Marxist intellectuals and surrealist poets and artists during the 1930s. The Dalsaces' politics put them in danger when the Germans occupied Paris in 1940, but the doctor and his wife managed to strip the house of its furniture and hide it before hastily leaving France for America. The Germans tried to requisition the house but gave up when they couldn't figure out how to turn on the heat or work the fixtures.

After the war, the Dalsaces returned, and the house remained in the family until recently, when an American collector bought it, restored it, and now lives there with his family. Visits are possible but are limited to small groups, with architects and architectural students given priority.[4]

The Maison de Verre has a lovely and very private garden tucked in behind, but it is difficult to linger here—the tour group moves on. Instead, there are several inviting pocket parks nearby, including the charming but rather difficult-to-find **Square Récamier**, located just off Rue de Sevres, at the end of what used to be Rue Récamier and now is a pedestrian walk. Surprising because of its lushness, this small park dips down and around in pleasing levels and curves, providing a pleasant place to rest as well as for children to play (especially in the sandbox at the far end).

Nearby are two other inviting parks, Square Boucicaut and Jardin Catherine Labouré. With Square Boucicaut, you are in the heart of **Le Bon Marché** territory, the first department store in Paris, which was founded by Aristide Boucicaut in 1852. In what turned out to be a classic rags-to-riches story—or at least, one that started humbly—young Boucicaut, the son of a Norman hatter, made his way to Paris and worked his way into a position of some responsibility at a small store before joining with another businessman in 1852 to open the Left Bank shop that they called Le Bon Marché, meaning "the good deal."

This was a modest venture, for this entry-level store was small and sold only linens and notions. But Boucicaut was a man of vision and soon made fundamental changes, introducing fixed prices as well as a policy of exchanges and refunds—novel practices that appealed to the practical side of the women who shopped there. He also invested heavily in newspaper advertising and introduced seasonal sales. Yet as Emile Zola later recognized, in *Au Bonheur des dames* (*The Ladies' Paradise*), female shoppers were especially enchanted with the delightful ambiance that Boucicaut's Le Bon Marché offered. For in this agreeable place, they could browse amid a wide range of tempting merchandise, displayed in an appealing manner. Immersed in this pleasantly seductive atmosphere, buyers eagerly bought, and Le Bon Marché quickly profited. By 1860, Boucicaut had increased the store's annual income from 500,000 francs to five million.

Boucicaut progressively transformed Le Bon Marché into a *grand magasin*, or department store, and others, including Le Printemps and La Samaritaine, soon followed, offering the lower prices that mass production and bulk buying made possible. Now, like La Samaritaine, Le Bon Marché is part of the luxury-oriented LVMH group and appeals to those with money and a taste for the high end of fashion. But whatever the contents of your purse, it costs nothing to window-shop there, and little more to purchase the makings of a lovely lunch in its food emporium, to enjoy at the park across the way—named, of course, for the store's founder.

Square Boucicaut is a popular place, given its location, but it is large enough and filled with enough greenery and flowers to accommodate the crowds. Its paths are curved and its terrain attractively landscaped in hillocks and terraces. And having been founded back in 1873, its trees and shrubbery have that wonderful established look. Even on the hottest days you will find plenty of shade to shelter under.

Jardin Catherine Labouré is a less shady destination, but nonetheless a charming and expansive walled garden, hidden off busy Rue de Babylone. Formerly an orchard belonging to a convent, it is named for a young nun who had visions of the Virgin Mary in the convent's chapel. This grassy expanse still has many apple and cherry trees as well as a grape arbor and a community vegetable garden—a pleasant surprise in the heart of Paris.

Further to the west is one of my favorite places, the **Peace Garden** of the headquarters of **UNESCO**, the United Nations Educational, Scientific and Cultural Organization. Unfortunately, this lovely spot has become difficult to get into, in our age of high security. Word has it that entry is possible via a reservation at the institution's restaurant, but I have not tried this—my visits took place in a less bulwarked age. But I'll proceed with my story anyway, in the hope that you will find your way in.

To begin at the beginning, let's return to precisely 8:15 a.m. on a hot and sunny August 6, 1945, when a B-29 Superfortress with the unlikely name of *Enola Gay* unleashed its atomic cargo on Hiroshima, leveling the city and killing 130,000 people. Three days later, another Superfortress dropped an even more powerful atomic bomb ("Fat Man") on Nagasaki, instantly vaporizing it.

In the town of Urakami, on Nagasaki's outskirts, the largest Roman Catholic church in Japan collapsed into a pile of scorched rubble, crushing Father Saburo Nishida and numerous parishioners inside. It had taken thirty years to build this Romanesque-style cathedral in Urakami, a town where Christianity (introduced by Portuguese traders) had thrived for centuries, even during periods of persecution. By the time "Fat Man" annihilated it, the Urakami cathedral had become one of the largest Christian churches in the Far East.

Now this beloved church was totally destroyed. But as the devastated survivors combed their church's ruins, they found an unexpected ray of hope—a fragment of a sculpted angel that had miraculously survived. Her torso had crumbled into dust, but her head and wings remained intact. Even her lovely face was still recognizable, although the bomb's blast had marred one of her eyes, making her appear—on first glimpse—as if she was crying.

Since 1976, when the town of Nagasaki parted with her to honor UNESCO's thirtieth anniversary, this treasure—known as the Nagasaki Angel—has been sheltered at UNESCO's Paris headquarters. Nagasaki's gift was both deeply moving and extraordinarily fitting, for since its inception, UNESCO has dedicated itself to promoting international peace. Even its headquarters, located near the Eiffel Tower, is a tribute to international artistic cooperation. The unusual Y-shaped Secretariat and its smaller accompanying buildings are the product of three architects (French, Italian, and American), while some of the leading artists of the twentieth century have contributed to the buildings' décor.

Pablo Picasso, an impassioned opponent of war, contributed a huge mural (*The Fall of Icarus*), while his fellow Spaniard Joan Miró created stunning ceramic decorations (*Wall of the Sun* and *Wall of the Moon*). Near Picasso's mural you will find a tapestry by Swiss-French architect and artist Le Corbusier, while a walk in the piazza to the west yields a wealth of fine art, including sculptures by Henry Moore (British), Alexander Calder (American), and Alberto Giacometti (Swiss).

But it is the beautiful garden to the east that provides the most touching tributes to peace, including the Nagasaki Angel herself. Here, in utter tranquility, a Japanese water garden adjoins a Square of Tolerance, dedicated to slain Israeli prime minister Yitzhak Rabin.

The small Square of Tolerance, with its thought-provoking olive tree, offers a quiet place for meditation, but it is the Japanese Garden of Peace that truly refreshes the soul. Here, in this small masterpiece by Isamu Noguchi, water cascades, ripples, falls, drips, or lies completely tranquil in small ponds carefully dotted with water lilies and perfectly placed stepping stones. Follow a succession of walkways and bridges to the garden's far end, where a mosaic mural by Jean Bazaine (*Water Rhythm*) continues the theme.

Then return to the top of the garden and its Fountain of Peace. For it is here, nestled against a wall that you will find the tiny Nagasaki Angel in all her tender beauty. A more poignant and powerful plea for Peace on Earth is difficult to imagine.

Not far from this memorial to peace is another poignant memorial, the **Place-des-Martyrs-Juifs-du-Vélodrome-d'Hiver**, a moving monument to the victims of the infamous roundup of Jewish men, women, and children in the summer of 1942, during the German Occupation of Paris. Crammed together in the Vélodrome d'Hiver, or Vél d'Hiv (a covered cycling arena), thousands of Jews, including more than four thousand children, suffered from brutal heat and lack of water, sanitation, or food while the Nazis and their French collaborators prepared to ship them to the death camps.

Since then, the Vél d'Hiv has been demolished and, some years afterward, this memorial was erected near the site of the atrocity. The memorial itself, in a garden that rises along the Seine, between the Eiffel Tower and the Bir Hakeim bridge, portrays a group of Jewish victims, including parents sheltering children, a pregnant woman, and an elderly man. Acknowledging the responsibility of France's Vichy government for these crimes against humanity, committed under its authority, the plaque concludes with, "Never Forget."

In quite a different mood, and in the shadow of the Eiffel Tower, is the woodsy garden of the **Musée du Quai Branly—Jacques Chirac**. The museum itself, dedicated to indigenous cultures from Africa, Asia, the Near East, Oceania, and the Americas, is a pleasant surprise—a strikingly modern building filled with wonderful discoveries. Here one is carried along a path that flows naturally from one geographical region to another, opening quite a different view of humanity from what one usually sees in large European-oriented museums. Stuffy it is not, and its outdoor garden is especially eye-opening—one wall entirely covered with growing plants, and the extensive garden forming a kind of natural wilderness—one that nonetheless is carefully planned and tended. This is a spot that draws picnickers as well as those simply wanting to rest their weary feet. But for those wanting a bit more, the museum has a pleasant café as well as a rooftop restaurant run by the Alain Ducasse team, with superb (albeit expensive) views of the Eiffel Tower.

Nature, in its most fantastic forms, takes shape nearby—down Avenue Rapp—in one of the most extraordinary façades you could hope to find. The architect, Jules Lavirotte, also designed its neighbor, at 3 Square Rapp, but it is his creation here, at **29 Avenue Rapp**, that is truly mind-blowing. An example of Art Nouveau architecture at its most flamboyant, this doorway is truly amazing. Lavirotte wanted to break with the classical restraint of the past, and he certainly achieved that here, letting his imagination run wild with the curves, floral motifs, and fantasy that characterized Art Nouveau—a style that had a short but influential life from around 1890 to 1910. Ceramic decoration played a central role in Art Nouveau, and the work of the ceramicist Alexandre Bigot at this address won a prize for the best façade of 1903.

Lavirotte built other Art Nouveau–influenced structures in Paris, and following his trail, let's head across the Seine to the Monceau quarter.

Parc Monceau. © M. McAuliffe

CHAPTER NINETEEN

~

Floral Fantasies

Following Art Nouveau architect Jules Lavirotte across the Seine, let's head for **23 Avenue de Messine**, at the corner of Rue de Messine, on the Monceau plain. Built in 1907—just a few years after Lavirotte's over-the-top structure on Avenue Rapp—this building's façade is just as filled with floral fantasy but executed with considerably more restraint. The result here, and in its adjoining building at 6 Rue de Messine, is less startling and certainly more beautiful.

The 23 Avenue de Messine structure was one of Lavirotte's last buildings in Paris and was the result of teamwork, as was always the case with Lavirotte. Here, he relied on Auguste Dondelinger for the elaborate ironwork of the balconies, and on Léon Binet for the lovely tangle of floral sculptures ornamenting the stone façade.

Like Lavirotte's Avenue Rapp façade, 23 Avenue de Messine was a prize-winner, but overall it was far better received—and has continued to be so in the succeeding years. A more mature Lavirotte created something of lasting beauty here, rather than what now looks a bit like a joke.

Paris is filled with museums, and some of the smallest gems can get over-looked, overshadowed by the Louvre and the Musée d'Orsay. One of these is the **Musée Jacquemart-André**, housed on nearby Boulevard Haussmann in a grand Haussmann-style mansion dating from the last days of the Second

Empire. It regularly hosts some eye-catching special exhibitions, but its permanent collection of Italian art and the mansion itself are a treat.

Edouard André was heir to a banking fortune, and with his wife (the painter Nélie Jacquemart), he amassed a remarkable collection of fifteenth- and sixteenth-century Italian art. The childless couple then arranged to turn the collection, along with the mansion, into a museum following their deaths. Even at those times when it is without a special exhibition, the Jacquemart-André mansion is well worth a visit just to see its state apartments, its winter garden (with a spectacular staircase), and the wealthy couple's breathtaking private apartments.

And then there is the café, which spreads outside in fine weather onto the garden courtyard—a favorite destination for many Parisians, whether for tea or an elegant lunch. It took me many years before I explored this fabulous mansion, and I wish I had discovered it earlier.

The Monceau plain has a long and involved history, dating from the Middle Ages and before. Eventually, these lands came into the hands of the Orléans family, a collateral line of French royalty that, in 1830, provided France with King Louis-Philippe. It was Louis-Philippe's father, Philippe, duke of Orléans, who in the 1770s created a dreamy landscape garden here, complete with colonnaded pool, winding paths, and numerous miniature temples and follies. The creation of the Farmers-General Wall intruded along the garden's northern edge, but its customs barrier was disguised as a circular rotunda in the form of a tiny classical temple, and Philippe claimed its upper story for his own use.

Philippe, who attempted to reinvent himself as a champion of the common man during the Revolution, renamed himself Philippe Egalité and even cast his vote for his cousin Louis XVI's execution. But Philippe soon followed his king to the guillotine, losing his lands in the process. These were returned to his family after the Restoration of the monarchy, but Napoleon III confiscated and nationalized them after seizing power in 1851. Still, due to a plethora of complexities, by the time Baron Haussmann cast his eye on the park, half of it still belonged to the Orléans family, while the other half belonged to the state. As a result, Haussmann found that to continue his citywide rebuilding plans in this area, he would have to make a major purchase on behalf of the city.

It was now that the rising banker and land speculator Emile Pereire stepped in, to prevent Haussmann the embarrassment of having to deal with the ousted royal family. This led to an amicable agreement, and in gratitude, the city sold Pereire a large chunk of the land not needed either for the new Boulevard Malesherbes or for what Haussmann already envisioned as a smaller, but still sizable, public park. The Pereire brothers used the land they received from this deal to build the elegant residential blocks that now typify the Monceau plain.

One of these is the luxurious mansion of the Camondo family—Jewish bankers and philanthropists, originally from Spain, then from Venice and Turkey, who moved to Paris in the late 1860s. Their first mansion in Paris, built soon after their arrival, served as the domicile of Emile Zola's blatantly nouveau speculator, Saccard, in *La Curée* (*The Kill*, or *The Spoils*). Zola likens "the kill" to the reward given to the dogs after a successful hunt, and there were a lot of spoils to be handed out in Napoleon III's Paris. There is no question of where Zola's sympathies lie (or do not lie) in his vivisection of the Second Empire's new Babylon, and his description of the house that Saccard builds, overlooking Parc Monceau, is a peon to vulgarity. Among its sculptured swags of flowers and branches can be seen "balconies shaped like baskets full of blossoms, and supported by great naked women with straining hips, with breasts jutting out before them." Around the roof runs a balustrade punctuated by "urns blazing with flames of stone." And the structure's interior is even more laden with gilt and display. The money practically clinks as one walks through this *nouveau riche* paradise—and that was the idea. As one of Saccard's guests remarks, at a suitably sumptuous dinner: "You see, everything is fine so long as you make money by it." While another guest grandly observes, "Let those brawlers of the [political] opposition say what they will; to plough up Paris is to make it productive."[1]

As it happens, this original mansion at 63 Rue de Monceau no longer exists, for in 1911, a new generation of Camondos replaced it with a far more elegant and classically inspired model, patterned after the Petit Trianon at Versailles. This is the structure that still exists today, exactly as it was lived in by the Camondo family through the 1930s (including their up-to-date kitchen and luxurious bathrooms). Tragically, the Camondo heir was killed in aerial combat during World War I, and his sister, along with her husband and children, were deported and murdered in Auschwitz during World War II. Bequeathed by the last Camondo to the city of Paris, the mansion is now the **Musée Nissim de Camondo** and is open to the public. Wander through and immerse yourself in the mansion's sumptuous setting, which showcases the family's extensive collections of eighteenth-century art, china, and furnishings. It truly is extraordinary.

Almost next door is the **Musée Cernuschi**, the Museum of the Asian Arts of the City of Paris, with a collection second only to that of Paris's nearby

Musée Guimet. The man behind the collection, Henri (Enrico) Cernuschi, was a wealthy Italian who got in trouble back home in the mid-1800s for supporting the Italian Republic and the Italian unification movement. After fleeing to Paris, he became a prominent banker, amassing a considerable fortune as well as a significant art collection, which he housed in this mansion. Having no heirs, he bequeathed both collection and mansion to the city of Paris, which has opened it up, free of charge, to the public. It's as much of interest for the lifestyle it so vividly illustrates as for the collections themselves.

Both the Musée Cernuschi and the Musée Nissim de Camondo border the eastern entrance to **Parc Monceau**, the fantasy-infused landscape garden begun by Philippe, duke of Orléans, and turned into its present form by Baron Haussmann. It is an elegant garden-park, frequented by the nannies and children of the surrounding mansions as well as by those who work in nearby areas and come to relax (or run laps) during their lunch breaks. Children come to ride the old-fashioned merry-go-round or feed the ducks in the colonnaded pool, and everyone strolls the paths that wind through lawns and flower beds, over a picturesque bridge, and around a grotto that supports a small cascade and stream that in turn leads to both bridge and pool.

Elements of Philippe's original fantasy remain, including that colonnade and pool, but Haussmann, with the aid of Adolphe Alphand, Gabriel Davioud, and Jean-Pierre Barillet-Deschamps, turned it into the jewel-like garden that Claude Monet painted and that, many years later, we see today. Over time, the trees have grown magnificently, and although a devastating storm two decades ago toppled several of them, most thankfully survived and continue to shade Monceau's winding paths and bowers.

Parc Monceau has four entrances, each guarded by a massive gold-embellished wrought-iron gate designed by Davioud (he also is responsible for the design of the iconic Paris public benches we see today). The main gate faces north, at the Rotonde de Chartres—the tollhouse designed by Claude-Nicolas Ledoux for the Farmers-General toll wall. This charming little building, which acquired a dome during the nineteenth century, once housed customs officials on its ground floor, while Philippe d'Orléans reserved the top floor for a personal retreat. Now it accommodates restrooms, but the building itself is still the loveliest of the four Ledoux tollhouses that have survived.

This wall was hated from the outset, for Parisians had grown accustomed to a city without walls ever since Louis XIV tore down the extensive wall hemming in the Right Bank, making way for the Grands Boulevards that followed. But this act, popular with the people, stymied the royal tax collectors, who now could do little to prevent Parisians from bypassing the toll-gates. After a century of missed revenues, the royal solution was simple and dramatic: a new wall around Paris, this time one whose sole purpose was to buttress the royal tax collectors, or tax farmers, called the Farmers General. This Farmers-General Wall went up in a hurry in the 1780s, ringing Paris with more than fifty tollhouses linked by a wall ten feet high and more than fifteen miles in circumference. Much of Paris's population was devastated by this turn of events, which sent prices soaring.

Oddly, those responsible for the wall seemed to think that Parisians would find their new constraint more acceptable—even a matter of civic pride—if it appeared to be a magnificent work of art, a kind of "garland" around Paris. They could not have been more mistaken. Instead, the very grandness of the numerous neoclassical tollhouses designed by Ledoux, one of the foremost architects of his day, stirred up an extraordinary degree of anger and resentment. Even aficionados of neoclassical architecture, such as Thomas Jefferson (who served as American minister to France during the 1780s), heartily despised them. Not surprisingly, the people of Paris destroyed many of these hated "temples of commerce" during the opening clashes of the Revolution. Only four of these controversial tollhouses have survived.[2]

Just outside Parc Monceau's northern gates is the entrance to the Monceau Métro station, with its sinuous cast-iron walls, Art Nouveau lettering, and lights like floral pods that seem to sway at the end of their long cast-iron stems. This was the creation of a young man named Hector Guimard, who was just starting to make a name for himself when those in charge of creating Paris's new Métro system chose him, in 1900, to design the system's many entrances.

It was an audacious choice. Guimard had trained at Paris's Ecole Nationale des Arts Décoratifs as well as at the Ecole Nationale des Beaux-Arts, where he earned a reputation as a rebel and, chafing at academic restrictions, failed to take his diploma. But his remarkable talent, coupled with a lively scorn for the mundane, soon attracted the attention of those with wealth and avant-garde taste. By the late 1890s, Guimard had emerged as a man to watch, with commissions to plan and build several mansions in Paris's wealthy sixteenth arrondissement.

What the Métro's commissionaires wanted was something elegant but light, with iron (a nod to Eiffel's famed constructions) and glass (including ceramics) as the preferred materials. Guimard had rivals for the job who were far more conventional and who had the support of the municipal council, but he seems to have benefited from powerful backers within the Métro commission itself. Whatever actually happened behind the scenes, Guimard's plans were finally approved in early 1900—just in time for the world's fair.

Guimard's models, all in a distinctly Art Nouveau style, varied from simple enclosures to the full-scale stations at Etoile and Bastille, both now demolished. In between was a type known as the "dragonfly," because of its glassy resemblance to dragonflies' wings. Two of these gauzy "dragonflies" still exist—at Porte Dauphine and the Abbesses station in Montmartre (the latter moved from its original placement at the Hôtel de Ville).

But it was Guimard's simple shelter that was most frequently used on the Métro's earliest lines. This structure, with open walls of cast iron rather than of solid stone, adapted well to the narrow sidewalks and typical crowding of urban Paris. Today, Guimard's Métro entrances have become some of the city's most best-known images.

By the end of 1900, eighteen stations on Line 1 had opened, and more would soon follow. It looked like a dream commission for young Guimard. But his hair-trigger temper and keen sense of self-worth soon got him in trouble, which began while he was supervising the placement of his entrances to the Métro's new Line 2 (which followed the semicircular path of the old Farmers-General Wall around the northern side of Paris). At first it was a question of money, but it soon became a question of artistic control. Guimard's employer, the Compagnie du Chemin de Fer Métropolitain de Paris, or CMP, now claimed that Guimard's projects belonged to it, to be directed as it pleased and by whomever it pleased. Guimard was aghast. How could his style, the "Style Guimard," be implemented by anyone else? Angrily, he took action to block building sites for his entrances to Line 2, and the CMP responded by suing him.

After much acrimony, Guimard and the CMP definitively broke in 1903. According to this agreement, Guimard was paid a favorable sum in return for ceding artistic rights to the style he had developed. As it turned out, his "Style Guimard" could indeed be implemented by others, and Guimard's very reliance (much like Gustave Eiffel before him) on prefabricated modular construction made the handoff easier.

The CMP finished installing Line 3 that year with Guimard-inspired entrances but without Guimard's input or oversight. Since Guimard had only partially overseen the installation of Line 2 entrances, due to disputes with the CMP, Line 1 remained the only line whose entrances bore the stamp of direct Guimard oversight. After 1904, the CMP would turn in an entirely different architectural direction for its entrances, using Marie-Joseph Cassien-Bernard to build the classical entrance for the Paris Opéra, a site that had loomed as a major sore point between Guimard and those who feared a Guimard-style entrance in front of this bastion of conservatism. With Guimard gone and Cassien-Bernard installed in his place, this battle was over before it even began.

But Guimard does not seem to have suffered from the imbroglio—at least, not financially. Not long after, he married an American heiress, and even though the Art Nouveau movement soon faded, his financial worries were over. He and his wife lived for many years in Paris, in the Guimard-designed Hôtel Guimard. They only departed Paris just before the outbreak of World War II, when (motivated by the fact that Guimard's wife was Jewish) they sailed for safety to New York.

In the years since, Guimard's style may have gone out of fashion, but his indelible imprint on Paris remains. Much to the relief of those who love them, his surviving Métro entrances are now protected as historical monuments.

Parc de Bagatelle. © J. McAuliffe

~

CHAPTER TWENTY

Western Vistas

One of my favorite days in Paris starts at Hector Guimard's gauzy-winged "dragonfly" entrance to the **Porte Dauphine Métro,** at the end of elegant, tree-lined Avenue Foch. This Art Nouveau treasure, recently refurbished, is a beauty—its delicate glass overhang shimmering in the sunlight, while its ceramic walls glow a deep floral orange, contrasting with the soft greens of the painted wrought iron. This is one of Guimard's masterpieces, and it is a treat to be here, looking westward toward the **Bois de Boulogne.**

It's but a short walk from the Métro into this huge parkland, crossing the busy roundabout and past the elegant Pavillon Dauphine. This inviting spot, with its yellow awnings and broad terrace, dates from the turn of the century and continues to host the well-known and the well-heeled. Then down the shaded Route de Suresnes to the **Lac Inférieur,** or Lower Lake, following the same route those open Belle Epoque carriages and their famed beauties took all those years ago.

A first glimpse of water is of a fringe of palm trees and a cluster of rowboats hugging the near shore. This lake is manmade but unintentional, the result of a mess up at the outset of Napoleon III's efforts to turn this former royal forest into a huge park for the people of Paris. Napoleon III had in mind something like London's Hyde Park, which he had admired when spending long years of exile in England. Even before he seized power as emperor, he arranged for the transfer of these lands to the city free of charge, on condition that they be turned into an area for public walking and relaxation. Then he set workmen to digging a curving watercourse, modeled on Hyde Park's

Serpentine. It was, in theory, a pleasing idea. But by the time Georges Hauss-mann arrived on the scene (as newly appointed prefect of the Seine), it was clear that those in charge had seriously underestimated the newly dug river's gradient, which left the upper portion dry while the lower level had become a swamp. Taking the situation in hand, Haussmann decided to divide the river into two lakes separated by a waterfall. This was not what the emperor had in mind, but nonetheless it was a happy solution that has worked well to this day.

Strolling clockwise, as I always do here, you will see familiar signs of Paris on your left, including a nice view of the Eiffel Tower. Years ago, Marcel Proust strolled here, and he dined on the first of the two islands on your right, in a restaurant that still exists—the Chalet des Iles. You reach this by a little ferry that chugs back and forth at your summons (you can take the ferry without a meal reservation but will have to pay a small fee). A bridge links the two islands, and at the end of the farthest is the picturesque Kiosque de l'Empereur.

In springtime, along the lakeside, you will see birds nesting and chicks taking their first plunges into the water. There are multiple benches along the way, some of them partially hidden in bowers that have grown up over the years—a great place to bring a book to read or to enjoy a second crois-sant. At the lake's end, you will see the waterfall that marks the place where the two lakes join. Climb to the top and enjoy the view before returning to complete, or almost complete the circuit. I say "almost complete," because I always branch off partway, to cross along the edge of the park surrounding the elegant Pré Catelan restaurant and head for the **Parc de Bagatelle**, that delicious trifle concocted during the last years of Marie Antoinette.

Legend has it (and legend may be right) that the Comte d'Artois, younger brother of Louis XVI and future Charles X, bet Marie Antoinette that he could replace the hunting lodge that already existed on the spot with a far finer structure, complete with gardens and grounds, within sixty-four days (the date when they would all return to Paris after a spell elsewhere for hunting). Hundreds of workmen carried out this ridiculous wager, which the young man won. The result, which must have pleased the queen, is a lovely little pink mansion surrounded by magnificent grounds that have been con-siderably refined since Marie Antoinette's day.

The Parc de Bagatelle is known especially for its roses, and it is a treat to wander among the hundreds of varieties that bloom here from late spring until frost. But I also come for the iris, which have their own exquisite gar-den, as well as the arbored and boxwood-edged kitchen garden—a dream of an old-fashioned kitchen garden that would make even non-gardeners yearn.

Beyond is an outdoor restaurant (expensive), the little pink mansion itself, and a vast expanse of lawn, as well as a series of follies that are yours to discover. In addition, there are ruins of a medieval abbey and several grottoes, as well as three truly impressive cascades. Regular visitors have their favorites spots, and mine is a small pond under a low-hanging tree, where my husband and I eat our picnic lunch and watch the carp and the ducks.

A truly peaceful way to spend an afternoon, before returning (via bus, along the Allée de Longchamps) to Porte Maillot and the city.

Of course, en route back, you can always stop at that wonderland for children, the **Jardin d'Acclimatation**, starting with the tiny train that choo-choos back and forth from the entrance. The rides are not splashy but inventive, and adults without children are welcome—provided they pay a small entrance fee. Unfortunately, few without children take this opportunity, and it's a shame. This truly is a lovely garden spot, and it's a pleasure to wander around and through it. The voices of children having fun adds to the ambiance.

Not far from this attractive playland is a newcomer to the Bois de Boulogne, the winged Frank Gehry–designed building that houses the **Fondation Louis Vuitton**, informally known as the Musée Vuitton. The museum's permanent collections are fine enough, but they have to work overtime to compete with Paris's major museums as well as with the building itself, which clearly is the star. People climb in and out of its sail-like structure, breathless with admiration (and perhaps the climb). In addition, there's a terrific water feature, a cascade that rolls right down to and under a portion of the building. The permanent collection may not be worth the trip, but recent special exhibitions have been terrific. That, and the promise of an architectural wonder is enough to draw many to this far side of Paris. On a lovely day, one can visit here and afterward walk over to the nearby Jardin d'Acclimatation or the Parc de Bagatelle to make a day of it.

Heading south from Porte Maillot along the western border of Paris, there is a relatively unknown pocket park with an unusual feature. It is the **Square Lamartine**, and it is the proud possessor of one of the two remaining artesian wells in Paris.

As you by now know, Parisians over the centuries have resorted to a variety of efforts to bring suitable drinking water—in fact, any water at all—to their doors. The Seine has never been a sufficient or satisfactory source for the city, and centuries after the Gallo-Romans brought in water via an aqueduct from the south, and medieval monasteries constructed a network of aqueducts from the hills of the north, massive hydraulic pumps operated for a couple of centuries from two bridge across the Seine. Of course, your average Parisian took to digging wells—a fairly likely prospect on the Right Bank, where the water table was close to the surface, but where it suffered from contamination. But it was the industrial nineteenth century that came up with the most daring solution to the problem. With sublime optimism and an unfettered can-do spirit, several entrepreneurs proposed to tap into the pristine aquifer that lay deep below the city's surface.

The idea was that this aquifer, caught between layers of impermeable rock and clay, could be reached by drilling. Unlike a regular well, an aquifer—if tapped in just the right place—spurts upward. The trick is to find that right place, the low point in the aquifer's basin, where the water is under the greatest pressure. This pressure forces the water up and out—the more pressure, the better.

Artesian wells have been around for a long time, but it was only in the nineteenth century, when the new industrial age made deep drilling possible, that their potential became truly appreciated. By this time it had become clear that Paris was sitting at the center of a huge geological basin containing an aquifer of formidable proportions. Prodded by the inspector general of mines and the mayor of Paris, the municipal council approved a large sum to tap this underground reservoir by drilling a series of artesian wells within city limits.

The first was in the fifteenth arrondissement, at the present-day intersection of Rues Valentin-Haüy and Bouchut. Work began on the Puits (well) de Grenelle in 1833 and continued through innumerable hardships and accidents until 1841, when—at a depth of 538 meters—a sudden whistling sound pierced the air, and a column of water dramatically shot up, inundating everyone and everything in the vicinity. After more than seven tough years, it was a moment of glory.

Following this grand success, more artesian wells were planned throughout Paris, the next being in Passy, at present-day Square Lamartine, to supply the artificial lakes and streams of the nearby Bois de Boulogne. Work on the Puits de Passy began in 1855 and went smoothly, thanks to modernized equipment and invaluable knowledge gained from the Grenelle enterprise. Still, it took six years before water gushed here.

Two more wells followed: one at Place Hébert, in the Chapelle quarter, and the other on the Butte-aux-Cailles, where the little river Bièvre was now too small and polluted to provide for the growing quarter. And so in

1863, drilling towers for both wells went up, although it would be many years before they reached the deeply buried aquifer.

By this time, it had become obvious that the Paris aquifer was not inexhaustible. Over the years, output from all of Paris's artesian wells had declined, with each additional well noticeably depleting the force and flow of the others. In the meantime, Baron Haussmann and Eugène Belgrand had established a grand system of aqueducts and reservoirs for the city that was making artesian wells unnecessary. The last artesian well in Paris, drilled for a swimming pool in the Vaugirard quarter, was completed in 1929. By this time, its near neighbor, the well of Grenelle, had dried up and was simply covered over.

The well at Place Hébert has similarly been covered over, with its water now flowing into a nearby swimming pool. The water from the Butte-aux-Cailles probe also flows into a swimming pool, but fortunately, this well and that of Passy still exist—at least, in the form of fountains. Usable fountains. Those four pipes at the Butte-aux-Cailles structure (located in **Place Paul-Verlaine,** just south of Place d'Italie, 13th) are in fact spigots, which release generous amounts of water drawn from the pristine aquifer below. The one at Passy, in Square Lamartine—a slab of stone with two large spigots—is similarly generous, and residents of both neighborhoods regularly line up with empty bottles to fill.

Bring a cup or empty bottle with you when you visit but be forewarned—the water is warm. It also has a strong mineral taste and a whiff of sulfur. But it is good for you, and in this day of designer water, it represents one of the rarer brands you could hope to find.

⌒

The city's light rail, the RER, runs along this western edge of Paris, occupying what used to be the tracks of the Petite Ceinture. At the Muette station, the little building that once served as station for the Petite Ceinture has been turned into an upscale restaurant, appropriately named La Gare.

You are now at the eastern point of the **Jardin du Ranelagh,** named after an eighteenth-century pleasure garden in London that featured a public dance hall. A Frenchman thought the idea a good one and introduced it here to the denizens of Paris. But time and events eroded the place's attractions, and by 1860, when Baron Haussmann took it over, it badly needed rejuvenation. Haussmann, as he did throughout Paris, transformed it into the public park it is today.

Shaded by a wealth of old chestnut and beech trees, the Jardin du Ranelagh is presided over by a statue of La Fontaine, the famous poet and writer of fables. Here he is looking benevolently down on the characters of one of his most well-known stories (derived from Aesop's Fables), "The Fox and the Crow"—complete with the cheese that the fox wangles from the crow by flattery. It's a beautiful area, and you'll find a simple old-fashioned (and unautomated) carousel near the far end, where children ride wooden horses and try to catch the rings with sticks. My carousel days are over, but I like to select some ice cream or sorbet at nearby Pascal Le Glacier (17 Rue Bois-le-Vent), some of my favorite ice cream in Paris, and enjoy it as slowly as possible in a comfortable spot here beneath the trees.

At the park's western edge is the **Musée Marmottan-Monet**, housed in the stately mansion once owned by the Marmottans, father and son. Their wide-ranging collections, from pre-Renaissance to Empire, include a wealth of paintings by Claude Monet and other Impressionists, especially Berthe Morisot. The museum's most famous attraction is Monet's *Impression Sunrise*, the work that gave its name to the movement. The name, by the way, originated with one of the group's detractors, who had howled in derision at this painting and inadvertently labeled Monet and his colleagues for the ages.

After the Marmottan son's death, the Académie des Beaux-Arts inherited the building and its collections, opening them to the public. Lovers of Impressionist art regularly make their pilgrimage here.

⁓

The sixteenth arrondissement, home to wealthy Parisians, is not unexpectedly home to some adventurous architecture, including the Art Nouveau creations of Hector Guimard.

But en route to Guimard's early masterpiece, the Castel Béranger, let's stop in at an unexpected hidey-hole, the **Maison de Balzac**. Honoré de Balzac, renowned for his novels and short stories, was also a man frequently short of cash. He seems to have chosen this out-of-the-way garden pavilion as a place to work without interruption on some of the novels of his massive *Comédie humaine*, as well as hide from his creditors. When you see this spot, you will understand. The small house with its tiny rooms is set on a narrow terrace midway between the roads high above and below it. As Balzac explained, in an 1844 letter to his future wife, Mme Hanska: "This is why I must have a quiet house between courtyard and a garden, . . . because it is my nest, my shell, the safety wrapping of my life!"

To access Balzac's nest from Rue Raynouard, you will find a reception pavilion with a choice of stairs or elevator to take you down to the house and garden. There's plenty in the small house to interest Balzac lovers, including the desk where the master labored, as well as the kitchen with its vintage wood-fired stove and Balzac's beloved walking stick. But most visitors will be taken with the location and its garden, for it is a charming spot, with a romantic free-flowering garden and a small lawn tucked against the steep rise behind. Adjoining the garden is now a café-tearoom, with tables inside and out to enjoy the view—one that includes much more than in Balzac's day, most especially the Eiffel Tower.

Any writer, in any state of solvency, would love to work here.

Castel Béranger, Hector Guimard's striking Art Nouveau masterpiece, was the young architect's breakthrough creation, launching not only his career but also the Art Nouveau movement in France. Even more than a century later, it stands out for its sheer audacity—a kind of dream vision on steroids.

Erected at no. 14 on the fashionable and otherwise staid Rue La Fontaine, this striking building won first prize in 1898 for the most beautiful façade in Paris, but it roused hostility as well, earning it the derisive name "Castel Dérangé." Not a private mansion, this was from the outset an apartment building, painted in tones of sepia and aquamarine and sheathed in a dizzying mix of glazed brick, carved stone, cast iron, copper, wood, and stained glass. Consistent with Guimard's vision, each of the original thirty-six apartments was unique, and the building's exterior boasts a visual explosion of exaggerated curves, bow windows, overhanging turrets, and ornamental ironwork stretched into fantastical shapes—from seahorses to what appear to be devils' masks. Best of all is the front door, a visual extravaganza that announces *le style Guimard* from the doorstep.

The style introduced to Paris by Baron Haussmann just a few years earlier had been one of classical restraint, even monotony. Today, Paris's "Haussmann buildings" are much admired and even beloved as quintessentially Parisian, but contemporaries were less enthused. As one journalist bluntly put it, these new houses of the Second Empire were "cold, colorless, as regular as barracks and as sad as prisons in the middle of streets aligned like infantrymen, . . . lamentable in their regularity." Another contemporary described these structures as "half palace half barracks."[1]

Guimard felt much the same way, and his Castle Béranger landed in 1890s Paris like a bomb, shattering past architectural ideals and declaring in no uncertain terms the opposite of all that Haussmann had established. Order and symmetry were out; sinuous curves and assertive individuality were in. Or at least they were for a while. But *le style Guimard* quickly fell out of favor, and by 1910, when Guimard built his **Hôtel Guimard** (122 Avenue Mozart) following his marriage to Adeline Oppenheim, it was far more restrained. Its wrought-iron balconies still had the characteristic Guimard curves, and the inclined elevator (to save space on the upper floors) was a distinctly Guimard feature, but the entire tone of the mansion is one of sedate beige. Those looking for another Castel Béranger at this address will be disappointed. Similarly, Guimard's **Hôtel Mezzara** (1911), at 60 Rue La Fontaine, is relatively classical in tone—the outcome of Guimard's evolution in the face of changing tastes and times.

~

This corner of Paris contains a wealth of important private dwelling places, especially Le Corbusier's seminal **Villa La Roche** and adjoining **Villa Jeanneret**.

Swiss-born Le Corbusier, who began life as Charles-Edouard Jeanneret, arrived in Paris in 1917, during some of the most difficult months of World War I. Committing himself to Paris and to the new spirit that already was emerging in the war-torn city, he gravitated to avant-garde art and theater productions while attempting to establish himself as a painter. Failing at that, he transitioned into architecture where, despite his lack of formal credentials, he slowly began to make a name for himself.

The name, though, changed. In 1920, Jeanneret and his partner, Amédée Ozenfant, first published their magazine, *L'Esprit Nouveau*, to promote "artistic balance and mathematical order" as a means toward a fulfilled life. In particular, Jeanneret and Ozenfant extolled the beauty and timelessness of "cubes, cones, spheres, cylinders, and pyramids."[2] It was now, as a pseudonym for the new publication, that Charles Jeanneret came up with the name Le Corbusier. By his own account, he had derived it from the name of an ancestor, a Monsieur Lecorbesier, who had been one of the few truly successful and prosperous members of Jeanneret's family. Jeanneret may simply have liked the sound of the name and its association with *le corbeau* (the raven or crow), given his own crow-like profile. Yet whatever the name's source, it gave Jeanneret the opportunity to reinvent himself.

That same year, Le Corbusier's young second cousin, Pierre Jeanneret, arrived in Paris laden with prizes and accolades from his studies in Geneva to study architecture at Paris's Ecole des Beaux-Arts. Initially, Le Corbusier was contemptuous of the young man, but he quickly grasped his cousin's abilities and potential. Eventually, Le Corbusier made Pierre Jeanneret his partner.

If you are interested in Le Corbusier's architecture, you may want to take a look at his **Maison Ozenfant**, the residence and studio that he designed for Amédée Ozenfant at the corner of Avenue Reille in the Montsouris quarter (14th), between the reservoir and the park. Dating from 1922, this is a very early example of Le Corbusier's work, and in this slim, upward-thrusting edifice topped by a double-peaked roof of angled skylights (now gone), Le Corbusier incorporated the most modern of amenities, including a garage (an unusual provision in 1922) and a full-size bathroom for the housekeeper as well as similar provision for the owner. After all these years, the Villa Ozenfant remains clean lined, airy, and inviting.

Soon after (in 1923), Le Corbusier began construction for his wealthiest client to date, the Swiss banker Raoul La Roche. Situated at the end of a small cul-de-sac (10 Square du Docteur-Blanche) on the outskirts of Paris's sixteenth arrondissement, the **Villa La Roche** (now housing the Fondation Le Corbusier) was designed to showcase Raoul La Roche's art collection, including works by Léger and Lipchitz as well as several fine Picassos and a Braque that Le Corbusier and Ozenfant had bought for La Roche at auction.

As it happened, Le Corbusier's brother, Albert Jeanneret, had just married a well-to-do widow, who commissioned a Le Corbusier–designed house adjacent to La Roche's, where she and Albert and her two daughters would live. The site was small and strangely shaped, giving Le Corbusier many headaches, but when completed, both edifices were revolutionary in materials (concrete and machined materials) as well as design. For the Villa La Roche especially, Le Corbusier created a magnificent space: a soaring interior atrium with balconies and a sloping ramp connecting the floors through a spacious gallery. A portion of the building rests on *pilotis*, or pillars, and it culminates in a roof garden. In addition, Le Corbusier designed or selected all the furniture and interior fittings, including the curtains (a blend of flannel and cambric), the lighting fixtures (supplementing natural lighting), and floors made of special rubber instead of wood parquet.

But hiring Le Corbusier was not something to take lightly: the architect demanded a great deal from his clients. "You must renounce the things you have learned," he told them, "in order to pursue truths which inevitably develop around new techniques instigated by a new spirit born of the profound revolution of the machine age."[3] Unquestionably, Villa La Roche was a triumph, but it sorely tested relations between architect and client, and it led to the breakup between Le Corbusier and his friend and partner Ozenfant as well (among other sins, Ozenfant had made substantial changes to the installation of La Roche's art collection that Le Corbusier had overseen).

If you are interested in Le Corbusier's architecture from this early period, you may want to look up two other structures of his in Paris: the Salvation Army's **Cité de Refuge**, a large multistoried homeless shelter in the thirteenth arrondissement, underwritten by the Princesse de Polignac, and the **Fondation Suisse** in the Cité Internationale Universitaire de Paris, at the southernmost edge of Paris. Most important, though, is his **Villa Savoye**, located just outside of Paris, in Poissy. Conceived as a country house for Pierre and Emilie Savoye, the villa embodied the culmination of Le Corbusier's 1920s concepts for private housing: a free, non-load-bearing façade; horizontal bands of windows; an open interior plan; attractive roof gardens; and *pilotis*, or posts, rising up and supporting the whole, with reinforced concrete at the structure's heart. Located just a short train ride from Paris, the Villa Savoye is open to visitors.

And then there was modernist architect Robert Mallet-Stevens, whose collection of six houses line the small **Rue Robert Mallet-Stevens**, located in the heart of this architectural wealth. We are fortunate to have this physical evidence of Mallet-Stevens' brilliance, because this prolific designer of buildings, homes, and interiors, as well as film sets, ordered that his archives be destroyed upon his death. Unfortunately, his wishes were honored, and as a result, Mallet-Stevens has pretty much disappeared from view. But take the short walk from Le Corbusier's Villa La Roche or Guimard's Hôtel Guimard and Hôtel Mezzara to see a very different architectural vision from that of Le Corbusier. The Hôtel Martel, at 10 Rue Mallet-Stevens, is especially striking.

You can find, with some persistence, another view of a striking Mallet-Stevens structure—the Villa Noailles, a remarkable villa built for the Viscount and Viscountess de Noailles, which still exists in the hills of southeastern France. During the late 1920s, these two wealthy leaders of Paris's avant-garde invited American surrealist painter and photographer Man Ray to make a film of the Villa Noailles, including its art collection and houseguests. Man Ray (who did not hesitate to accept a midwinter invitation to the Riviera) came up with a twenty-minute film that he called *Les Mystères du Château de Dé* (*The Mysteries of the Château of Dice*), inspired by Stéphane Mallarmé's poem "Un coup de dés jamais n'abolira le hazard" (A Throw of the Dice Will Never Abolish Chance).

The film begins with two masked people tossing dice on whether or not to leave Paris. It then portrays their auto trip southward (in a vintage 1920s car on similarly vintage roads) toward the Noailles' villa—a striking modern structure whose cubic form originally made Man Ray think of Mallarmé's poem, which in turn inspired the dice theme. After the travelers depart, the film cuts to the mysteriously empty villa, which it slowly explores. People suddenly appear, their identities hidden by masks, and cavort until they fall asleep, accompanied by the caption, "A throw of the dice will never do away with chance." The travelers at last arrive at the villa and happen on a large pair of dice on the grass, which they roll, asking if they should stay or go. The dice answer that they should stay, and the travelers entwine and gradually become fixed and white, like a marble statue. The film then closes on an artificial hand holding a pair of dice.

Weird, yes, and even spooky, but remember that this was at the height of the surrealist movement, and Robert Mallet-Stevens and his buildings were at the heart of the 1920s avant-garde. Take a few moments to get to know him better.

From here it is not far by bus (no. 72) or Métro to take you across one of the Seine's wide loops to the suburb of Saint-Cloud. There, at the far side of the bridge, you can climb the hill to what used to be the Château de Saint-Cloud and now is the **Parc de Saint-Cloud**.

The château, which once was a royal residence, was destroyed during the 1870 Franco-Prussian War, leaving vestiges of gardens and fountains in a lovely spot overlooking the Seine and Paris. Of the fountains, the most dramatic by far is the **Grande Cascade et Jets d'Eau**, a kind of Niagara of fountains, which flows, burbles, and yes, cascades on certain Sunday mornings, usually in June. It's a magnificent spectacle, created more than three centuries ago at the bidding of Philippe d'Orléans, younger brother of Louis XIV, who took possession of the property and conceived of this cascade as a "theater of liquid crystal." In those days, the brother of the king could and did create such spectacular diversions, and the huge and complex structure that forms the many fountains, terraces, and basins of this supernova of cascades truly creates a theater of water as it crashes downward.

In the summer months, other fountains remaining from the now-disappeared château make a pleasant place to stroll, especially for the panoramic view of Paris, complete with the Eiffel Tower and the tethered hot-air balloon that regularly makes its ascent from Parc André-Citroën, across the Seine. But my favorite spot requires another climb, which takes you to a terrace, then to a small pond with a tiny island, surrounded by ancient specimen trees—a truly peaceful place to rest or read, enjoying this gift from past centuries to our own.

And it is here that I will leave you, to enjoy the peace and the beauty of this spot, and to continue your own explorations of the secret gardens, hidden places, and stories of Paris.

~

Notes

Chapter One: The Heart of Paris

1. Erlande-Brandenburg, *Notre-Dame de Paris*, 212.
2. See chapter 18.

Chapter Two: The Latin Quarter and Beyond

1. André Langevin, *Paul Langevin, mon père*, 13.

Chapter Four: Along the Seine

1. Paul, *The Last Time I Saw Paris*, 16–18.
2. Ionesco, *The Bald Soprano & Other Plays*, 8–9.

Chapter Five: Ancient Byways

1. John Rewald, *History of Impressionism*, 31.
2. Manet to Antonin Proust, as recorded by Proust, in *Manet by Himself*, 28.
3. See chapter 17.

Chapter Six: Dangerous Times

1. See chapter 15.

Chapter Eight: An Imperious Queen

1. Schopp, *Alexandre Dumas*, 486.

2. Bernhardt, *Memories of My Life*, 132–34.

3. Gertrude Stein, *Autobiography of Alice B. Toklas*, 31–32; Leo Stein, *Appreciation*, 157.

4. Leo Stein, *Appreciation*, 171.

5. Gertrude Stein, *Autobiography of Alice B. Toklas*, 53.

6. Richardson, *Life of Picasso: The Prodigy*, 417.

7. Gertrude Stein, *Autobiography of Alice B. Toklas*, 53, 57. Picasso made her a gift of the work, which now hangs in New York's Metropolitan Museum of Art.

8. Beach, *Shakespeare & Company*, 102.

9. Beach, *Shakespeare & Company*, 215.

10. Beach, *Shakespeare & Company*, 415.

11. Hemingway, *Moveable Feast*, 28; Beach, *Shakespeare & Company*, 32.

12. James Laughlin, founder of the publishing house New Directions, quoted in Will, *Unlikely Collaboration*, 69.

13. Will, *Unlikely Collaboration*, 70.

Chapter Nine: Montmartre

1. Contamine de Latour's reminiscences appeared in the August 3, 5, and 6, 1925, issues of the French journal *Comoedia*. From Orledge, *Satie Remembered*, 26.

2. See chapter 15.

3. Orledge, *Satie Remembered*, 26.

4. As told to his son, Jean Renoir (*Renoir, My Father*, 197).

5. Gaby Casadesus, *Mes noces musicales: Gaby Casadesus, Conversation avec Jacqueline Muller*, 15.

6. Aymé, *Le Passe-Muraille*, 19.

7. Olivier, *Loving Picasso*, 170.

8. Olivier, *Loving Picasso*, 178.

9. Leo Stein, *Appreciation*, 175; Flanner, *Men and Monuments*, 134.

Chapter Ten: Montparnasse

1. Salmon, *Montparnasse*, 127.

2. Kiki, *Kiki's Memoirs*, 228–32. In 1920, Victor Libion retired, selling his beloved Rotonde, which went on without him.

3. Chagall, *My Life*, 103.

4. Kiki, *Kiki's Memoirs*, 84.

5. Kiki, *Kiki's Memoirs*, 126. Other previously impoverished residents of Montparnasse recalled similar experiences (*Kiki's Memoirs*, 254).

6. Man Ray, *Self-Portrait*, 116.

7. Varenne, *Bourdelle par lui-même*, 168, 169.
8. Goncourt, 17 September 1868, in *Journals*, 141.

Chapter Eleven: Lost River

1. Champigneulle, *Rodin*, 14.
2. Champigneulle, *Rodin*, 42.
3. See https://www.paris-historique.org/arche-de-passage-de-la-bievre.

Chapter Twelve: Into the Marais

1. See chapter 18.
2. Mozart, *Mozart's Letters*, 88, 116.
3. See chapter 7.
4. See chapter 18.
5. See chapter 16.

Chapter Thirteen: Points East

1. See chapter 7.
2. Carmona, *Haussmann*, 288.
3. Haussmann, *Mémoires*, 917.

Chapter Fourteen: Onward and Upward

1. See chapter 15.
2. See chapter 7.

Chapter Fifteen: From the Heights

1. Samson, *Chopin*, 80; Szulc, *Chopin in Paris*, 79.
2. James, *Parisian Sketches*, 35–36.

Chapter Sixteen: Grande Croisée

1. The office of mayor of Paris would not be reestablished until 1977.
2. Haussmann, *Memoires*, 825.
3. Voisin, *Men, Women and 10,000 Kites*, 104–5.
4. Haussmann, *Memoires*, 1072.
5. Its closure for renovations in 2023 will be a big disappointment to many. These will take between three to seven years, depending.

Chapter Seventeen: Welcoming the World

1. Carmona, *Haussmann*, 356.
2. Harvie, *Eiffel*, 97–98.
3. Goncourt, *Journal*, 2 July 1889, 347–48.
4. Monet to Armand Fallières, 7 February 1890, in *Monet by Himself*, 132.
5. Monet to Clemenceau, 12 November 1918, in *Monet by Himself*, 252.
6. Geffroy quoted in Wildenstein, *Monet*, 1:410.
7. Gold and Fizdale, *Divine Sarah*, 78.
8. Matisse to the Museum of the City of Paris at the Petit Palais—Musée des Beaux-Arts de la Ville de Paris, 10 November 1936, in *Matisse on Art*, 124.
9. See introduction, 1.
10. Julie Manet, *Diary*, 6 and 8 October 1896, 100, 104.
11. Coppée quoted in Montens, *Paris*, 140.
12. Haussmann, *Mémoires*, 928–29.
13. See chapter 12.

Chapter Eighteen: Eiffel Tower and Beyond

1. See chapter 17 for more on Eiffel and his tower.
2. Cocteau, *Souvenir Portraits*, 126–27.
3. Butler, *Rodin*, 507.
4. For visits, contact l'Association des Amis de la Maison de Verre at: mdv31@orange.fr.

Chapter Nineteen: Floral Fantasies

1. Zola, *La Curée*, 15, 18, 29, 27.
2. On the Left Bank, twin buildings—the remains of the old tollgate, the Barrière d'Enfer—still stand at Place Denfert-Rochereau, where one now serves as an entrance to the Catacombs, and the other to the Musée de la Libération de Paris–Musée du Général Leclerc–Musée Jean Moulin. On the Right Bank, the small rotunda at the entrance to Parc Monceau marks what once was the Monceau toll barrier, while far to the east, in the Place de la Nation, two columns dramatically mark the old Barrière du Trône tollgate (twin buildings flanking these columns once served as offices and lodgings). Most striking is the Rotonde de la Villette, at the foot of the Bassin de la Villette at Place de la Bataille-de-Stalingrad. This massive rotunda guarded a convergence of northern routes into Paris, including the old Roman road to the sea.

Chapter Twenty: Western Vistas

1. Pinon, *Atlas du Paris Haussmannien*, 87.
2. Nicholas Weber, *Le Corbusier*, 177, 179.
3. Nicholas Weber, *Le Corbuiser*, 203.

Bibliography

Adams, William Howard. *The Paris Years of Thomas Jefferson*. New Haven, Conn.: Yale University Press, 1997.

Agulhon, Maurice. *The Republican Experiment, 1848–1852*. Translated by Janet Lloyd. New York: Cambridge University Press, 1983.

Andia, Béatrice, ed. *Les Enceintes de Paris*. Paris: Action Artistique de la Ville de Paris, 2001.

Aymé, Marcel. *Le Passe-Muraille*. Paris: Gallimard, 1943.

Ayral-Clause, Odile. *Camille Claudel: A Life*. New York: Abrams, 2002.

Baker, Jean-Claude, and Chris Chase. *Josephine: The Hungry Heart*. New York: Cooper Square Press, 2001.

Baldwin, Neil. *Man Ray, American Artist*. New York: Da Capo, 2001. First published 1988.

Balzac, Honoré de. *Père Goriot*. Translated by A. J. Krailsheimer. New York: Oxford University Press, 2009.

———. *Eugénie Grandet*. Translated by Marion Ayton Crawford. Harmondsworth, Middlesex, UK: Penguin Books, 1955.

Beach, Sylvia. *Shakespeare & Company*. Lincoln: University of Nebraska Press, 1991. First published 1956.

Beaumont-Maillet, Laure. *L'Eau à Paris*. Paris: Hazan, 1991.

Benton, Tim. *The Villas of Le Corbusier, 1920–1930*. With photographs in the Lucien Hervé collection. New Haven, Conn.: Yale University Press, 1987.

Berlanstein, Lenard R. *The Working People of Paris, 1871–1914*. Baltimore, Md.: Johns Hopkins University Press, 1984.

Bernard, Philippe, and Henri Dubief. *The Decline of the Third Republic, 1914–1938*. Translated by Anthony Forster. New York: Cambridge University Press, 1988.

Bernhardt, Sarah. *Memories of My Life: Being My Personal, Professional, and Social Recollections as Woman and Artist*. New York: D. Appleton, 1907.

Bertaut, Jules. *Paris, 1879–1935*. Translated by R. Millar. Edited by John Bell. London: Eyre, and Spottiswoode, 1936.

Bertin, Célia. *Jean Renoir: A Life in Pictures*. Translated by Mireille Muellner and Leonard Muellner. Baltimore, Md.: Johns Hopkins University Press, 1991.

Berton, Claude, and Alexandre Ossadzow. *Fulgence Bienvenüe et la construction du métropolitain de Paris*. Paris: Presses de l'Ecole nationale des ponts et chausses, 1998.

Birmingham, Kevin. *The Most Dangerous Book: The Battle for James Joyce's Ulysses*. New York: Penguin, 2014.

Bonthoux, Daniel, and Bernard Jégo. *Montmartre: Bals et cabarets au temps de Bruant et Lautrec*. Paris: Musée de Montmartre, 2002.

Bougault, Valérie. *Paris-Montparnasse: The Heyday of Modern Art, 1910–1940*. Paris: Editions Pierre Terrail, 1997.

Bourdelle, Antoine. *Bourdelle: Dossier de l'Art 10* (Janvier-Février 1993).

Bradbury, Jim. *Philip Augustus: King of France, 1180–1223*. London: Longman, 1998.

Bredin, Jean-Denis. *The Affair: The Case of Alfred Dreyfus*. Translated by Jeffrey Mehlman. New York: George Braziller, 1986.

Bresler, Fenton. *Napoleon III: A Life*. London: HarperCollins, 1999.

Brinnin, John Malcolm. *The Third Rose: Gertrude Stein and Her World*. Reading, Mass.: Addison-Wesley, 1987.

Brombert, Beth Archer. *Edouard Manet: Rebel in a Frock Coat*. Boston: Little, Brown, 1995.

Brown, Frederick. *Zola: A Life*. New York: Farrar, Straus & Giroux, 1995.

Bury, J. P. T., and R. P. Tombs, *Thiers, 1797–1877: A Political Life*. London: Allen & Unwin, 1986.

Butler, Ruth. *Rodin: The Shape of Genius*. New Haven, Conn.: Yale University Press, 1993.

Cachin, Françoise. *Manet: Painter of Modern Life*. Translated by Rachel Kaplan. London: Thames and Hudson, 1995.

Capellanus, Andreas. *The Art of Courtly Love*. Translated, with notes and introduction, by John J. Parry. New York: Columbia University Press, 1990.

Carbonnières, Philippe de. *Lutèce: Paris ville romaine*. Paris: Gallimard, 1997.

Carmona, Michel. *Haussmann: His Life and Times, and the Making of Modern Paris*. Translated by Patrick Camiller. Chicago: Ivan R. Dee, 2002.

Carrière, Bruno. *La saga de la Petite Ceinture*. Paris: Editions La Vie du Rail, 1992.

Carter, William C. *Marcel Proust: A Life*. New Haven, Conn.: Yale University Press, 2000.

Casadesus, Gaby. *Mes noces musicales: Gaby Casadesus, Conversation avec Jacqueline Muller*. Paris: Buche-Chastel, 1989.

Cazelle, Raymond. *Nouvelle histoire de Paris: de la fin du règne de Philippe Auguste à la mort de Charles V, 1223–1380*. Paris: Diffusion Hachette, 1972.

Chadych, Danielle. *Le Marais: Evolution d'un paysage urbain*. Paris: Parigramme, 2005.

Chadych, Danielle, and Charlotte Lacour-Veyranne. *Paris au temps des* Misérables *de Victor Hugo*. Paris: Musée Carnavalet, 2008.

Chagall, Marc. *My Life*. Translated by Elizabeth Abbott. New York: Da Capo Press, 1994. Republication of 1960 edition.

Champigneulle, Bernard. *Rodin*. Translated by J. Maxwell Brownjohn. London: Thames and Hudson, 1999.

Charters, Jimmie, as told to Morrill Cody. *This Must Be the Place: Memoirs of Montparnasse*. Edited and with a preface by Hugh Ford. Introduction by Ernest Hemingway. New York: Collier Macmillan, 1989. First published 1934.

Christ, Yvan. *Eglises de Paris*. Paris: Diffusion Française, 1956.

Clanchy, M. T. *Abelard: A Medieval Life*. Oxford, UK: Blackwell, 1999.

Clemenceau, Georges. *Claude Monet: The Water Lilies*. Translated by George Boas. Garden City, N.Y.: Doubleday, Doran, 1930.

Clément, Alain, and Gilles Thomas. *Atlas du Paris souterrain: La doublure sombre de la ville lumière*. Paris: Parigramme, 2001.

Cocteau, Jean. *Souvenir Portraits: Paris in the Belle Epoque*. Translated by Jesse Browner. New York: Paragon House, 1990. First published 1935.

Cooper, Duff. *Talleyrand*. New York: Grove, 1932.

Couperie, Pierre. *Paris through the Ages*. New York: George Braziller, 1971.

Curie, Eve. *Madame Curie: A Biography*. Translated by Vincent Sheean. Garden City, N.Y.: Garden City Publishing, 1940.

Dalí, Salvador. *The Secret Life of Salvador Dalí*. Translated by Haakon M. Chevalier. New York: Dover, 1993. First published 1942.

Debussy, Claude. *Debussy Letters*. Edited by François Lesure and Roger Nichols. Translated by Roger Nichols. Cambridge, Mass.: Harvard University Press, 1987.

Descouturelle, Frédéric, André Mignard, and Michel Rodriguez. *Le Métropolitain d'Hector Guimard*. Paris: Comogy editions d'art, 2004.

Douglas, David C. "Medieval Paris." In *Time and the Hour*. London: Eyre Methuen, 1977.

Dubois, Isabelle. *Le 4e Arrondissement: Itinéraires d'histoire et d'architecture*. Paris: Action Artistique de la Ville de Paris, 2003.

Duby, Georges. *The Chivalrous Society*. Translated by Cynthia Postan. Berkeley: University of California Press, 1977.

———. *France in the Middle Ages: From Hugh Capet to Joan of Arc*. Translated by Juliet Vale. Oxford, UK: Blackwell, 1991.

Dumas, Alexandre, père. *La Reine Margot*. New York: Oxford World's Classics, 2009. First published 1845.

———. *The Three Musketeers*. Translated by Lowell Bair. New York: Bantam Books, 1984. First published 1844.

Duval, Paul-Marie. *Paris antique: des origines au troisième siècle*. Paris: Hermann, 1961.

Ellmann, Richard. *James Joyce*. New York: Oxford University Press, 1982.

Erlande-Brandenburg, Alain. *Notre-Dame de Paris*. Translated by John Goodman. New York: Harry N. Abrams, 1998.

Evanson, Norma. *Paris: A Century of Change, 1878–1978*. New Haven, Conn.: Yale University Press, 1979.

Fawtier, Robert. *The Capetian Kings of France, Monarchy and Nation: 987–1328*. Oxford, UK: Hassell Street Press, 2021.

Ferruolo, Stephen C. *The Origins of the University: The Schools of Paris and Their Critics, 1100–1215*. Stanford, Calif.: Stanford University Press, 1985.

Fitch, Noel Riley. *Sylvia Beach and the Lost Generation: A History of Literary Paris in the Twenties & Thirties*. New York: Norton, 1985.

Flanner, Janet. *Men and Monuments*. New York: Harper, 1957.

———. *Paris Was Yesterday, 1925–1939*. New York: Viking, 1972.

Fulcher, Jane F., ed. *Debussy and His World*. Princeton, N.J.: Princeton University Press, 2001.

Gagneux, Renaud, Jean Anckaert, and Gérard Conte. *Sur les traces de la Bièvre parisienne: Promenades au fil d'une rivière disparue*. Paris: Parigramme, 2002.

Gillingham, John. *The Angevin Empire*. 2nd ed. London: New York: Oxford University Press, 2001.

———. *Richard I*. New Haven, Conn.: Yale University Press, 1999.

Gold, Arthur, and Robert Fizdale. *The Divine Sarah: A Life of Sarah Bernhardt*. New York: Vintage Books, 1992.

———. *Misia: The Life of Misia Sert*. New York: Morrow, 1981.

Gold, Penny Schine. *The Lady and the Virgin*. Chicago: University of Chicago Press, 1985.

Goncourt, Edmond de, and Jules de Goncourt. *Pages from the Goncourt Journal*. Edited and translated by Robert Baldick. New York: New York Review of Books, 2007.

Gottlieb, Robert. *Sarah: The Life of Sarah Bernhardt*. New Haven, Conn.: Yale University Press, 2010.

Greenfield, Howard. *The Devil and Dr. Barnes: Portrait of an American Art Collector*. Philadelphia, Pa.: Camino Books, 2006.

Harvie, David I. *Eiffel: The Genius Who Reinvented Himself*. Gloucestershire, UK: Sutton, 2004.

Haussmann, Georges. *Mémoires: édition intégrale*. Vols. 1–3. Paris: Seuil, 2000. First published 1893.

Hemingway, Ernest. *A Moveable Feast*. New York: Touchstone, 1996. First published 1964.

Higonnet, Anne. *Berthe Morisot*. New York: Harper & Row, 1990.

Horne, Alistair. *The Fall of Paris: The Siege and the Commune, 1870–71*. Harmondsworth, UK: Penguin, 1981. First published 1965.

———. *Seven Ages of Paris*. New York: Vintage, 2004.

Hugo, Victor. *The Hunchback of Notre-Dame*. Translated by Walter J. Cobb. New York: Signet, 2001. First published 1831.

————. *Les Misérables*. Translated by Norman Denny. New York: Penguin, 1985. First published 1862.

Ionesco, Eugène. *The Bald Soprano & Other Plays*. Translated by Donald M. Allen. New York: Grove, 1958.

James, Henry. *Parisian Sketches: Letters to the New York Tribune, 1875–1876*. Edited by Leon Edel and Ilse Dusoir Lind. New York: Collier, 1961.

Jonas, Raymond Anthony. *France and the Cult of the Sacred Heart: An Epic Tale for Modern Times*. Berkeley: University of California Press, 2000.

Jones, Colin. *Paris: The Biography of a City*. New York: Viking, 2004.

Josephson, Matthew. *Zola and His Time*. Garden City, N.Y.: Garden City Publishing, 1928.

Journas, Georges. *Alfred Dreyfus, officier en 14–18: Souvenirs, lettres et carnet de guerre*. Orléans, France: Regain de lecture, 2011.

Kelly, Amy. *Eleanor of Aquitaine and the Four Kings*. Cambridge, Mass.: Harvard University Press, 1978. First published 1950.

Kent, Princess Michael of. *The Serpent and the Moon: Two Rivals for the Love of a Renaissance King*. New York: Simon & Schuster, 2004.

Kiki. *Kiki's Memoirs*. Introductions by Ernest Hemingway and Tsuguharu Foujita. Photography by Man Ray. Edited and foreword by Billy Klüver and Julie Martin. Translated by Samuel Putnam. Hopewell, N.J.: Ecco Press, 1996. First published 1929.

Klüver, Billy, and Julie Martin. *Kiki's Paris: Artists and Lovers, 1900–1930*. New York: Abrams, 1989.

Langevin, André. *Paul Langevin, mon père: L'homme et l'œuvre*. Paris: Les Editeurs Français Réunis, 1971.

Leroux, Gaston. *The Phantom of the Opera*. Introduction by John L. Flynn. New York: Signet, 2001.

Lewis, C. S. *The Allegory of Love: A Study in Medieval Tradition*. New York: Oxford University Press, 1958.

Lorenz, Philippe, and Dany Sandron. *Atlas de Paris au Moyen Age: Espace Urbain, Habitat, Société, Religion, Lieux de Pouvoir*. Paris: Parigramme, 2006.

Man Ray. *Self Portrait*. Boston: Little, Brown, 1988. First published 1963.

Manet, Edouard. *Manet by Himself: Correspondence and Conversation, Paintings, Pastels, Prints, and Drawings*. Edited by Juliet Wilson-Bareau. London: Macdonald, 1991.

Manet, Julie. *Growing Up with the Impressionists: The Diary of Julie Manet*. Translated and edited by Rosalind de Boland Roberts and Jane Roberts. London: Sotheby's, 1987.

Marchal, Gaston-Louis. *Ossip Zadkine: La sculpture—toute une vie*. Rodez, France: Editions du Rouergue, 1992.

Matisse, Henri. *Matisse on Art*. Rev. ed. Edited by Jack Flam. Berkeley: University of California Press, 1995.

Maurois, André. *The Titans: A Three-Generation Biography of the Dumas.* Translated by Gerard Hopkins. New York: Harper, 1957.

Maxwell, Elsa. *R.S.V.P.: Elsa Maxwell's Own Story.* Boston: Little, Brown, 1954.

Mayeur, Jean-Marie, and Madeleine Rebériioux. *The Third Republic from its Origins to the Grreat War, 1871–1914.* Translated by J. R. Foster. Cambridge, UK: Cambridge University Press, 1989.

McAuliffe, Mary. *Clash of Crowns: William the Conqueror, Richard Lionheart, and Eleanor of Aquitaine—A Story of Bloodshed, Betrayal, and Revenge.* Lanham, Md.: Rowman & Littlefield, 2012.

———. *Dawn of the Belle Epoque: The Paris of Monet, Zola, Bernhardt, Eiffel, Debussy, Clemenceau, and Their Friends.* Lanham, Md.: Rowman & Littlefield, 2011.

———. *Paris, City of Dreams: Napoleon III, Baron Haussmann, and the Creation of Paris.* Lanham, Md.: Rowman & Littlefield, 2020.

———. *Paris Discovered: Explorations in the City of Light.* Hightstown, N.J.: Princeton Book Company, 2006.

———. *Paris on the Brink: The 1930s Paris of Jean Renoir, Salvador Dalí, Simone de Beauvoir, André Gide, Sylvia Beach, Léon Blum, and Their Friends.* Lanham, Md.: Rowman & Littlefield, 2018.

———. *Twilight of the Belle Epoque: The Paris of Picasso, Stravinsky, Proust, Renault, Marie Curie, Gertrude Stein, and Their Friends, through the Great War.* Lanham, Md.: Rowman & Littlefield, 2014.

———. *When Paris Sizzled: The 1920s Paris of Hemingway, Chanel, Cocteau, Cole Porter, Josephine Baker, and Their Friends.* Lanham, Md.: Rowman & Littlefield, 2016.

Michel, Louise. *Louise Michel.* Edited by Nic Maclellan. Melbourne, N.Y.: Ocean Press, 2004.

———. *The Red Virgin: The Memoirs of Louse Michel.* Edited and translated by Bullitt Lowry and Elizabeth Ellington Gunter. Tuscaloosa: University of Alabama Press, 1981.

Miller, Michael R. *The Bon Marché: Bourgeois Culture and the Department Store 1869–1920.* Princeton, N.J.: Princeton University Press, 1981.

Monet, Claude. *Monet by Himself: Paintings, Drawings, Pastels, Letters.* Edited by Richard R. Kendall. Translated by Bridget Strevens Romer. London: Macdonald, 1989.

Montens, Sophie-Marguerite S. *Paris, de pont en pont.* Paris: Bonneton, 2004.

Morisot, Berthe. *The Correspondence of Berthe Morisot with Her Family and Friends: Manet, Puvis de Chavannes, Degas, Monet Renoir and Mallarmé.* Edited by Denis Rouart. Translated by Betty W. Hubbard. London: Camden Press, 1986.

Mozart, Wolfgang Amadeus. *Mozart's Letters: An Illustrated Selection.* Translated by Emily Anderson. Boston: Little, Brown & Co., 1990.

Musée de la Marine de Seine. *La Seine: mémoire d'un fleuve.* Paris: Societé d'Editions Régionales [1989].

Myers, Rollo H. *Erik Satie.* Rev. ed. New York: Dover, 1968. First published 1948.

Nichols, Roger. *The Life of Debussy*. Cambridge, UK: Cambridge University Press, 1998.

Norgate, Kate. *Richard the Lion Heart*. New York: Russel & Russell, 1969. First published 1924.

Olivier, Fernande. *Loving Picasso: The Private Journal of Fernande Olivier*. Translated by Christine Baker and Michael Raeburn. New York: Abrams, 2001.

Orenstein, Arbie. *Ravel: Man and Musician*. New York: Columbia University Press, 1975.

Orledge, Robert, ed. *Satie Remembered*. Translated by Roger Nichols. Portland, Ore.: Amadeus Press, 1995.

Paul, Elliot. *The Last Time I Saw Paris*. New York: Random House, 1942.

Pinkney, David H. *Napoleon III and the Rebuilding of Paris*. Princeton, N.J.: Princeton University Press, 1958.

Pinon, Pierre. *Atlas du Paris Haussmannien: La Ville en héritage du Second empire à nos jours*. Paris: Parigramme, 2016.

Pissarro, Camille. *Letters to His Son Lucien*. Edited by John Rewald, with assistance of Lucien Pissarro. Translated by Lionel Abel. Santa Barbara, Calif.: Peregrine Smith, 1981. First published 1944.

Planhol, Xavier de, and Paul Claval. *An Historical Geography of France*. Cambridge, UK: Cambridge University Press, 1994.

Plessis, Alain. *The Rise and Fall of the Second Empire, 1852–1871*. Translated by Jonathan Mandelbaum. New York: Cambridge University Press, 1987.

Pollack, Howard. *George Gershwin: His Life and Work*. Berkeley: University of California Press, 2006.

Power, Daniel. *The Norman Frontier in the Twelfth and Early Thirteenth Centuries*. Cambridge, UK: Cambridge University Press, 2004.

Power, Eileen Edna. *Medieval Women*. Edited by M. M. Postan. Cambridge, UK: Cambridge University Press, 1975.

Price, Roger. *A Social History of Nineteenth-Century France*. London: Hutchinson, 1987.

Quinn, Susan. *Marie Curie: A Life*. New York: Simon & Schuster, 1995.

Renoir, Jean. *Renoir: My Father*. Translated by Randolph Weaver and Dorothy Weaver. Boston: Little, Brown, 1962.

Rewald, John. *The History of Impressionism*. 4th ed. New York: Museum of Modern Art, 1973. First published 1946.

Rheims, Maurice. *Hector Guimard*. Translated by Robert Erich Wolf. Photographs by Felipe Ferré. New York: Abrams, 1988.

Richardson, John. *A Life of Picasso: The Prodigy, 1881–1906*. New York: Knopf, 2012. First published 1991.

———. *A Life of Picasso: The Cubist Rebel, 1907–1916*. New York: Knopf, 2012. First published 1996.

———. *A Life of Picasso: The Triumphant Years, 1917–1932*. New York: Knopf, 2007.

Robb, Graham. *Balzac, A Biography*. New York: Norton, 1995.

————. *Victor Hugo: A Biography*. New York: Norton, 1998.

Ruelle, Karen Gray. *The Grand Mosque of Paris: A Story of How Muslims Rescued Jews During the Holocaust*. New York: Holiday House, 2009.

Salmon, André. *Montparnasse: Mémoires*. Paris: Arcadia, 2003.

Samson, Jim. *Chopin*. New York: Oxford University Press, 1996.

Scheijen, Sjeng. *Diaghilev: A Life*. Translated by Jane Hedley-Prôle and S. J. Leinbach. New York: Oxford University Press, 2009.

Schopp, Claude. *Alexandre Dumas: Genius of Life*. Translated by A. J. Koch. New York: Franklin Watts, 1988.

Secrest, Meryle. *Salvador Dalí: The Surrealist Jester*. London: Weidenfield & Nicolson, 1986.

Sert, Misia. *Misia and the Muses: The Memoirs of Misia Sert*. Translated by Moura Budberg. New York: John Day, 1953.

Shattuck, Roger. *The Banquet Years: The Origins of the Avant Garde in France, 1885 to World War I; Alfred Jarry, Henri Rousseau, Erik Satie, Guillaume Apollinaire*. New York: Vintage, 1968.

Spurling, Hilary. *Matisse the Master, A Life of Henri Matisse: The Conquest of Colour, 1909–1954*. New York: Knopf, 2007.

————. *The Unknown Matisse, A Life of Henri Matisse: The Early Years, 1869–1908*. New York: Knopf, 2005.

Steegmuller, Francis. *Cocteau: A Biography*. Boston: Little, Brown, 1970.

Stein, Gertrude. *The Autobiography of Alice B. Toklas*. New York: Vintage, 1990. First published 1933.

Stein, Leo. *Appreciation: Painting, Poetry, and Prose*. Edited by Brenda Wineapple. Lincoln: University of Nebraska Press, 1996.

Stravinsky, Igor. *An Autobiography*. New York: Norton, 1998. First published 1936.

Stravinsky, Igor, and Robert Craft. *Memories and Commentaries*. New York: Faber and Faber, 2002.

Stuart, Andrea. *The Rose of Martinique: A Life of Napoleon's Josephine*. New York: Grove, 2003.

Szulc, Tad. *Chopin in Paris: The Life and Times of the Romantic Composer*. New York: Charles Scribner, 1998.

Thomas, Edith. *Louise Michel, ou La Velléda de l'anarchie*. Translated by Penelope Williams. Montréal: Black Rose Books, 1980.

Thomas, Gilles. *The Catacombs of Paris*. Translated by Diane Langlumé. Paris: Parigramme, 2011.

Thurman, Judith. *Secrets of the Flesh: A Life of Colette*. New York: Ballantine, 1999.

Tombs, Robert. *France, 1814–1914*. London: Longman, 1996.

Tuilier, André. *Histoire de l'Université de Paris et de la Sorbonne*. 2 vols. Paris: Nouvelle Librarie de France, 1994.

Unger, Harlow Giles. *Lafayette*. New York: Wiley, 2002.

Varenne, Gaston. *Bourdelle par lui-même: Sa pensée et son art*. Paris: Fasquelle, 1937.

Voisin, Gabriel. *Men, Women, and 10,000 Kites*. Translated by Oliver Stewart. London: Putnam, 1963.

Walsh, Stephen. *Stravinsky: A Creative Spring; Russia and France, 1882–1934*. Berkeley: University of California Press, 2002.

Weber, Eugen. *France, Fin de Siècle*. Cambridge, Mass.: Belknap and Harvard University Press, 1986.

———. *The Hollow Years: France in the 1930s*. New York: Norton, 1994.

Weber, Nicholas Fox. *Le Corbusier: A Life*. New York: Duffield, 1914.

Wildenstein, Daniel. *Monet, or the Triumph of Impressionism*. Vol. 1. Translated by Chris Miller and Peter Snowdon. Cologne, Germany: Taschen/Wildenstein Institute, 1999.

Will, Barbara. *Unlikely Collaboration: Gertrude Stein, Bernard Faÿ, and the Vichy Dilemma*. New York: Columbia University Press, 2011.

Wullschläger, Jackie. *Chagall: A Biography*. New York: Knopf, 2008.

Zola, Emile. *The Ladies' Paradise (Au bonheur des dames)*. Introduction by Kristin Ross. Berkeley: University of California Press, 1992.

———. *La Curée (The Kill)*. Translated by Alexander Teixeira De Mattos. New York: Boni and Liveright, 1924.

Index

Page references for illustrations are italicized

~

About the Author

Mary McAuliffe holds a Ph.D. in history from the University of Maryland, has taught at several universities, and has lectured at the Smithsonian Institution, the Barnes Foundation, and the Frick Pittsburgh. She has traveled extensively in France, and for many years she was a regular contributor to *Paris Notes*. Her books include *Paris Discovered, Paris City of Dreams, Dawn of the Belle Epoque, Twilight of the Belle Epoque, When Paris Sizzled, Paris on the Brink,* and *Clash of Crowns.* She lives in New York City with her husband and shares her insights and photos of Paris with her readers on her Paris Facebook photo blog (www.ParisMSM.com).